THE NEAR

AND

HEAVENLY HORIZONS.

FROM THE BRITISH PRESS.

"'The Near and the Heavenly Horizons' is a charming book. Madame de Gasparin has the touch of genius which has the strange gift of speaking to every one 'in their own tongue.'" —*Athenæum.*

"A book full of beauty and pathos."—*British Quarterly Review.*

"Be persuaded, reader, to get this beautiful volume. It is just the book for Sabbath afternoons in a Christian family."—*Eclectic Review.*

"The pictures of nature here are wondrous. This books speaks to the hearts of us all."—*Macmillan's Magazine.*

"These pages are like gossamer threads beaded with radiant dew-drops. The book ought to become extremely popular."—*The Witness.*

"The gifted author paints the ever-changing scenes of nature with marvellous delicacy and force."—*Leeds Mercury.*

"We have scarcely ever read a book with more enjoyment than its perusal has afforded us."—*Aberdeen Free Press.*

"A remarkable book—displaying marvellous powers of descriptive writing."—*The Scotsman.*

"This is a book to be enjoyed and revelled in rather than criticised. The reader who sits down to it will have a rare literary treat."—*The Scottish Guardian.*

THE NEAR

AND

THE HEAVENLY HORIZONS.

BY

MADAME DE GASPARIN.

"Earth by Heaven, and Heaven by changeful Earth
Illustrated, and mutually endeared."—WORDSWORTH.

NEW YORK:
ROBERT CARTER & BROTHERS,
No. 530 BROADWAY.
1865.

CONTENTS.

THE NEAR HORIZONS.

INTRODUCTION, ... 3
LISETTE'S DREAM, ... 6
THE THREE ROSES, ... 26
THE TILERY, ... 48
THE HEGELIAN, ... 67
THE SPRINGS, ... 83
A POOR BOY, ... 97
THE GALLEY-SLAVE, ... 120
THE DOVECOT, ... 128
MARIETTA, ... 146
THE SCULPTOR, ... 154
THE ARBOUR, ... 165

THE HEAVENLY HORIZONS.

THE HEAVENLY HORIZONS, ... 177

PART I.

TO WHOM I SPEAK, ... 181
OF WHOM I SPEAK, ... 196
THE AUTHORITY ON WHICH I REST, ... 202
THE PARADISE WE FEAR, ... 221

Part II.

THE SUPREME TYPE: A RISEN SAVIOUR, ... 231
THE SLEEPLESSNESS OF THE SOUL, ... 242
PERSONAL IDENTITY, ... 253
THE ETERNITY OF LOVE, ... 265
THE RESURRECTION OF THE BODY, ... 276

Part III.

THT WHOLE CREATION SIGHETH, ... 287
THE COMING OF CHRIST, ... 296
NEW HEAVENS AND NEW EARTH, ... 303

THE NEAR HORIZONS.

THE NEAR HORIZONS.

INTRODUCTION.

"Una donna soletta, che si già
Cantando, ed iscegliendo fior da fiore,
Ond'era pinta tutta la sua via."

—DANTE.

THE night is far spent; many of the stars that shone in the sky have disappeared behind the mountain, the dawn pales those that remain. My thoughts revert to the early hours of evening, and rest on some simple figures whose path my steps have crossed. From those hours rise spring-tide emanations, rise I know not what scents, what dewy freshness that revives my heart. The figures I speak of are not all young, not all beautiful; no; they have merely the charm of reality. Their sober, simple outline stands out after the manner of the old masters from a clear and transparent ground.

I am one of those who love the things that are past; things that, quitting as it were our terrestrial region, rise to mid-heaven in a limpid atmosphere that lends them an infinite charm.

About to emerge into the brilliant light of day, I linger for an instant; my gaze follows shadows soon to be effaced; profiles, some frank and fair, others a little sad; these singing on in their spring, those dreaming on in their winter; some full of mystery, others very simple, and such as we see every day. And there are landscapes too; sometimes two trees and a few leaves, vividly green against the blue, like those in which Perugino framed his holy families; sometimes the thick forest, the vigorous growth of the July grass, the woodland songs, the flowers in full blossom.

It is all this that I would contemplate, muse on a little during that short uncertain hour which folds back its veil before the splendours of the morning.

There is nothing here for utilitarians, nothing for so-called realists, for lovers of the dramatic, for acute connoisseurs; nothing, indeed, I believe, for any but me and those like me—dreamers, satisfied with little, whom a great poem scares, but a flower half-opened, a holiday bee, a rustic outline, can throw into infinite reverie.

If this once begins, there is hardly any end to it. It is not a series of pictures, it is still less romance. What, then? Truly, I do not know. It is that unknown something which sings within, the wide undulations of whose voice expand as we advance, and sometimes blend ideal melodies with the most common details of the most prosaic life. It is that something which is artist too; whose pencil can, while our bodily eyes turn from the grocer's shop to the tavern at the corner, flash out upon us the green of the meadow, the darker green of the forest, the ruddy gold of the sunset, the pale gold of the sunrise, passing over the spirit of life with the spirit of poetry. And it is, besides, that hidden poet who, as we are moving on wearily through life as it has been made to us, keeps repeating in the depths of our soul strange words, words replete with wild harmony, words that the gentleman with whom you are chatting would hardly understand, nay, that you yourself, alas! in your common-sense business hours, would treat as mere fancies, although they charm you, soothe you, transport you into serene regions where you would live, where you would gladly die.

It is just this that I have to impart to you. The hand will be inexpert, the voice often trembling; the poor poet, frightened at his own boldness, will perhaps stop short; the play-bill is promising, the piece poor. What matters it! The reader is the true author. I may stammer; your genius will sing: I may let you fall on the way; your imagination, light-winged messenger, will bear you further than my steps could reach.

Every book is, in fact, a journey; a journey in which we find little more than we ourselves bring; the richly provided, richly acquire. I do not possess very much; if you have kindliness, some love for God's nature, the dower of capacity for simple pleasures, come, let us take our way through this meadow, by the side of that stream; we two together, our fortune is made.

LISETTE'S DREAM.

IT was by that very meadow, and by that stream, I took my way, one fine May morning.

The grass was thick and tall, the starry primroses were over, the blue clusters of the squill withered long ago, the last petals of the fruit-trees were lost in the thicket as they fell,—the summer gained the victory over the spring. But this had not been without some sharp encounters; *tussles*, as our peasants say.

The blackthorn, the first, had had many a *tussle* then with drifts of soon melted snow, the hawthorn with cool showers that soaked the red twigs of the hedges, the cuckoo and the blackbird with a return of cold winds blowing over the scarcely unfolded leaves; but, spite of storm and frost, the April days—beautiful lengthening days, pressing back with both hands the shades of morning and evening—had marched on young, triumphant, crowned with lilacs; while, at the touch of their fingers, the hedges, the apple-trees, the ground, burst into blossom. And now summer was at hand; her warm breath was already felt on the buttercup-covered meadows; while, from the neighbouring mountains, from the snowy summit of the Jura, came still a keen, reviving breeze, the virgin kiss of the departing spring.

In our country each flower in succession has its own absolute reign. The sun, looking through the windows of the fantastical dwellings assigned to him in almanacs—the sun, according as he inhabits the sign of the Ram, the Bull, the Twins, or the Scorpion, covers our valleys, far as eye can reach, with white crocuses, then yellow primroses, then hyacinths, then lilac-tinted cardamines, then golden ranunculuses. There is almost always one sheet of colour, splendid in its uniformity. It is true that in March, by the hedge side, balmy violets and fumitories; along the brooks, and at the foot of the oak-trees, rosy white anemones; do what they can to blossom in tufts. The observant eye may, indeed, detect them in their nests, but they do not affect the general aspect of the valley, which always presents a dazzling carpet of one single shade, till towards the end of June it is enamelled with every hue, radiant with every kind of brightness, each flower opening, displaying itself, scattering fragrance on its own account.

There is, indeed, in May—at the very time I was taking this particular walk—a short season when green is the dominant tone; a harsh, crude, uncompromising green, without any softening touch of red or yellow, or any delicate silvery light. This green is somewhat oppressive, I might almost say sad.

It was so that morning. The grass I walked on had such a glaring brightness; the leaves of the hedge, whether hawthorn leaves, sweetbrier, willow, or alder, were all so varnished and brilliant, you could hardly look at them. On the mountain side, the bright verdure of the beech so prevailed over the sombre foliage of the pines, spread so lustrously and positively on every side, rose so boldly up to the pasture-land, itself so decidedly verdant too, that, apart from the cupola of snow upon the very summit, one could see nothing but this intense green, which seemed to repress thought.

And yet there were the walnut-trees, the great walnut-trees, which were not green. They, at least, protested;

opening out, at the extremity of their smooth, whitish branches, bunches of purple and aromatic leaves.

Then there was the brook, whose perfectly pure waters ran over a now smooth, now stony bed, sometimes encountering a little moss-covered block, round which they broke, singing those eternal songs that ears like mine could listen to by night and day.

Then, again, there were the bees; young bees, of a lighter brown, a more delicate velvet; inexperienced, lost in some flower-chalice, intoxicated and overtaken, far from the hive, by the dew and the evening chill.

Ah! how many of those thoughtless ones did I save, fishing them out from the eddies of the brook, in a large leaf or the hollow of my hand! How many I collected at sunset, wings wet, benumbed, half dead, placing them in some warm shelter, safe from the lizard, or else on some dry bough looking to the east, that the early rays might restore them to life! How many I took back to the hives, and tried to get them admittance there! Alas! it is the same with bees as with us; the ladies of the hive came out, felt the intruder all over, turned her round and round, and pushed her out of their community. The more suffering the creature, the more severe the reception; while the latest comers, those belonging to the last swarm of the last hive, boldly thrust the victim through with their stings; then, dragging her by her legs to the edge of the platform, let her fall into the field of death below, amidst the drones, their defunct husbands.

Whether it was owing to the green or the drones, I know not; but that morning I went on my way sadly. The glory of the spring did nothing for me.

Do you know hours when the demon of analysis, the bad angel of our age, brushes against you with his cold wings? Do you know what it is to explore your affections, your thoughts, and to say of them all, What do they profit?

The young are more subject to this complaint than the old. Which of us has not descended those desolate slopes, has not seated himself weeping in that sterile valley, which the sun has forsaken, has not remained there, counting his wounds, finding a fatal pleasure in saying to himself that all is over, that happiness is wrecked, faith extinguished, faculties weakened, tenderness dead; that life, like a faded flower, has let fall petal after petal, and that there is nothing more to be done but to let old age come, and then death.

At such times it seems as though we were wandering in one of those ruined planets, those extinct worlds whose lurid light still traverses the sky. Then we see things as they are, or rather as they would be, if the wondrous brightness of day, if perfume, harmony, blue atmospheric depths were all taken away from us, and our earth left bare. Everything becomes dry, hard, resolvable into problems, the positive solution of which destroys our last illusions. The task which charmed me with its time-speeding magic, it has no use, teaches nothing, is worth nothing! Those melodies which wafted me into realms of serenity, they are flat, monotonous, wearisome! My pencil, nothing either! My friends, my beloved, that image closest to the heart; oh, it is here that the abyss yawns; here there is dead silence, and the demon speaks in his doubting voice:—Your father, your child, your wife! you are their treasure, you are the breath of their soul, the days they live away from you are days of heaviness; if you are late, they are anxious; if you suffer, they are sad; if you died, they would die too? No! they would not die; they could do without you! You believe yourself essential, you are not; you believe that you give happiness, others would give more; you think that were you taken out of their life, that life would be shattered. Not so. It would resume its course, would pass through other regions, other flowers, to blossom under other skies. The thought of you, passionately cherished at first, would recede towards the distant horizon, would remain suspended there, and only rare intervals and hours of sadness would lead them back to you.

No one is indispensable to any other; there is but one thing imperishable, and that is the need we have of being happy at any cost.

We have more vitality than the hydra. Cut, cut away, lop off here and there, strew the ground with our limbs, leave only a bleeding trunk; it will writhe, then it will stanch its wounds, then it will glide into some new path, under the leaves, amidst the grass, it will find some shady retreat, and it will live.

This is worst of all, to own to ourselves that we can be mutilated and yet survive; that after such severance the wound can close; after the thunderbolt the sky grow clear; that with the heart torn out we may walk on without any unbearable pain; that failing a life interpenetrated with love, we can create for ourselves a narrow quiet existence, where mere mind or matter prevails according to individual temperament, that the day may come when we honestly confess to be better off after than before the storm, and to journey on more comfortably alone; a day when a horrible egotism may sit a victor on the ruins of all our past. This is the supreme misfortune; to find ourselves at last alone, self-contemplating, self-satisfied, self-conscious that self is our all in all. This is the source of mortal disgust and sovereign disdain.

I was going along, a bitter smile upon my lips, a bitter

indifference at my heart, reduced to despair, as negation after negation fell on me like blows from an axe; when I chanced to raise my eyes and saw the country, saw it magnificent, exuberantly fresh; saw the barley fields that promised harvest, the young bunches of grapes that promised the vintage; saw the tufted fields, the orchards, laden with fruit, the bees and the butterflies flying off in quest of pillage, the peasant going to his work. The earth is beautiful, I said to myself, the earth is good! Then I raised my glance up the mountain side, higher than the beeches, higher than the pines, higher than the chalets, than the pastures, up, up to the snow, up to that sparkling cupola whose white outline sharply cuts the deep blue sky, up to that region of Paradise! O ye heavens, ye are great and glorious! My God, thou art the mighty One, the Eternal!—Love! It is only that which I have been ignoring all this while! The love of God, the love which came down to us, the love which defies time and space, the immortal, imperishable love Thou hast put into the heart of man!

Our years will pass, our faculties fade, our loved ones depart; nothing of us will remain save poor old withered bodies that drag themselves into the sunshine; all will die. No, all lives, love though buried beneath the snows of age, love glows unextinguished. It breathes in wordless prayers, it looks back to cherished memories, forward to the land of promise. The cheeks are wrinkled, the lips wear a smile the vigorous call childish, the eye is dull; we seem to have merely a pale effigy, aimlessly wandering amidst a new generation. Do not think so; below the surface there are tears, strong hopes, there is a whole vast world, there is a human heart, there is the Infinite.

Nothing that has ever truly lived is lost, nothing useless; not a sigh, a joy, or a sorrow which has not served its purpose. Our tears are numbered, the fragrance of our innocent pleasures mounts heavenward as a sweet-smelling savour. Let us take courage; honest labour, upright thoughts, healthy emotions endure. Let us give, love, become as little children, so shall we reach self-forgetfulness, that supreme possession, that dominion over the universe.

Yes, so it is; in our day there are young people who are old, having exhausted everything; who are indifferent, sceptical, weary as a traveller at nightfall. And there are old people who are young, ready-witted, with sparkling eyes and energetic hearts, easily pleased, open to innocent enjoyments. And such as these,—this spring blossoming so near death, this union of simplicity and native dignity, this green intellect, this indulgent benevolence, this ready cheerfulness, have a charm for my nature which almost excites emotion.

It was just such an old woman as this that I was going to see.

Before entering the village, I stopped a little on the hill. On one side, the valley stretched out in its green attire very far below to the blue lake; further still, full of vapour, to the white Alps. On the other side, behind the village, the mountain sloped down to the highest houses, all dotted with beech and fir, with orchards intermixed; and as I had climbed to some height, I found those trees still blossoming which had done flowering below.

There was no longer that glaring green which had thrown me into such a strange train of thought. The dome of the apple-trees rounded itself rosy-white, relieved here and there with crimson buds; the pear-trees rose in silver pyramids, immaculate, almost hard in their brilliancy. There was an infinite variety of hues. The branches, laden with garlands, surrounded with humming bees, stooped down into the grass; the topmost flowers kissed the lowest; not a leaf dared to shew. The hawthorn displayed all around its small stars spotted with purple stamens; through its gaps you saw roofs; bright panes of glass; and on the hill, near those lazy rocks sunning themselves up there, blackened spaces shewed where the woman had been beating out the hemp last autumn.

The goats were just setting out for the mountains; little boys driving them along the wood-paths; you could hear their bells; a kid, perched in the middle of a bush, gave a startled glance at the grand procession, then returned eagerly to nibble the young shoots about him. The peasants were all at work in the country; the village was deserted.

How charming a village is! how charming those fountains, with wooden basins! if the village be rich, with stone ones, with the water trickling down and running over.

In the evening, the cows come heavily by, drink slowly, and return to their stalls, scattering sparkling drops from their cool, wet muzzles. The pleasant smell of hay is wafted from the open barns. Women come and go, and wash vegetables at the fountain; men, seated before their houses, sharpen their scythes, and fill the air with metallic notes; children sing and dabble, and heap up handfuls of fine sand; hens seek their food with that little, anxious, monotonous cluck, that protest of a good housewife, who sighs each time she puts by a millet seed; cocks, proudly thrown back on their tails, send forth a warlike cry, which gets repeated by all the sultans near.

But on the day I speak of, it was morning; the village was silent; you only heard beneath a heap of fagots, in some mysterious corner, the self-complacent cackling of the laying hen.

To reach Lisette's house, (it was to her I was going,) I had to pass through a barn. Now, barns give me untold satisfaction; I feel at home in them; my heart expands. My hand is scarcely on the latch of the little door, with its two separate halves; my foot has hardly touched the floor, covered with newly-mown grass; I have hardly inhaled the perfume of last year's hay, heaped up on both sides of me, when I feel a perfect flood of happiness. Am I related to the cattle? Perhaps so; to those oxen, for instance, whose noses are pushed right and left through the open rack, into the hay-loft, enjoying as well as I the sweet smell of the new grass. I have not the least objection to claim kinship; but so it is, that my heart leaps again, and I thank God, who has made meadow, skies, oxen, barns, and me. Everything is beautiful, everything is wondrous! Life is an ineffable gift: death, a triumph. Men are brothers: the poor, precious friends. To give pleasure, to dry tears,—it is heaven on earth! Ah! for once good-bye to analysis; this is not to be defined, scarcely to be understood; it is a sudden radiance, the illumination of the soul; it is a hymn that bursts out at once in all directions. I have often thought that woods, fields, nests, moss-covered hollows, sent up just such an anthem to the Lord.

Having passed through the barn, here we are at Lisette's, in her dark, flagged kitchen, with a large chimney, into which the fowls sometimes adventure themselves; then we pass in her bright, cheerful room, with a window looking on the street. It is here Lisette is to be found.

Close to the lighted stove, (for it is still cold, and one is glad of fires in the morning, before the sunbeams shine through the cloudy panes of glass,)—close to the stove, sits Lisette's old husband, half sleeping, half musing, his hands resting on the iron pot about to boil, his head on his hands, his white knitted cap drawn over his eyes.

Generally, when he sees me, Lisette's husband rises, stretches himself, scratches his forehead, says—"One must be looking after the cows," and goes away.

I think that his wife and I—taken in combination, that is to say—weary him. His wife is a thinker: he can excuse this, as long as she is silent; when I arrive, we talk. This worthy man, who, during the whole of his fourscore years, has discerned little more than the four seasons succeeding each other; hay-time, harvest, vintage, then ploughing and sowing, then finally death, repose, not to say annihilation,—this good man of ours mistrusts us. He perceives vaguely that we speak a strange language; thoughts stir there which disquiet him, questions that embarrass; a certain consciousness of inferiority comes over him,—he never has it at other times. The humble old woman has never been aware of the keen intelligence, the depths of thought within her. "Stuff and nonsense!" mutters the good man to himself; opens the door, and disappears.

Lisette, as well as her husband, has run her fourscore years or thereabouts. Lame of one leg, but erect and well made, there she is on her old, straight-backed arm-chair. Pretty children—her grandchildren—surround her, formidable hunches of cake in hand. "Just go and play out there in front," says she; and they disappear, like a flight of starlings.

There is nothing now in the room but the bed with chintz curtains, with great blue branches, on a red ground; some walnut chairs, well polished; the stove, the table with turned legs, the great press, carved in a former age, and the old woman seated near the window, close to her pot of green marjoram, close to her rose geranium which bushes out in a cracked earthen pan.

Poor as are the adjuncts, the figure is charming. Slender, as I said, rather thin, with noble features, a pale complexion, colourless without being withered; gray hair almost hid under a cap of the thick lace our great-grandmothers used to wear; black eyes, as young as they were at twenty, soft, limpid eyes, which look into, and allow you to look into the soul. A smile completes the face. It is not an inadvertant, it is not a triumphant smile; it is a smile in which blend such freshness, such exquisite delicacy, such sweet graciousness, that, once seen, it floats eternally in the memory. I shall be laughed at, but I have never seen more than one mouth that reminded me of Lisette, and that was the mouth of the Joconda. Lisette's had the same sudden brightness, and ineffable fascination, *minus* the wild flash, *plus* the angelic goodness.

Lisette was a spiritualist; there are such in villages. She had been an excellent manager in her day; had baked, fed her cattle, worked hard in hay-time. She had taken her part in the vintage, wielded the rake, dug the garden, spun enough to fill all the presses in her cottage from top to bottom. On washing-days, the hedges round were rich with her treasures; no one more apt to labour, more prudent as to expense, but while her arms were employed her brain was active. And now that all she could do to amuse herself was to mend clothes, or wind thread, thought had got the upper hand.

Lisette had a soul; she was conscious of it, nay, she was anxious about it. This is not common in our days, in the country any more than in towns. Lisette belonged to that austerely brought-up generation, kept under by their fathers—grand, grave men, who governed by a look, without waste of words. They had strong natures, and lived soberly in their sheltered nooks. No network of good roads joined, as now, hamlets to villages, villages to cities. Local papers had scarcely an existence. Ten years might pass without a new book drifting into their dwellings. Nevertheless, the peasant read on Sunday winter nights; read the Bible, that history of nations, that philosophy of the heart, that divine poetry, that speech of God to man; and he made his children read it, their little fingers following each word, and that generation, growing up thus beneath the shadow of Judea's palm-trees, in direct relation to the God of heaven, fed on faith, early subject to duty, that generation had a character at once gentle and courageous, calm and reflective, poetical and ideal, such as our age most certainly will not transmit to its children.

Lisette had grown up under that system, had breathed the very air of the East. For her, Ruth and Naomi, Sarah, Moses, and Rachel who would not be comforted, were personages more living, more real than the great Napoleon and his twelve marshals.

She had no very distinct recollection of the Revolution of '89; its terrible echoes had but faintly shaken the mighty wall of the Jura. All the noise made in France, the days of July; many other glorious days; insurrectionary cannonades; popular cry of a Republic; acclamations of the Empire,—all these died away on the moss of the forests, in the thick tangle of the beech-trees. The winter blasts through the pines had a louder voice, an eternal wail that prevailed over them all.

Above the beautiful region she inhabited, and beyond the limits of her actual life, a world had opened out to

Lisette, even from her earliest days. It was the Hebrew world. There the camels and caravans of the Ishmaelitish merchantmen passed through the desert; there Hagar wept under the palm-tree; there the transparent waters of the Red Sea stood on a heap; there more golden sheaves and richer ears of corn waved on the fields of Bethlehem beneath a softer breeze which had kissed the pomegranates in blossom. There, too, smoked Mount Sinai; there stood Moses, his face bright with mysterious radiance, breaking the tables of the law before the dancing and delirious people.

Even as a child, when she used to take the cows to feed in the forest glades, the wild strawberries having been once gathered, and small gardens planted here and there, Lisette would sit down beneath some spreading pine, on the smooth surface made by its falling spikes, her eyes wandering from the black to the brindled cow, and in that wood-enclosed pasture she would begin to dream. She dreamed of Jacob's flocks, of Leah, of the wondrous ladder; with the intense gaze of her soul fixed on the depths of past ages, deriving thence the simple faith, the fresh purity of the time when man was young upon the earth. She spoke to God; God spoke to her.

Had an angel, palm in hand, appeared before her there under the great pine, it would not have surprised her; she would have prostrated herself; would humbly have laid her basket of strawberries at his feet. Oh, if it might but have been!

How often Lisette had steadily contemplated the infinite sky, to catch some golden beam descending on her straight from Paradise! If the juniper bush that shadowed her strawberry plants had suddenly kindled with supernatural flame, Lisette would have approached as did Moses;

putting her shoes from off her feet, she would have received the divine command with a simple heart.

Was Lisette then a visionary? By no means; she had too much common sense for that. With her bodily eyes she never saw anything but the fields, the cows, and the blue sky overhead; but she believed, moved, and lived calm and thoughtful in the realm of faith.

Her piety had a touch of austerity and timidity; there was a reserve about her which rather reminded you of the women of the Old Testament than of the New. She had a great fear of offending God; she loved from afar, very humbly, reverence almost veiling love. Brought up rather on the precepts of Moses than the revelation of Christ, you would have taken her for one of the Israelitish women who followed Miriam when, sounding the cymbal with a triumphant hand, she celebrated Pharaoh's defeat. Or again, she resembled that Shunammite intent on hospitably receiving the servant of the Lord: modest, with burning heart beneath all her reserve, who, when her son died, laid him on the prophet's bed, then boldly went to seek the man of God, and say, "Did I desire a son of my lord?"

Lisette's serious aspect, serious and serene, recalled those times. She possessed fervour, judgment, veneration; beneath her gray hairs the ingenuity of her girlhood; a clear mind that saw death coming, a delicate conscience, that mere honesty did not satisfy; a native intelligence always turning over grave problematical questions. She teased no one, nor agitated herself; everything in her was sober and sagacious; only when she spoke of her end, her smile was rather sad, and with a most loveable shake of her head, she would say—"Well, I hope indeed—but can God really forgive me?"

Now, Lisette's sin, you may well believe, was no crime

it was the sin of us all—your sin, alas! and mine; petulance, a warm temper, a few hasty words, many years spent without much thought of God; a heart unapt to lay hold on Him; easily turned away.

The majority call this virtue. Not so Lisette; she saw things too clearly. Her searching, logical mind was not one to be lured by a toy, or satisfied with a show. If diverted a moment, it was sure to return.

Lisette had never trifled with that deep need of holiness, that thirst after truth which kindles sooner or later in all elect souls. She was incessantly occupied in contemplating the mystery of death, and of what comes after it.

" Do this and live," cried to her, from the summit of Sinai, the voice that thundered amidst the lightnings. " Only believe!" said the voice which speaks from the bleeding cross.

Lisette believed, hoped, loved; but her pale face, turned towards the desert, bore the impress of a holy terror; her heart dared not expand; she sat trembling on the threshold of Eden, and sometimes saw the flaming sword of the cherubim turned against her.

It was of this we were conversing.

She shewed me the awful Jehovah; I pointed her to the God of Abraham: she spoke to me of sin; I spoke to her of pardon: she said to me, I have erred too much; I said to her, He has suffered more.

Do not be alarmed, I am not going to treat you to theology; not that I despise it, but I should be awkward at it,—Lisette, too. For my part I hold in reverence all who lead a life of thought, theologians as well as others. To eat, drink, sleep, dress well, and to-morrow die, has never prepossessed my fancy much,—nor Lisette's either. To go through life like a great burly drone, knocking up against flowers, burying his proboscis in their cups, without looking or wondering at anything, without even inhaling the perfume of the blossoms he pierces, then, when evening comes, to die congealed beneath the leaves, or to be killed in a matter-of-fact way by a bee who has done with him,—whatever may be said for it, neither Lisette nor I find any sense or any poetry in a course like this. But dreamers—I do not mean by this empty dreamers; I mean the dealers with ideas, those who go digging into some rich vein, deep down in the mine, or soar on daring wing beyond the skies,—these, however poor their condition or their outward man, we—Lisette who knows none of them, and I who know but few—hold these to be true sages, great poets. In fact, it is just they who take the world in tow. Not easy-going people, elastic, satisfied with themselves and with all else, because seeing little beyond their particular peck of oats; but souls with vigorous griefs and mighty joys, men of the day-time, who want light everywhere, who prefer suffering to a truth-haunted sleep, who feel themselves travellers, pilgrims, wrestlers, always under arms, on the march, in the battle; often bruised, harassed, losing courage, but sometimes visited by such fulness of joy, believing so boldly what they do believe, reigning so absolutely in the realm of soul, sowing so richly the soil they tread, conquering so triumphantly the adverse circumstances barking at their heels, that as we see them pass we feel that they are indeed the masters, the living men, and all others slaves, dead!

I say all this to explain Lisette to you. She was a domestic creature, easy to live with, peaceful, smiling, especially to children; a superficial observer would have taken her for the type of serenity. But inwardly in a very ferment of thought, satisfied with difficulty, never satisfied with false reasoning. And as she knew nothing of society, politics, or science, the great problem of Eternity hung ever motionless before her, one side lit by faith, the other shadowed by doubt.

"I am sad," said Lisette to me. "Listen; you will laugh, but I have had a dream."

"Dreams are liars," answered I, foolishly enough.

"Oh, dear no! Dreams are not all true, I know, yet Joseph dreamed; Pharaoh saw the seven fat, then the seven lean kine come out of the rushes of the river; it was God who made him see them."

"Yes, God can employ"——

"The Lord has many messengers," she broke in; then she shook her head. "It has left a gloom upon me."

"Come, tell it me, Lisette."

"You will laugh; but it 's no matter, I am going to tell it.

"I was walking in a meadow, towards evening; the sun was down, the plants drooped, clouds of dust rose from the road,—a wide, smooth road; much quality went along it, coaches, riders, merchants, gentlemen, men walking behind their cows, poor people, too—a crowd like a fair. They all went one way; I did not trouble myself about where it led, did not seem much to care, it was as though I understood without knowing—I am tiring you."

"Not at all."

"Old people are slow."

"Take your time."

"I had not chosen that road, yet I went with the rest. I walked on the grass easily enough, though I was in a great hurry.

"On one side, under the thorns, I saw a rough path; one of those mountain tracks full of brambles and stones, felled trees that one had to stride over, roots on a level with the ground in which the foot caught. There was no crowd there; every now and then some heavily-laden traveller, some woman, looking harassed and sad. They sat down, or rather all but fell; then they looked to the top of the hill, took courage, rose, settled their baggage better on their shoulders, and bending under it, dragged on amongst the stones.

"The others, those on the highway, had not taken any notice of me; these gave me sad looks, but said nothing. I was uncomfortable; it seemed as though they were mourning over my fate. As for me, badly off as they were, I did not pity them, never thought of doing so.

"I said to myself, Suppose I go to them! I did try. I went aside, and got upon the path; the stones rolled down. I felt weary, as if I had been beaten; I hurt my foot against a pebble, and returned to the meadow. Then those in the path looked at me more sadly than before, and went on.

"I had a weight at my heart. But evening was closing in; there was nothing for it but going on, though as I went I trembled. A fear came over me. All at once it broke upon me that we were all going towards death. Then I tried to get back into the path; but there was no longer any path, any travellers, only the great green meadow stretching far as eye could reach, and I was walking alone in the middle of it.

"I beg your pardon!"

Lisette was in tears! Then she recovered.

"At the end of the great meadow, I saw a beautiful dwelling; a square house, very large, very high, not one side larger or higher than the other. This house was of gold, bright as the sun at noon; the grass went close up to the walls; the setting sun shone through the clear windows, and fell upon it

"A great rush of joy came over me! I was happy! No one had told me so, but I knew quite well that this dwelling was the Paradise of God. When I came close to it, I looked for the door; there was none on that side; there were only the large windows, with their bright panes, transparent as water, the red sunset darting through them. I went round the house; no door. I went round again; none. There was only the grass and the windows. I felt, searched about. Fear came over me again. At last I returned to the front, and looked up. Behind one of the windows of clear glass, I saw an old woman like myself, only handsomely dressed in black silk, with white hair, and a severe, though sweet look, sitting up and knitting. She went on knitting, without seeing me. She looked very happy. I cried out, or seemed to do so. Then she turned towards me. 'You have made a mistake,' she said; 'you did not take the right road. You will not get in, my daughter.' Then, with a calm face, she took to her knitting again; and as for me, I fell dead."

You are inclined, perhaps, to laugh; if you had seen Lisette, you would not have been so. She was pale; fear, that fear of God which hath torment, had got hold of her. She turned and re-turned her dream in her mind. She could not treat it lightly; she was too pious for that. She could not pray; the servile dread of the slave paralysed her heart.

"Lisette," I said, "you have told me a dream; I will tell you a story, a very short one.

"One spring day in Judea, just as the corn was ripening, a crowd was coming out of the city. With much tumult and loud cries, they were leading three men to execution. Of these three, two had killed, stolen, pillaged; they were thieves: the other had announced God's pardon; it was Jesus.

"They nailed them to the cross. One of the criminals insulted Jesus; the other, suddenly struck, said—'Dost thou not fear God? as for us, we are punished justly; but this man!' Then turning to Jesus,—'Lord, remember me!' He got in safe, Lisette! What road, then, had he taken?"

Lisette kept a solemn silence; a divine light dispelled the shadows on her brow.

"Neither the highway, nor that terrible mountain path, had he, Lisette?"

Lisette looked at me; her beautiful black eyes shone; the sweet, pure smile played round her mouth. "He believed," she said.

That day we philosophised no more.

Her husband came back; the children ran in; the hens popped their beaks in at the half-opened door. Lisette returned to her winding; I to the road that led down into the valley.

At the present time, many winters have passed since Lisette entered the golden house.

Does she knit on, from age to age, impassive in her beatitude, by the side of that matron with the silver hair? I do not think so; I believe her living, active in heaven as on earth. All anxiety over, immutable happiness, supreme life, reveal their mysteries to her ardent soul.

THE THREE ROSES.

THREE roses early faded on earth; three roses which bloom in heaven.

They were three; their name was Rose; they died before they were twenty.

They belonged to the same family; were, I believe, cousins; but they hardly, if at all, knew each other, because of their difference of age. When one was being carried to the grave, the other, flaxen-haired and laughing, was playing in her spring-time along the roadside.

I.

I saw the first when she was quite a child. She lived with her father, her mother, and a brother younger than herself, in a farm on the border of a wood.

We shall not have to go far into the wood. I only want you to know that the farmhouse was spacious, well-built, turned full towards the east; with a roof that projected like a cowl, as though the better to protect the family; that a splendid row of hives filled the garden with their humming; that the garden itself had rose-trees that were a perfect spectacle, red poppies, heart's-ease, marigolds; that the vine, with its golden leaves, had crept to the granary; and that the wood of planted oak-trees—venerable oaks, their stems lost in the coppice below—was the home of all the bees in the country. They formed a great aviary, open to the sky,—where, from daybreak, blackbirds whistled, and tomtits, chaffinches, wrens, robin-redbreasts, and the whole tribe of vocalists, kept up such a chatter that the nightingale, though he bred there, had some difficulty in maintaining his supremacy. However, when he did set to in good earnest, you heard no one else. He filled all the forest nooks with his loud gushes of song.

There is one exquisite hour in an oak-wood; that particular moment in spring when the underwood is all green, while the old trees are not yet fully out. At their feet there is an inveterate entanglement of honeysuckle, elder-bushes, clematis,—all vigorous, full-grown, in the first glory of their first leaves, with tall plants intermingled; while above, at a great height, spreads the light dome of the mighty trees. Look where you will, it is luminous; there is above you, rather a green cloud—an emerald transparency—than decided verdure. The very atmosphere is green; green seems floating in the air, blending with the blue of the sky. There are none of the intense tones of summer; none of the warm colouring, the broad, massive touches of July; everything is distinct, everywhere there is shade; and against the soft green of the young foliage you can trace the bold outlines of the dark trunks and the gnarled branches of the oaks.

In these woods, Rose and her brother gathered glorious nosegays; in April, of the periwinkle, which covered the ground with its blue stars; in May, of the lily of the valley, which hides itself beneath the brambles, and grows in the shade over the roots of the old oaks. Oh, delight of being there well concealed! of creeping along in spite of a thousand scratches! and while the nightingale dwells upon some wondrous note, all the other birds warbling too, of looking for, step by step, then suddenly coming upon, a very show of select treasures! "Are not there lots of them?" "Shall I shout to my brother?" Conscience deliberates; meanwhile the hand is busy; it gathers, gathers. There they are, those darling lilies! pure, modest flowers! There they are! very straight, very strong; with their little reversed urns, the lowest in blow, the highest in bud. There are others on the mountains; delicate, differently shaped, more ethereal in their perfume; but they are not the true lily of the valley; the genuine, the old-fashioned, the lily of the valley of our songs, of our grandmothers. So they are left; the wood-pea too, with its changing colour, the orchis, everything but the lilies are left. The fingers can scarcely close over the bunch gathered. What a smell of spring! the very ideal of freshness! You would say that it contained all the magic of the month of May; the clear sky, the young foliage, the birds' song.

Little shouts are interchanged.

"Have you found some?"

"Yes."

"A good place?"

Silence.

There is no pursuit where selfishness shews itself more plainly than in this pursuit of lilies of the valley. One is silent. To say *no*, would be a falsehood; to say *yes*, would be to lose one's prize. So we make all the haste we can; if scrupulous, we murmur something very vague indeed; and the treasures secured, we slip away, far away, to some other fragrant hiding-place, all covered with white bells.

In this manner Rose went through the wood; and when she reached the high ground, where the lilies do not venture, she got uneasy, and called her brother, who came, with trousers torn, and three poor sprigs in his hand.

"All that!" she said, and then shewed her great bunch.

"Oh!" sighed the little fellow; and his poor flowers dropped from his fingers. Then they walked on that short, smooth, elastic mountain sod, which spreads itself out, as it were, at random.

This open ground belongs to no one in particular; it is a common, where on Sundays old and young walk, in the week, sheep graze,—a hall of verdure, shaded here and there by some ancient oak; neither field nor meadow, only turf, trees, mountain flowers; a place of which no one says, "It is mine," "It is John's," "It is Peter's,"—it is the domain of the poor, of children, of all; it is the one little spot which Poetry, driven out by potatoes, may claim as her own.

Rose wandered there, arranging her nosegay; her brother trotted and gambolled about. Neither of them looked at the Alps on the horizon, or the blue lake in the distance, motionless in the midst of its green cup. They did not listen to the bells that were ringing—that grave harmony, dilating in the air; they hardly felt the morning breeze careering over the country; the sloping turf, that grew wilder, and began here and there to be dotted with pines; the great mountain blocks, the hamlets surrounded with orchards; the scattered houses of various styles;—all this, that would have delighted a painter, they were hardly aware of. They walked on at random, wrapped in a ray of soft yellow light, apparently unconscious of the magical scene around.

And yet it is these May delights; this free breath of the woods; it is the scent of the pine, the perfume of the lily; the skies of our valleys, shut in by the peaks of our Alps, the dark sides of Jura,—it is all this, on the plains of laughing Italy, which rises to the heart of our sons, and causes them to desert or tc die; it is this, too, which, in the midst of cities, comes and whispers to them I know not what enchanted words, which tarnish all the luxury around, and make their tears flow.

On Sunday, the court of the old manor-house was opened to the village children. Rose and her brother ran off there in haste, through vineyards and meadows. That was the place for amusement! Good people, those people of the manor-house; no pride about them,—visionary, letting every one have his own way.

The children in troops—there were at least sixty of them —seated on benches, under the shade of great plane-trees, their legs hanging down, and swinging to and fro to mark the rhyme, sang plaintive songs. Verse followed verse—simple, and rather sad—accompanied by the monotonous music of two fountains; then the children darted off all at once, like a flight of starlings, no one knew why, and formed great circles, enclosing the whole court, singing catches—"*C'est le chevalier du guet; c'est un beau château,*" &c.—which were still plaintive, so surely is there melancholy at the root of all things, even of pleasure. Suddenly the circle would break up; then came wild races, screams, joy in simple existence.

Rose, a little frightened, played by herself in a corner, making discreet little springs and jumps of her own. Her brother threw himself into the midst of the games and dances, and, shaking his curly head, bounded as the lambs bound amongst the wild thyme.

When evening came, all went home again; the others in troops, these two alone. Rose and her brother passed timidly, for it was nightfall—under the white church, under the cemetery. The moon, shining in the sky, accompanied them with her soft glance. They quickened their step as they got near the wood.

Here are the gardens! here are the beans! here are our cabbages! They recovered their voices; nay, the brother returned home like a hero, bellowing out in his deepest tones some rough vintage song. Once at home, there was the bright fire, the mother, and they recounted all the wonders of the manor-house.

One Sunday, neither the brother nor the sister came.

The boy was stretched out in his little bed, at the foot of his parents' large one. Beside him sat his father, gloomy, hollow-eyed, and speechless. The mother was on her knees, raising her child. Rose looked on, wondering and silent.

Death was hovering round the child's brow. His complexion was not livid, his features were not drawn; but by the glory spread over the face, by the eye swimming in ethereal brightness, you knew well that he was about to go.

"Mother, mother!" he said, looking through the open window at the sky. His mother leaned forward, and grew pale. "Mother, I see beautiful angels! Do you see them, father?" Then he stretched out his arms, and passed away.

Years, too, passed away.

Rose was growing up. She was a young girl—handsome, sensible, sedate, leading a retired kind of life. You met her sometimes when they were thinning the vines, her petticoats tucked up, a load of vine leaves lightly balanced on her head. With one finger she steadied it; the branches, with their indented leaves, fell round her, veiling her slight figure; she walked with that firm, modest, active step, which carries young working girls to their home. If you happened to stop her for a moment, her cheeks crimsoned, she looked at you innocently, then returned a few timid words, neither bold nor awkward: then went on her way, and you asked yourself what wood-nymph had brushed you by with her robe.

Her eighteenth birthday came; the village band came too, one fine July twilight, after the harvest was over.

The violins came, scraping; they were heard from a distance; they came all through the village, through the wood; the young men walking after them, then the girls.

"I'll run away!" said Rose.

"Simpleton!" returned her mother, half through timidity, half for fear of any talk.

The clarionet sounded gaily, the notes dropped off like pearls, capered with a shrill falsetto, which made the woods laugh again. Rose was agitated; she felt her feet dance under her. Her heart beat, her eyes shone, and yet she could have wished herself on the very top of the mountain—far away!

The band came nearer, the playful character of the tune was distinctly heard—an old-fashioned German waltz, an irresistible measure. Yet Rose was inclined to cry; it was as though the peace, the ignorance of her youth, were flapping their wings as they flew away.

Soon you could distinguish laughter, you heard the rustling of leaves, you saw the procession come winding through the branches.

"Mother, the beautiful angels!" What voice at that moment repeated those words to the heart of Rose? Why are mournful images so often conjured up by a burst of laughter? Rose drew back.

"Mother, tell them not."

But her mother, a simple creature, was not given to take the initiative; and, besides, Rose was eighteen—ought she not to go with the rest? if she kept apart, folks would say that she was proud. And here was the band, here were the young men and the girls deploying at the door.

"Now then, Rose, we are come for you. The whole village, you see. You can't think of affronting us!"

And as Rose seemed to shrink, two or three of her young friends came forward from the rest.

"Come, Rose!" they said, taking her aside. "We are going, as you see; don't vex the others; if you knew how good-naturedly they have all come for you! Can there be any harm in amusing ourselves a little?"

As they were talking, they led her on. The band followed at a little distance, then the young men, then, further off, the girls. Soon they found themselves under the oak-trees, on the fine mountain-sod. They began to dance. Was Rose happy? There were, indeed, a few moments of rapture. All made much of her; every now and then she had fits of flattered vanity. And yet she was ill at ease. She recalled her little room, her evening hymn on the garden bench, while the moon rose slowly behind the oaks, her silent walks with her mother, the freshness of the fields on the border of the wood. I do not know whether she prayed or not. Sundays do not end well so.

At intervals there were others of the same kind. Rose found little pleasure in them.

Young girls that Jesus has once visited may, indeed, wet their lips at the cup of idle pleasure; they cannot drain it. One who has enjoyed long communing with God, who has fed upon the strong meat of Scripture, who early in life has bravely fought with the enemy—that lion greedy after his prey—such a one is not long detained by false pleasures. She finds there too many snares, too many disappointments await her; she sighs too much for blessings lost.

For the world—what I mean by the world, is not to be confounded with the gaiety that befits youth, with fresh laughter and innocent meetings, the radiance, the harmony, the frank outbursts of healthily happy hearts. No; it is frivolity, dissipation with its sad commonplace of paltry jealousies, spiteful comments, over-excited vanity. It is the heart departing from God, saying to the Father, "Give me my portion, that I may enjoy it at my ease far from Thee."

Rose, uneasy and dejected, was doing this.

The Angel of Death touched her.

It was a tedious illness, with unexpected changes for the better, then sudden relapses; yet Rose had again found happiness. Long weak, then confined to bed; peace shone upon her brow. She went slowly down youth's flowery slopes; she went the way of all the earth, but heaven had opened to her. A little sad at leaving her father and her mother, she had a fund of secret joy in her heart. But this had not been won without some struggles—some efforts to clutch again at life. There were days when earth seemed beautiful, Death cold,—when that unknown thing, the passage between the two, frightened her. These days came to an end, others rose radiant, when heaven was so near, the hand of Jesus so strong, that the young girl seemed to walk on lightly, modestly, and firmly, as when in former evenings she followed the homeward path, her head crowned with vine branches, and bathed in the glow of sunset.

One night, the last, she asked—she, who would suffer anything rather than wake her father and mother—asked them both to sit up with her.

"See, father; see, mother, I am going away. God has

been very good to me. Ever since that Sunday I was unhappy in myself. If I had got well, perhaps I should have gone back with the rest. Where I am going God will keep me. It is very beautiful there. Do not cry. You will come there, father; you will come there, mother."

That was all. Rose had never been much of a talker. She was "close," as our villagers call it.

When, the night nearly spent, two struck on the old wooden clock; when the first streak of morning, rather a pallor than a light, glided in the east between the Alps and the sky; when came that shudder of the dawn which detaches so many lives; that dubious hour, when watchers by the sick feel their eyes grow heavy; that mysterious hour when the dying cease to struggle, and the unseen hand cuts the thread,—Rose, with one bound, leapt from her bed.

"Father, your arm!" she cried. Then she walked up and down, trembling, supported by her father, who had waked with a start out of his sorrowful sleep. Rose stood still before the window which looked to the east; the earliest blackbirds were beginning to sing in the wood; she saw the reddening horizon; wonder was painted on her face, something of timidity, too; but the prevailing expression was happiness.

"Is it *that*, father?"

Her father clasped her tightly, then carried back the body to the bed.

Two evenings later, the white dresses were again seen winding through the wood paths, under the oaks.

In the farmhouse, on the bed, reposed the most beautiful corpse it was possible to see.

The young girls entered silently, crowding in at the end of the little room, near the door, looking on with wide-opened eyes; the youths stood without.

Rose had on her Sunday dress; her first communion veil was thrown over her head, leaving her face bare; the features were marble, the eyes half open, the expression grave, almost austere; only the hand of Jesus had impressed on them the peace of heaven. Her hands were crossed. Above them, on her breast, God's book, which had consoled her; at her feet, the white crown which her young companions had brought.

The mother made no ado, nor the father either. Not but what their anguish was great, but it was God's doing. God ripens and destroys the crops; God gives our bread and takes it away. He knows why; He is our Father; what have we to say?

They placed Rose in the coffin; they put the garland on it; the youths carried the bier; the young girls followed; this time without violins, without clarionets, they took the road to the wood.

Three Sundays after, on the turf, not far from the churchyard, the young people were dancing.

II.

The first Rose faded, another came. A white rose; one of those roses with a foreign perfume; a hot-house rose that our winters kill.

Even as a child she was peculiar; liable to bursts of immoderate mirth and immoderate depression; at both these alike, her father, a discreet, deliberate man, frowned. Her mother took her part in her father's presence, but secretly she scolded her too.

Awkward at her work, unpractical in daily life, Rose would wander about dreamily; sometimes she had fits of laughter; sometimes she shut herself up unsocially in a solitary corner, with lips compressed and a gloomy expression. She grew up amidst reprimands; but she preferred her mother's lectures to the tacit discontent of her father, a worthy but austere man, who truly loved her.

Her parents were tolerably well off, but still they had to work. As for working in the fields, this Rose plainly could not do that; tall, slender, pale as she was, with preternaturally large deep eyes, a transparent aquiline nose, the nose of a princess, and fair hair which surrounded her with a golden halo. They determined to make a lady of her; she was one already.

At school she was no better off than at home. She had to learn; she went on dreaming.

At last—

"My girl," said her father, "we have had enough of masters; your portion has been spent on your education; you have lots of learning, gain your bread, my child; you could not, or you would not, do so in the field; take to teaching in your turn."

Rose left home. Very hard the life of a stranger in a strange house! There are mother's kisses, mother's scoldings for the children; there is nothing of the kind for the governess. She is looked at coldly, and if she has faults one remarks them to one's-self, one does not tell her of them.

Rose suffered less, though, than in her village life. She was in the midst of the great world of which she had so long dreamed Still hers was an unsocial, reserved nature, with wants that earth does not satisfy. She expected too much from life, when disappointed she shrunk within herself, and silently turned her proud head away. She did not succeed in practical matters, went from one family to another, earned little, spent much, being generous to the poor, and self-indulgent too. Sometimes she returned to her father's, discontented, taciturn, dressed like a fashionable lady. Her father was cold in manner to her, her mother gave her good advice, and Rose went away again.

She had an upright heart, a straightforward mind, the purity of crystal, only there was the secret frown of a constant depression on her brow; telling of a missed vocation, of a wasted life. One spring she returned ill, but, as her cheeks were very rosy, and her eyes flashed bright, her father did not take much notice of it. Besides, Rose got soon tired of the village. The forest had nothing to say to her—she had not, as a little child, gathered strawberries in July along its fragrant borders. The meadows were gloomy; she had never with her sisters driven thither in October the red cow, the black, the brindled. The Jura! oh, that dark Jura! it was like her discontented father, it made her shiver.

Rose, though an invalid, took another flight; she went to a hot climate, which speedily kills the delicate.

When she returned, December had cast its winding-sheet over the earth. She was taken out of the carriage half dead. This time her father felt how ill she was, and how much he loved her. They took her into the best room, her mother gave her her own large, green-curtained bed. Rose was colourless, worn out by a hollow cough, but sometimes fever flushed her face; it bloomed as the Alps do at sunset, only to look like them the paler afterwards; her large eyes and her abundant hair were all that remained to her.

I do not know what was going on in her soul, but I believe that there was a great conflict there. She remained stiff, haughty, reserved. She was quite aware that she must die, but death dissatisfied her as life had dissatisfied;

God was accomplishing His own work in her quite alone; later it became evident He was leading her apart along those rough paths where He leaves us in full sight of our own selves, a prey to our own will, our own desires, till broken down we fall on our knees, arms outstretched, calling loudly on Him who saves.

As for visits, Rose cared little for them; besides, her young acquaintance, being afraid of her, kept back. Her father, who had been moved just at first, relapsed into silence; dying, his daughter suited him no better than she had done when well. There was no expansion; there were no caresses. Rose seemed frozen; a kiss would have dissolved the ice, but she did not offer one, and no one else dared to do so. She laid the blame of her unhappy existence on all around her; on her father, the village, on God, who had made her as she was. As to whether she regretted life or feared to die, no one could say; she listened to the Bible, to prayer, to everything with closed lips, her large eyes flashing out of their sunken orbits. Only her mother, watching narrowly, sometimes saw great tears suddenly gather there and overflow; then she would clasp her in her arms. Rose only turned her head away, buried her face in the pillows, and answered nothing. Her father murmured: "My daughter, my daughter!" A thrill would pass through her weak frame, a transient light; then Rose, sad, with brow paler than ever, but lips still closed, would resume her proud look and dream on in silence.

No one had dared question her as to her faith. "She believes," her mother would say; a mother's eye can see to the bottom of the heart.

There was an unnatural stillness in the air. In that quiet room, entered and left so noiselessly, where meals were taken at regular hours, where in the evenings the father sat reading to himself by the lamp-light, while the mother sewed, there brooded a deeper sadness, a more intense woe than bursts of weeping ever expressed.

The darkest despairs are the most silent; and it was one of these which the heart of Rose concealed; no disappointed love, no foolish hopes deceived. No; but let her thoughts turn where they would, from her first days to her last, she could not find one happy moment, not one! And now where was she going? What would be her fate in presence of that God from whom she had asked nothing, had received nothing? In her hours of pride, indeed, she tried to contend with Him, but her daring only left her more desolate,—the darkness thickened, she was appalled at herself.

One evening it was getting dark, the wind was driving the snow-showers along the deserted streets; you heard nothing except the wooden shoes of some belated frequenter of the public-house. It was cold, gloomy; the lamp was not yet lighted; the father was musing, his back against the stove; the mother, with her elbow resting on the window, watched the falling flakes, one side of her face whitened by their reflection. Rose was motionless in the large bed, breathing unevenly; she seemed dozing.

All at once, "My father, my mother!" Could that, indeed, be Rose's voice? had it such touching inflexions?

"Come, come, dear father, and you, mother, too!"

Her father staggered; he felt as though something heavenly had lighted in the room, his limbs shook as he approached the bed; the mother was kneeling there already. Half raising herself, Rose was looking at them; oh, never in her best days had she looked at them so; her trembling hand sought theirs!

"Pray, pray, my father! Father, forgive me. I love you! Oh, what good it does me to tell you so! I could not before. . . . . I have been a bad daughter, my father, proud, exacting; I have not made you happy. . . . . Kiss me, mother; my father, my father!" and she clasped him in her arms.

Her father and mother wept; her father most; there was a something of remorse, a more intense tenderness wringing his heart.

"Poor child!" sobbed the mother; "must thou, then, indeed go?"

"Say blessed child, say redeemed! O my mother, this is the first happiness I have ever known! Jesus has found me! Mother, it is sweet to die!"

What kisses, what forgivenesses were exchanged! what fervour of heart kindled between these three poor souls who had believed they did not much love each other! Their daughter, so beautiful, so gentle, so dutiful; their daughter, as they had dreamed her, was actually there, their arms were round her, their eyes fed upon her face,—and she was about to die.

But as for her, an ineffable rapture filled her heart. Heaven awaited her; earth, before relinquishing, lavished on her all its treasures. In an instant, like one who gleans in haste, her hand snatched all the richest sheaves. A moment is as a thousand years to one about to enter on eternal day. She had reaped all; she regretted nothing. Of the love of her father and mother, nothing henceforth could ever deprive her; the love of her God shone round about her. In this glory she departed.

The Lord has sudden unfoldings, such as these, for souls long closed. For beaten-down stalks He has looks which ripen into a golden harvest; He has warm rains for parched-up ground; He has royal compassions, at which the hosts of angels break into hallelujahs of praise that ring from heaven to heaven.

III.

They had all been working hard: in the meadows getting the hay in; in the vineyard, cutting the leaves; in the fields, tying up the sheaves. July was drawing to a close.

"I don't know," said the mother to me, "what ails my Rose. She has fretted too much for the father; she has over-tired herself. It will be no harm though, I am sure." But evidently her heart was heavy.

On the morrow, the doctor paid a visit to the little room. One reached it by a wooden staircase outside the house; the window got all the sun, and looked on a small garden. A young girl sat there sewing away as fast as she could,—a slender form, with a fair, innocent face. Her mother was standing a little behind her.

When the doctor entered, the young girl looked at him in amazement, rose, blushed deeply, then suddenly dropped down again on her chair, in all the bashfulness of sixteen.

She had never left her mother; had never been to dances; never run about the roads in the evenings, hand in hand with other girls, singing rounds as long as the moonlight lasted; not that she was unsociable, or proud, but she knew better things than these; and then she loved her mother, she mourned her father. To sew in her little room, to weed the garden, cut the vines, make hay, beat hemp in autumn, go to church on Sundays, sing hymns, return to sit on the benches of the school, where, as a child, she had been taught to love God,—these were her delights.

These delights were so true and holy, that never face beamed with more serene brightness than did hers.

But this visit of the doctor wearied her. She sick, indeed! Certainly she felt tired, she did not eat; but was that any reason for bringing that fine gentleman here?

I have always thought that the scene, put, just as it was, upon canvas, would have produced one of those touching pictures for which amateurs pay their weight in gold. The doctor, a man in the prime of life, with lip defined by a delicate moustache, bright brow, keen eye, firm and smiling mouth, was examining the young girl. Rose was seated in the full sunlight, she cast her long-lashed eyelids down; sometimes, though, she raised them, and then her limpid glance was fixed on the doctor without any timidity; her mouth was almost severely grave, only when some sally of his made her mother laugh, a smile, gayer than a sunbeam, passed over her lips, then a deep flush rose to her cheeks; then again she sat stiff and motionless, as though she were about to have her portrait taken.

The visit over, the doctor left. The mother, who was uneasy, followed him into the kitchen.

"She may recover," said the doctor.

"She is very ill, then?"

"She may recover."

The prescription written out, he left, walked on some way, then, turning to me, he said, "But she will die."

I often saw her after that, that rustic Rose,—that sweetbrier of the woods, that never opened out fully save to God and to her mother.

Her soul had the transparency of a crystal; she had its sharp angles too, something which might have been a little hard, but that her native sweetness, and the humility of the Christian softened it down. Truth came nakedly from her lips. She told you what she liked, and what she did not like, without any circumlocution. She only knew the yea, yea, nay, nay, of the gospel, and with that she had so much graceful ingenuousness, cordial affection. Hers was one of those individualities mightily developed by the Bible; uniting all the simplicity of the village, the inexperience of her age, and of her retired way of life, with extremely delicate perceptions, keen discernment, and great knowledge of her own heart. She shewed sometimes the blank amazement of a bird that has just left the nest; she cast a stupified glance upon what of the world came within her notice; at other times she would utter some deep saying that a master-mind might have gladly claimed.

Rose was no maker of speeches, but when one brought her flowers or fruit—for the time soon came when she could not gather any for herself—her face lit up, her pretty teeth sparkled; she would say, with a blush, "It is too much," then look at her mother, and one felt that for such a look one would willingly despoil orchard and garden.

There are hours of fugitive joy, there is an efflorescence of happiness on pale faces, which infuses heavenly felicity into one's heart; how one blesses God when one has been the means of calling these forth! what deep disgrace to do this so seldom! and yet how slight a thing may have the desired effect.

Rose suffered tortures; death had to wrestle with all the strength of sixteen. She did all she could to conceal them, but it was hardly possible; it was as though she were broken on the wheel. At such times she would clasp both her arms round her mother's neck, and hide her face in her breast; then she would raise herself, and look into her eyes with her clear, confiding glance. Her mother turned away, and wept.

Never were there greater sufferings in any poor body, never greater peace in any soul. It was one of those easily detached lives that the Lord just touches and which fall off like a vestment. This mother was a widow, this daughter was in all the brilliancy of her first youth, they loved each other, and yet they tranquilly advanced—the one torn to pieces, but submissive; the other a little sad, but composed—towards that turn in the road where they had to bid each other farewell. It was done simply, without much speaking, without any transports. The daughter saw plainly that she was going to die, the mother had known it long. Rose had asked no questions, her mother had kept nothing back; they walked on side by side, day after day; the last day would come when God pleased.

These hidden existences are nearer to heaven than ours. These lives, which unfold so quietly, are better prepared for a sudden close. They have not so much to leave, they are more accustomed to receive everything, good and bad, directly from the hand of God, the soul's relations with Him are more simple, the habit of obedience more strongly formed.

There was nothing triumphant about the departure of Rose. Some deaths are glorious; hers advanced quiet, modest, a little austere like herself, at times illuminated with rays from above.

Neither mother nor daughter troubled themselves about an earthly future. Her mother would say—

"Afterwards, why, I shall be dull enough; but I shall not be alone, nor long in this world."

Then Rose would look at her. "He will not forsake you, mother."

She had always pretty children about her—the children of a brother and sister settled in the village. Little boys with merry faces, very noisy fellows, but quiet there; a cradle, and under green cloth curtains a fresh little face, smiles without a cause, and mottled hands, beating the coverlet. Then the brow of Rose would flush with vivid light, her eyes swim in ecstasy, her heart bound high; you would have taken her for one of Perugino's Madonnas; she had the same pure outline, the same repressed ecstasy, the same fulness of holy love.

Flowers, too, charmed her, and she always had them in profusion; wild flowers, gathered by her former companions, and stuffed into great burly jars; in April the periwinkle, in May the lily of the valley, in June the honeysuckle, in July the sage, the pink, the red poppy, with the corn-flower, the sweetbrier, the mignonette, mixed with a few green ears of corn. Rose would take them one by one, and look at them long. "They are beautiful—they are sweet! . . . . Last year I used to gather them myself, great aprons full of them." Then she grew silent; then suddenly raising her eyes, and looking at her mother, "You must not cry, mother, I'm not fretting over myself."

And yet Rose had her heart-sinkings, had hours when her heart turned back towards life. There would come across her images of health, of pleasure, even of those noisy pleasures which she had refused. But this did not last. "I am very wicked," she would say; she clasped her hands: her calm returned.

One day, quite confused, she said, "Could you believe it, mother? I am thinking of my white frock, my first communion frock! I have only worn it once, mother. . . . You will put it on me, will you not?"

The mother, with wrung heart and closed lips, stood at the foot of the bed, ardently looking at her child.

"Will they give me the crown? the beautiful crown, with

roses, orange flowers, and hawthorn?" . . . The tears ran silently down the mother's face. "You will keep it, mother?"

This was the last sigh after earthly things; afterwards came on the agony, afterwards the Lord drew near; the young girl felt her heart beat with holy impatience to depart; happiness overflowed her; always sincere, she did not exaggerate the strength of her faith; but she was in haste—her eyes shone.

The hour struck—it was in the night; with a voice still firm, looking at her young friends gathered round her bed, sad and aghast: "Give your hearts to Jesus," she said; then let her head fall on her mother's breast. That was all.

When the morning came, the village awoke. It was baking day; at dawn the oven-tenders came to call the women, by tapping against the window panes; the oxen went heavily along to the fountains, the mowers betook themselves to the meadows, the children to school; the larks singing deliriously rose into the light of the beautiful sun.

On earth there was nothing changed, only a mother that wept; nor was anything changed in the little room, only a beautiful white crown, framed and glazed, was suspended on the wooden partition close against the bed.

THE TILERY.

IT is an outlandish house, situated far from any village; a man and his wife live there, young people, quite alone, but for three children, boys. This man and his wife make tiles. Their dwelling nestles at the bottom of a little valley by the side of a brook. The tenants of the tilery—for it does not belong to them—have for their solace, on their right, a view of the wood which slopes down to the stream, very thick on the crest of the hill, with oaks that emerge from the rest of the verdure; less dense, towards the low ground, single trees standing out, and plenty of brambles between them. To the left, our good people, from their deep hollow, may contemplate at their ease ground which rises in great undulations like a natural park; hollowed here, swelling there, devoid of trees, up to an old castellated dwelling which stands on the highest of these rounded slopes, and looks down at them through its few windows. Beyond, the Jura cuts against the sky, with its lofty dome, black at the base, still clearly defined, but becoming almost ethereal at its summit. A little more to the north, and slightly receding, as if the better to throw out the sombre hues of the mountain, a wide amphitheatre of rocks opens out in broad, bold masses, with picturesque yellow clefts, and forms an abrupt barrier, crowned through its whole length by an edge of firs, standing out like delicate etchings against the sky.

You think such a dwelling as this melancholy, but it is

not so; retired, out of the way it certainly is, but so much sunshine smiles there, so many light-winged dragon-flies dart to and fro under the leaves that shade the brook; so many blue and yellow butterflies sport in the meadows; so many birds sing in the woods; you inhale such fresh breezes there, you are so firmly planted in the very heart of nature as God made it, that positively I never go there without feeling that I would willingly remain.

You may reach the tiler's house either by the valley or by the wood. This morning I take the valley, scarcely knowing why.

Have you any time to lose? I have for my part. We shall see the valley by and by, since that is the way we are to go, but we may take our time, there is no hurry. Come first with me up this steep path, and let us walk a little in the wood.

This break-neck path would be the delight of a painter, with its red surface, ravaged by the rains, falling rather than descending from the plains above, with a bristling hedge on one side, on the other a green field. When a shepherd with his flock rears himself up there at the top in seeming gigantic proportions, walking with crook on shoulder, while the air is filled with plaintive bleatings; or again when the sheep, spread out like a white avalanche, with black spots, the picture is complete; one of those exquisite scenes, not taking much in, indeed, not aiming at sublimity, but presenting at a given moment a few of those simple effects, these humble, nay, trivial incidents, over which colour, accuracy, and purity of style throw an ineffable charm.

After the path comes the plain, arid enough, half common, half poor pasture. The soil is clayey, the sun beats down on it fiercely; there are no bees flying about, no grasshoppers jumping there, no juniper bushes to shelter the thrush; it is one of those torrid zones which one traverses, looking out for some green to rest one's eyes on. The valley which opens out below, the one we are going to take by and by, opportunely offers the silken show of its culture to our gaze: the pink spikes of the sainfoin, the golden rape, the purple clover, the waving barley, and meanwhile a keen air, a north wind that has been sifted through the forest, passes through the burning atmosphere, and fans our faces.

Here first we come upon the pines; they grow in clusters, little grassy pathways winding round their stems. They have sown themselves at various heights, and according as they spring from the level where we stand, or rear themselves from the slope which sinks down to the valley, they reveal from root to crown a deep intensity of green which absorbs the sunlight, or they only shew their pointed summit sharply outlined on the landscape.

On the other side of the valley, now hidden, now disclosed, you see the cottages of the nearest village ranging themselves along the top of the hill, and with the slender spire standing out against the dark mass of the Jura;—you might almost think they leant up against it, you would say they were a white carving on a black ground,—but for the transparency of the atmosphere, but for a certain aërial perspective, certain limpid vapours, rather air rendered visible than mist, which surround them with light, and convey the impression of a strip of unseen level ground between the village and the mountain.

There are hours, evening hours, when the sun, concealed behind the ridge of the Jura, darts such a glory of rays between its rounded shoulder and the rock battlements; when such streams of light pass through that spacious opening, when the serrated outlines of the amphitheatre are so royally bright; when that side of the mountain which hides the sun melts into such solemn tones, that the soul remains wellnigh overpowered in presence of one of the grandest spectacles of nature.

But now the sun is in the east; it is rising higher and higher, each tree casting a long far-spreading shadow on the earth.

The pines are in flower. Do you know the flower of the pine? I fancy that it was from it that the old gods of Olympus used to extract the odorous resin with which they perfumed their nectar. The pines, far as the eye can reach, lift up their little wax candelabras—virgin granulated wax. Each branch bears its own; it seems as though the forest were preparing some marvellous illumination for the fairies, and when a puff of wind comes, and the boughs swing slowly, the golden dust of the pollen floats around in soft clouds, and sinks gently down upon the moss.

But we are still walking on this debatable ground, which has suddenly widened out; on the clayey soil where grow a few sparse cereals bending to the breeze.

The forest, the real forest, lies before us. Do you wish for songs? let us go under the old oaks. Do you prefer silence, with a vague stir in the air? let us keep below the pines.

First of all then, under the oaks. There, where the grass grows, and brambles interlace; where the sweet-brier stops up the way, and creeping plants abound; there along that shining track where footsteps have trodden down the vegetation.

There it is that you are fairly lost; there that exhale all round nameless perfumes, fresh emanations of the earth, of the old trunks, of the young foliage. The very light is green, the shade all interpenetrated with sun. Not a breeze, except every now and then indeed a mere puff, you know not whence, which just lifts the branches, wafts here and there still sweeter scents, then dies away, and leaves you half intoxicated with perfume.

What charming mysteries there are in these nooks! Millions of insects, all dowered with intelligence, dressed for a festival, displaying, between the blades of grass, the purple, the ebony, the ultramarine of their elytra, their armour of malachite and gold, delicate antennæ, and little feathered crests. There are artizans among them, who lead a hard life, hewing, sawing, storing night and day. There are idlers who go to and fro, climb to the top of a stalk, look upon the world below, move right and left without any particular purpose; take things as they find them. There are thinkers, too, motionless for hours beneath a sunbeam. There are busybodies who fly in haste, make sudden starts, long journeys, and prompt returns without very well knowing why. There are musicians who, for hours together, go on repeating their monotonous song. There are swarms of ephemera waving hither and thither in some brilliant spot, neither too high nor too low, seeking no sustenance, in a very ecstasy of life, light, and harmonious motion.

It is good to be here. The path glides under the bushes; flowering branches strike against your face. As you advance, a low cry, a rapid flight, reveal to you nests that your hand sets gently rocking as you divide the branches before you. From every nook burst the brilliant notes of the *maestri* of the wood. Redbreasts, blackbirds, chaffinches, wrens—all except the nightingale, who finds the cite too wild; except the lark, who prefers the open sky of the fields; except the quail, who hides her brood in the hay;

—all at the top of their voice; all with throats proudly distended, sing, trill, call! It is a glorious fulness of harmony, which affects you like the vibrations of the sunlight.

Marvellously fresh is the song of the blackbird. In spring infinitely varied in its tones, it gets shorter as the summer advances, until, by the time his nestlings are hatched, he loses his notes one after the other, and remains cut short, rather quizzical, rather embarrassed, and a good deal amazed that he can go no further. And while the blackbird whistles at random on the top of a great oak-tree, the redbreast, perched below on some thick bush, throws off a very rain of diamonds and pearls, scatters in the air his crystalline notes all full of light and fancy. Lower yet, beneath the brilliant concertos and bravura songs, there are murmurs more intimate and charming still; the whispered talk of an enamoured pair; the chirping of the mother to her young brood. The rest is a mere affair of display; here there is soul; here there are endless narrations, little cries of joy, sage counsels, innocent surprises; sometimes, but rarely, bursts of anger; lovers who lose themselves in ineffable repetitions, children who speak all at once, and little melodious beatified sighs, as if a bird's heart was not large enough to hold so much happiness.

And now we reach the clearing—a wide space, twilight; no more brushwood, only luxuriant grass; here and there an old oak, with rugged trunk and strong knotted branches. A wide dome circles above; all round stands the green wall of the wood; at intervals a stray sunbeam; within it a fly passing to and fro; absolute stillness and calm. We have left the wood-songs in the coppice; the cuckoo's plaint alone is to be heard afar, from one hiding-place to another; here it comes to us muffled,—does not trouble the silence.

A dead tree is lying in the shade; it is cool here, let us

seat ourselves. Fit retreat for a philosopher; fit occasion for communing with one's-self. Commend me to these green studios, these sylvan fortresses, this deep isolation. What enterprises the soul enters on here! what deeds are planned, what mighty things are done! how the world gets shaken, overturned, made and remade at one's will! If you have a fancy to be king, emperor, great Mogul, or only the first poet of the age,—to be any kind of genius whether in music, painting, rhyme, or reason,—go and seat yourself a while on the prostrate trunk in the forest glade. You will see all the glories of the world pass before you; you will engage in terrible battles; you will come in for some rude blows; nothing is to be conquered without trouble; but I know not how it comes to pass, you will always be the hero, always the victor. As for me, inveterate idler that I am, I think of nothing. There are people who dream, and know what about; some idea or other is always running in their head; some image moving before and beckoning them on; for me, nothing of the kind. I lie at full length under the branches, I inhale the aroma, I look at the lacework of trees against the sky; I admire the mysterious harmony of green with blue; I rise as high as I can into the infinite azure depths; I feel that existence is sweet; my soul floats suspended in ether; I am neither asleep nor awake, only it seems to me that I have some comprehension of the immensity of God.

Oh, liberty, liberty! to live the healthy life of the woods; to encamp in the forests like those gipsies who have left that red rag hanging on that shoot of sweet-brier; to see the sun rise between the leaves; to see the moon march on through the oak-trees; to come in for the dew of morning; to wander without hindrances; to be satisfied with little! There is so much hard work in our stone houses, so heavy a load of care, so many difficulties in moving a finger, so much bondage to custom, such crooked artificial natures, so little aptness for true enjoyment; and here, two steps off, is absolute independence, self-possession, free motion, existence such as God created it in Eden!

Nay, we are no longer in Eden: we are in a land of pilgrimage; a land of toil, with great clods to break, hollows to fill up, fallow ground to till; by and by will come the rest of evening. No, we are no longer in Eden; these traces of the axe in the forest glade tell it me too plainly.

My tall, beautiful oaks! Have not they been cut over, laid low on the ground, with all their foliage, in the glory of their summer! Have they not had glaring spaces, awkward gaps made in them; have not their secret retreats been profaned, the mysterious hiding-places of the squirrel laid bare! When I see these mutilated trunks, this reddened wood from which the sap is flowing; when I see the glade gain upon the wood, the pasture on the glade, the arable land on the pasture, I say to myself, that the time is coming, is at hand, when, in our country, you will seek for the forest in vain.

Despoiled of their woods, of their fruit-trees even—for everything is turned into money—will our valleys and hills, bare as my hand, lit up by one same sun, washed by one same rain, swept by one same wind, be more beautiful, be worth more? Let wise heads determine; but for my part, I have great confidence in the wisdom of God. No rills without woods, no birds without branches, no music without birds. I do not speak of our harvest devoured by insects. But is it nothing to have beauty, grace, melody everywhere? What sort of a race will remain to you when you have weaned it from poetry? People will go on working, eating, drinking, saving money, it is true; but no more noon-day rest beneath the walnut-tree, no more hawthorn wreaths snatched in passing, no more walks in the wood on Sunday evenings, no more strawberries gathered at the foot of the mountain in those green nooks, shut in by pines; the moon in rising will shine no more through the tall pear-trees, no more lily of the valley will be gathered in great handfuls to perfume the little cottage-room all the week through.

Does man live by bread alone? Jesus has said that he does not, that he has need of the Word of God as well. With the exception of the one Book, written by His supreme hand, I know few of such sovereign power; I know few words as penetrating, few that so effectively touch the heart, as do the simple influences of a nature untouched by our hand.

As for me, these words contain a large part of my life. As a child I followed the steps, now, alas! effaced, of a grandfather, a mother, and many others. These dusky avenues have heard many a cry of joy; many a fine story, lasting as long as we were in the forest, has unfolded itself along these winding paths. What fun it was when all the party chanced boldly to plunge into a swamp! What delight when, the great drops of rain falling one by one, we took refuge under the shelter of the oaks; the earth exhaling its healthy perfume; every opening in the leaves becoming a gutter, then the branches bending, then the shower turning into a cataract; we were wet through, we were, oh, how happy!

The forest is still the same. In the spring the bee-orchis displays her velvet robe at the foot of the great pines; in the summer, the pink, with slashed petals of gray hue, balances itself at the end of a slender stalk—singular flower whence exhales a perfume that makes the very heart faint. The shade is the same, the freshness great as ever,—that rarefied freshness through which floats a passing aroma that soon dies away again, like those wandering notes that rise in wide expanses of country, then suddenly lose themselves without one's knowing whence they rose or where they died away.

Nothing has changed; only I have been going on. Be it so; this immutable aspect of nature, the perennial character of seasons, flowers, birds' nests, I like it; it does me good. But some are soured by it, find in it almost an insult to our sorrows. It is no more so than the equable azure of the sky, the star-lamps kindled every night. It is the eternity of God's goodness, the eternity of youth; the eternal ideal affixed by the Lord's hand on creation's brow. And then are there not children, even while we are young; young lives while ours are declining; strong men rising round when we have to die? Is it not well that they should inhale the same flowers, rejoice in the same sunshine, quench their thirst at the same fountains?

This is why these blows of the axe upon the oaks resound so in my heart.

Let us return by the path under the pines.

Every soil makes its own tree, every tree makes its own fauna and flora, and, by a wonderful reaction, its own soil too. Here the ground is swept clean; brown, smooth, covered with dry, needle-like leaves; it is all that a brier can do to grow in open spaces. The stems rise tall and slender, armed at their base with small sharp branches; higher up, with bristling tufts, proudly indenting the sky. The air plays freely round; no deep shade, only the light is softened as it strains through. Sometimes a single pink, lost in the grass, sends out a transient emanation on the breeze. The roots of the pines, clothed with bark like the branches, intersect the path like irregular flights of steps. The walk, I know not why—is it the confirmation of the soil, or have the pines something to do with it?—has assumed a mountain character. The breeze is keener; the spirits grow more elastic. Behind the colonnade of trees you see the country spread out in different levels; now hollowed into wide valleys, now rising into plateaus, as far as the Alps. At the bottom, through the fields, the high road divides the district by a line that shines in the sun. It runs straight, then branches into rays, with thin threads, that lose themselves at the horizon. Far away, the Alps rear their frozen ramparts: the thick wood hides the Jura. You only hear the cry of the labourers, who, the moment the hay is got in, break up the ground to prepare it for autumn, their loud voices spreading over the plain; grating, mournful, like the voices of men who lead a hard life. They reach the pines, and break against them into a softened tremulous sound. Sometimes the bells of some small vehicle trotting along the road scatter little sparks of sound, that mingle with the trills of the cricket in the clover,—that is all. Above the forest you may see some night bird flying heavily along, escorted by all the winged hosts of the wood. Then what an outburst there is of hooting and screams of derision, till he is conducted into another canton! At your feet a travelling snail or adventurous cricket crosses the path, on his way to visit his relations in the fields.

It is not yet the season of grasshoppers. Later, they will leap in thousands wherever your foot treads, green as a July apple, or gray and earth-coloured, or brown with scarlet-lined wings; with their lively expression, their goat-like profile, and their prominent eyes, they will chirp away in the newly-cut grass.

Nor is it the time of fungi either; those grotesque creations which dot the wood with their vivid colours as soon as October has deflowered the glades. They are a singular race, and full of mystery. There are good and bad among them. I am not speaking of their poisonous properties, but of their outward shape and bearing. Some are delicate, milk-white, planted in circles, as if to mark the spot where fairies danced last night. Others are solitary, blackish, livid, treacherous-looking; planning some crime apart. Those purple, lined with orange, display their magnificent attire in the midst of a crowd of gray knobs, that stand round at respectful distances; pachas in their harems! These, bright as silver, smooth as silk, a satin dome above, ivory gills below. There are some rainbow-coloured, some of pale gold. Whence do they come; whither do they go! When the mists of autumn hung heavy on the earth, what sun purpled them, painted them sulphur-coloured, gave them their mother-of-pearl iridescence? Why does the cow who browses the latest plants, and munches up the frost-bitten leaves; why does the sheep wandering under the bare oak-trees, leave these untouched? I do not know why.

But the mid-day heat scorches the country; it is getting late, let us go down to the valley, for it is there, indeed, that our way lies, as you already know.

Here we are by the brook. We enter the intense shade cast by rocks, all clothed with wild cherry-trees, mountain ash, maples, and hazels. The flowering bramble hooks itself on to everything; the brook runs on beneath the willows between lichen-covered stones. Down there it is almost dark; a beautiful gloom surrounded by light. Sometimes the king-fisher skims the water with his wing; follows its course like a flash of blue lightning, too quick for the eye. An old pollard bends its stem across. Out of the middle of its crown shoots the young cherry-tree, sowed there last year by the hands of some child at play. The brook leaves the shade, crosses the road, widens in the sunshine. It is here that the young haymakers bathe their bare feet. Next it sets off running through the meadows, sometimes in sight, sometimes concealed beneath arcades of bushes.

There is no road through the valley, merely a track. On both sides are steep rocks, to the left clothed with brushwood, to the right with old oak-trees, flinging down festoons of wild vine, and balmy clematis. Then the rocks disappear, and the valley throughout its length is enclosed by the wood on the east, by the green rising ground to the west, with the Jura and the rocky amphitheatre closing in the horizon.

I do not know any retreat richer in flowers than this.

Not a breath of air. The sun darts fiercely down, but the grass keeps green, the murmur of the water, its fresh gurgle, its limpid whispers seem to spread moisture round. No seed is brought here by the hand of man; the birds, the wind, when it chances to pass by, are the only sowers.

There are successive flower-shows here, and each has its own one plant. Blue salvias; columbines, with their lovely hanging bells, that tremble every time a butterfly touches them in his flight; a profusion of yellow coronella, then small red starry pinks; and near the brook, the white feathery fragrant tufts of the meadow-sweet, with some green insect slumbering in their midst.

As soon as a cluster of alders bends over the water, the honey-suckle throws its night-scented tufts from stem to stem. Then beneath, you find secret bathing-places; little shady bays, where the current hardly stirs the leaf that hangs lowest.

Here at noon come the village youths, here cries of joy are heard, here the water is thrown up in fountains, falls in sheets, and dripping feet soak the meadow-grass.

But at this present hour there is perfect silence; the silence of mid-day in June. Only, beneath some wild pear-tree, you may see the mowers stretched at full length, their straw-hats over their faces, or their faces buried in the grass.

Onward. The fleece of the hemp is swelling, it is exquisitely sweet. The old bridge throws its arch from side to side; one stone has detached itself, perhaps thirty years ago; a willow grows on it, it lies in the water, moss-covered, like an emerald in the sun. I fall into a dream, the stone changes to an island, the sprigs of moss are palm-trees; I land—I am in the East! . . .

Onward still. The ground is wilder, has fewer flowers Reeds rattle; the valley narrows, the swampy soil shakes beneath one's feet. This portion of the forest, only half cleared, still amazed at the broad daylight, exposes its stumps to the sun. It is covered with tall, large-leaved plants. The brook glides over a clay bottom, grows wider, has no more sheltered creeks. A sudden turn, here is the tilery seated in its solitude.

It consists of little more than a shed, beneath which dry the tiles, a bit of a house opposite, under the same roof,—a low window, a door with a porch—and in front a bare garden, where grow some cabbage-stalks and some rows of kidney beans.

Not a creature about, the children have run away at our approach. No poultry; the small farmers, to whom the neighbouring fields belong, would not suffer them. No cow;

there is no hay for one. In the stable there is a goat, for which the boys go at nightfall to gather young shoots in the wood; there is an old horse, too, half blind, half lame, who gets harnessed to the old cart, and carries the tiles to the customers.

We will enter the kitchen; the floor is earthen; not much to be seen in it, just enough to prove most decided poverty. A few plates in the rack, a few iron spoons and prongless forks, a dinged saucepan, on the hearth nothing but a broken trivet. No flitches of bacon, no wreaths of sausages hung in the chimney; only a string of onions, and on the table an earthen tureen, where smokes some thin soup or other, and three pieces of black bread neatly cut. Yet everything is clean: the rush broom has been all round; the bareness is orderly, is not pitiable. Where destitution has got the upper hand, things are not so well arranged.

At the sound we make, the bed-room door opens gently, a man comes out—a puny figure, timid-looking, with a moist, kind eye, a rather slow, quiet manner, and a happy expression.

"Well, James."

"I beg your pardon, ma'am. We sent for you. She has been dreadfully ill; just now things are better."

"And the child?"

"Oh!" and James gave a simple kind of laugh; "the child! It will be like the others."

At that moment three chubby faces,—three curly heads, little rogues half undressed, furtively advance to the outside of the window, and look through at the tureen.

"Those?" James nods his head. "Very well, James, eat your soup; I have something to do here; you will come in by and by."

James is not in the habit of disputing, he stands still a moment, and beckons to the boys, who come in just as we pass into the next room. It is the bed-room, there is no other; bare as the kitchen; barer if possible; only it is very clean, very bright, and it has a boarded floor. Just at this moment, however, the light is a little obscured. James has hung up some old aprons in the windows. The red-curtained bed leans up against the wall; a walnut-wood cupboard, the family wardrobe, stands opposite; by the two windows are two chairs; no table; and that is all.

In the bed lie mother and child; she, as robust as her husband is weakly, with an eye as bright as his is subdued. A strong nature, with a wild light in her glance, something about her unusual, outlandish, like her house.

"This is how you behave, Jane? On the very point of death without letting people know!"

Jane lifted herself up with an abrupt gesture.

"It's like that always, but this time I thought the end was come."

Her voice was firm, her accent decided; it was only the trembling of her arm that betrayed her weakness.

"Why not get help?"

"Oh, if one got into the habit of it!"

"You have suffered a great deal?" Jane looked at me, the flash in her eye was her only answer. "And now?"

"I shall get well."

This woman will not die; each lying-in is torture, she goes through it; she measures herself with death, wrestles, shakes off his clasp, and eight days after you see her driving the old horse, who draws the old cart with the tiles.

James moulds the clay, and bakes these tiles. Jane takes them to the houses around; he remains quietly at home, she scours the valley; but she is never long away.

Jane is no talker, she walks on in silence by the side of her cart, her eye always a little wild, then she returns to her nest. When there are no orders, weeks pass away without either of them being seen.

"You did not forget God, Jane?"

"No."

Why should I repeat what passed in confidence between us? Jane's secrets, what she believes, what she hopes, what her soul holds within itself, belongs to her only. Besides, she says little. James came in; his look, when it rested on his wife, had a tenderness about it which stirred my heart. She turned, and their eyes met.

"He is a good man," said she, and I saw a tear gather under her eyelids.

"One does as well as one can," said James.

"You are lonely," I broke in, "so far from the village."

Both looked at me with an expression of astonishment.

"You are not dull?" Jane laughed, her white teeth lighting her face up. "If your pains were ever to get worse?"

"One has the doctor," replied the husband; it only takes about two hours to go for him."

"And two more to bring him back, which makes four. In that time Jane might sink."

"God will see to that," said Jane.

"And your children?"

"Oh, no fear for them!"

"Does not the day seem long to you?"

"No," said they, both at once. Then James went on—

"Look you, ma'am, we do very well. I have my tiles; she has her horse, her garden, and her spinning-wheel, and then there are the children. When winter comes, one reads a bit in the evenings; one takes a spell in the Bible, and one goes to bed early. Then there is the wood; in spring there is plenty of singing there. People are no good to us. They are such talkers in the villages, and so proud, too. We are but poor, and they would look down upon us belike. Though as for that, the year goes round, and we get on very well somehow."

Jane said nothing, but in her black eye you saw a light that was kindled by something more than her husband's negative happiness.

For him, fireside peace, silence, one day like another, with affection, sufficed. She loved too, somewhat indeed after the fashion of a wild animal, but she did love. She would not on any account have had a James of a different stamp, less gentle, less careful, less quiet. And yet, for her, this solitude included something over and above domestic happiness. Whether she distinctly understood this or not, I cannot say; but she felt it.

Here she breathed fresh free air, that wild poetry which passes through the forests on the wings of the morning wind; here she lived far away from the prose of frequented spots; the jokes, the grievances, the gossip of the village never jarred her. When she walked along by the old cart, and heard the grinding of its old wheels, there was an unconscious music within her heart that cheered her on. The notes of birds singing in the woods, the sound of distant bells, the merry voices of her children echoing softly from afar; the sweet scent of the meadows; the keen breath of dawn; the warm breeze of evening; the mountain, whether in gloom or radiance; the changeless blue of the sky, with its swift battalions of clouds;—all these went to swell that music of which we speak. And at night when she pressed her little nestlings close; when the dead branches flamed brightly on the hearth, lighting up the face of James as he looked at her with that innocent expression of his, Jane's heart glowed within her. Melted into tenderness, proud, and passionately happy, she would not have changed her lot with that of the Queen of England, seated crown on head on a throne of gold.

THE HEGELIAN.

ONE night in the month of May, but not therefore a beautiful night—for it rained in torrents—I was travelling in a diligence. It was in the year 1849, and there were then no railroads in Switzerland. The diligence, a great house on wheels, with its two coupés, an interior, a *rotonde*, cabriolet on the roof, seats here, seats there, rolled along, collecting everything and everybody, and, in its winding, river-like course, might be said, in geographical phrase, to *drain* the country between Neufchâtel and Bâle, at which last place it arrived on the second night.

It rained, I have said, in torrents. There was no place in either of the coupés. The cabriolet was out of the question. I had an aged relative with me, the Baroness Z., whom I was accompanying into Germany. We squeezed ourselves into the interior.

Nothing could be clearly seen. The rain was lashing the glasses; the leathern roof leaked; we could hardly distinguish our companions. I had upon my feet the great feet of a great burgomaster of those parts, with protuberant stomach built up to threefold elevation, and pendent chin of fit proportions hanging down to meet it. He took all things calmly, and with deep bass voice chuckled whenever a drop of rain from the leaking roof fell upon him. By his side sat some description of American, not much the gentleman. From time to time he drew from his pocket a long bottle, (of gin, porter, brandy, I know not—some alcoholic liquor,) and applied it to his lips; when he did not drink, he smoked. To the right and left were peasants and citizens lost in the shade: these came and went. The burgomaster was immovable; so, too, was the American. In one corner a man of lofty stature, and young, so far as I could judge, sat silent.

Infernal machines were those old travelling arks, where space and air were both denied to you; where your elbows were driven into your sides; where your legs were wedged fast amidst innumerable packages; where to draw a pocket handkerchief from your pocket was an affair tedious as diplomacy, and a great deal more laborious; where, during twenty-four hours, you had the face of your opposite neighbour, with its inevitably besotted, bewildered expression, jogging there ceaselessly before your eyes with the same idiotic movement. Infernal machines! for he must be good indeed who does not begin to feel very wicked in one of them.

The rain poured on incessantly. Impossible to open anything. The moisture from within tarnished the glasses; the mud from without splashed them. There was a sickening odour of stale wine, stale tobacco, old cheese, and old crusts; and there you sat amidst the snoring and the swaying to and fro of heads with great open mouths, which at some sharper jolt than usual, would suddenly shut themselves up, and then it was the turn of the eyes to open on you with their imbecile stare. We had neither thunder nor lightning; nothing but this incessant deluge. Looking out, one could just distinguish the roofs of houses dripping with rain, and the flooded road that spirted up under our wheels, and the great pools of water formed in the meadows. Thick clouds were drawn around us on every side, which added to the oppression of our atmosphere; and yet the cold—the cold of a sleepless night, the cold of the drenched earth and the pouring skies, and a carriage soaked with rain—penetrated the very bones, and made one shrink into one's-self.

The epoch we were in—it was 1849—was as cheerless as the scene which nature presented.

In France, Socialism was rising into power; in Germany, whither we were travelling, revolutions had taken place, or were hourly expected. My aged companion and relative was in great fear. I endeavoured to reassure her; but to me also everything looked black as night. I saw, through those gloomy showers, nothing but rising scaffolds; revolutionary scaffolds stood out upon my horizon in every direction.

At length the morning came—not with her scarf of gold, nor with roseate fingers; came in very simple robes—gray upon darker gray.

Pale as it was, the day had dawned. And see the power of light! In a moment the whole world changed its aspect. Order was triumphant everywhere, and, after all, a little conflict did no ill. And then it was the month of May, and this shower was falling upon the roofs of pleasant cottages—thatched roofs, where wild flowers grow, and which project kindly over the wall, securing a sheltered space round the house. The velvet moss, which had taken a new lustre from the rain, enlivened even the dripping thatch; the cottage windows, with their little round panes of glass imbedded in the leadwork, glistened out on us. These windows almost touched each other, and opened upon the well-stacked pile of logs. Moving in and out of the oval porch of carved wood, you saw the mistress and manager of all, her head covered with a scarlet handkerchief. The ducks and the geese quack around her with ceaseless movement of their tails. Further on, one sees the peasant himself, yawning and stretching himself before the barn-door. Even our enemy, the rain, seems to rebound gaily, and to dance upon the clean flag-stones which surround these pleasant homesteads. In the garden it falls on great globes of apple-blossoms and the gay cones of the lilac, and impresses on them an undulating and graceful movement. The tulips, proud as sultanas, quite unconcernedly let it glide down their gorgeous array; other flowers, with their petals thrown back, laugh as they shake off the petulant shower; the stocks and the wallflower embalm the air at every gust of wind.

Under the roofs the swallows sit motionless, with neck outstretched, upon their nests; or sometimes hazard a rapid zig-zag flight, skimming the soil, and, returning, perch upon their nests, and there, with tail close pressed against the wall, chat with their little ones, or fill their open beaks. The sparrows—more audacious, great thieves and great brawlers, red republicans underneath their brown feathers—laugh at all these cataracts of rain. They, perched upon the tiles—they choose always the best houses—let the rain rain, and wrangle on: with strong beak and raised head, eating of everything, and eating always, and stunning the neighbourhood with their cries.

And yonder the pigeons coo. They put out their slender heads from the holes of the dovecot; then, with great noise of wing, they pounce down on some clean space in the court below, where, promenading with their little, timid, rapid steps, they peck here and there at some grains escaped from the sheaf, their necks changing like the opal as they move, and in a moment, scared at nothing, take flight again in a body.

But more than all, the orchards shine out as we pass them, in spite of the pale day, and the dissolving clouds, and the moistened earth. Through it all the apple-trees and the pear-trees, in the magnificence of their blossom, shed a ray as of victory. The mind, at mere sight of them, fills with hope. Revolutions !—with those globes of roseate blossoms ? Scaffolds !—in a land where men can wander under such coverts, amidst such splendour of the spring ?

I know not why, unless it was to catch some sympathy for my own thoughts, that my glance now turned from the orchard to the interior of the diligence, which still went lumbering on. It did not penetrate to the American, for he was walled up in his cloud of smoke ; it glided past the burgomaster, stolid and imperturbable, and passing over sundry sleeping heads, rested in the corner on the youthful figure that I had hitherto rather divined than seen.

All night that figure had remained there enveloped in shade. It had not slept. From hour to hour a clear voice, resonant and firm, had been raised to ask of some one on the roof, or in the *rotonde*, or elsewhere, if all went well with them. The voice had been answered in the frank tone of the good comrade, yet with something too of respect. Strange ! that figure, motionless and pensive, and which was not regarding me, *destroyed* in an instant the peaceful train of ideas I brought to it for sympathy !

He was a young man, hardly thirty ; the forehead high, the face pale, the eyes very large, blue, and soft ; he had an air of thought, of candour, of determination, as if possessed by some fixed resolution. His mouth had a smile upon it ; a tawny beard descended in undulating lines to his chest. His stature was tall, his carriage lofty ; he had the air of command. There were no pistols, no poignard ; and yet I said to myself, with the invincible assurance of a sudden presentiment, 'This man is some captain, going to stir up battle on the other side of the Rhine.'

Such, in fact, he was.

What brought us into communication? What broke the silence between us? A nothing, a jolt of the diligence, the fatigue of my infirm relative, my anxious expression. He had the corner, which was the best place; he rose, and with a frank smile, and a thousand charming attentions, installed the baroness in it, put his cloak under and round her feet. We talked. The burgomaster, the American, and all the rest still slept on. Of what did we talk? Of the rain, of the spring-time, of the uncertainties of fate, of the revolutions everywhere breaking out. Here his eyes flashed.

"I am going there!" he said, throwing back his head, not with the air of a boaster, but of one rejoicing in some happy enthusiasm. "I am going there; into my own Germany! I re-enter my own country, and liberty re-enters with me."

"Are you sure to conquer?"

"I am sure to combat."

"The army of the State is numerous."

"Ours is more so; it is the nation."

"You do not hesitate to embroil your own country?"

"It must be!" For a moment he knit his brows, and seemed lost in thought; then, raising his head, he continued:—"Every one must have his fair place under the sun—or under the rain," he added, glancing with a smile at the window. "In fact, there must be bread for all, joy for all, leisure for all. There must be no disinherited children on the face of the earth; no longer must this man be corrupted by superfluous wealth, while this other is starving. Harvests ripen for all. The house of stone, good furniture, the easy and calm life, should be for all."

At this moment he encountered the frightened expression of the baroness.

"I am not a *Red*, nor a confiscator of other men's goods, though appearance, it seems, is against me. I am higher. I wish nothing but justice,—nothing but what God wills. I wish equality."

"Equality!" I exclaimed. "Since the days of Eden, it has not been known upon the earth. The day after you had made division of the spoil"——

"I divide no spoil; I want to prepare the earth; I want to remove all obstacles to progress; I want to open a great career to humanity, to that young humanity which aspires. It claims its share of happiness, its right to rejoice, and it shall have it."

"I fear that to the end of time there will be strong and feeble, the ugly and the beautiful, men honest and men vicious. What becomes of your equality?"

The Captain shook his head.

"These are old ideas," he said; "the rags left us by the middle ages. The world advances to a social revolution; it will leave its winter skin on the bushes of the month of May."

"But those others—the obstructives as you call them—will defend their old customs."

"I know it well."

"And then?"

"And then—we kill them."

This was said with a voice sad but inexorable.

"If they would trust themselves to us," he continued, "they should wither out in peace. This they will not, and they cannot do."

I contemplated with terror this melancholy smile, this sincere look, this insane goodness and candour, deluded by some horrible Utopia, decorated with flowers, and dripping with blood. An instant after, he resumed with a voice that slightly trembled, but which vibrated with an absolute confidence in himself—

"Whatever is born, must die. This is an eternal law. No level was ever made, that did not destroy flowers as well as weeds. Our social revolution will issue from the tomb. To arrive at universal harmony, we must stifle the discordant sounds."

"They will return from every side."

"No!"

This *no* was said simply with an overwhelming assurance.

"But," I replied, "these discordant notes, they are living men."

The Captain reflected; then, in a low voice, said—

"Yes, one hundred thousand heads."

"A hundred thousand heads rolling from the scaffold, and millions of women in despair, children and mothers."

"This morning were there no women in despair? no infants who wept on the earth? no fathers, or mothers, or poor people who died?"

"Some—yes—here and there."

"Everywhere!—on all sides of this desolated world, at every second there rises a cry of agony."

"It is a world accursed, which we men have ruined, have lost."

"That I do not believe."

"What! you do not believe yourself a sinner?"

"No!" This other *no* was pronounced with the same absolute certainty. A moment after he added, with a softer expression—

"I trouble, I alarm you. But see you not that death mows down generation after generation—a little sooner, a little later, what matters it? We all fall at our given hour; all as the ploughshare lays us in the furrow. A single war, the wars of your Emperor, have killed hundreds of thousands of men."

"I detest war."

"The cholera which has just broken out in London, in Paris, will cut down thirty thousand men in a day."

"That is God's doing."

"Well?"

"You are not God."

The Hegelian regarded me with his bland, inexorable look.

"I am God," he said.

I shuddered.

"I am God! My thought is a ray of the Divine Thought, my will is a part of the Supreme Will; the Great Heart which beats there above beats in me, in you, in all."

A burlesque idea will sometimes traverse the mind in its most serious moods. I could not help looking opposite with a smile at the burgomaster; the Captain followed my glance; he shrugged his shoulders, but continued with imperturbable calm—

"Yes, he also, as well as others—only somewhat more enveloped. We are all waves of the one ocean, from which we emerge, into which we sink. God! God is the world! God vibrates in every plant, in every insect, in the sun above us, in these drops of rain about us."

Then, returning to his own defence, he said—

"I have a right to do what I do. I shall die—that is very possible; others will die—that is certain. Humanity advances perhaps through destruction. Did not the Israelites traverse the Red Sea? A reviving humanity will flourish on a youthful earth, and the golden age will re-descend from heaven"

I, feeling all speech powerless to cope with so great a folly, did what the fashionable world will think very ridiculous, puritanical in short. I took out my New Testament, and gave it him. The Captain extended his hand, received it, looked at it, and as he put it into his bosom, he said, with a serene and radiant expression—the expression of one of the *illuminati*—

"I know it well—your Bible."

"If you know it, you have seen there the true law of universal love?"

Without answering me, he pursued his own thought.

"I have more than once studied its pages; I have penetrated its deeper and concealed meaning. It has an apparent, and it has a mysterious signification."

"It should be read with an honest, simple spirit. It was written for simple men."

A light flashed into his eyes. "You have the letter," he said; "we have the spirit."

After this we fell into a profound silence.

Miserable world, thought I, if ever God delivers it to such fallen angels as these!

The Captain broke the silence, and with a tone of kindness, in which, however, one traced the habitual exercise of authority, he said—

"We are approaching Bâle. Permit me to make a proposition. Madame is timid, and you will find Germany in flames. Let me accompany you. With me you will pass everywhere. I will leave you on the frontiers of Prussia; it will be for me only the delay of two days."

He made the proposition in simple good faith. Such self-negation, such complete candour and sincerity beamed in his countenance, that I could not but feel touched at his offer. Should I have done as much—I, the wiser one, who looked down on him in pity?

I refused it nevertheless. He insisted just as far as good breeding permitted. Then gathering together his cloak and some baggage, he called to the postilion. The diligence stopped, he descended, his companions grouped themselves around him; with a rapid movement, full of energy, and a sort of poetic fervour, he waved his adieu to us, cast one look up into the skies, then struck off across the plain to gain the Rhine.

I was bewildered. This candour of a child, with this delirium of pride, this kind soul with this inexorable hardness! God at once adored and denied! What an abyss!

Terrible creatures these ideologists!

To spare some trouble to an aged woman, this man would willingly have traversed two hundred leagues, and this same man, coldly, with that beautiful smile upon his lips, would send a hundred of his fellow-creatures to the scaffold. Just now, to save us from some anxiety, he would have risked for himself the danger of delay; and if, four days hence, we should be brought before him as *obstructives* to human progress, he would order our decapitation without the least remorse. He would not even find it necessary to harden his heart against us. No. From the depths of his Absolute, from the centre of his Eternity, he is indifferent to the tears of the day, and the death of a transitory generation. Proud fatalist, with a calm, untrembling hand, he would baptize the earth with blood, contemplating the gay futurity that is to advance crowned with roses.

Truth! Truth! thou indeed art worth all we suffer for thee. Truth, thou savest us from madness; without thee we should be tossed like a dismasted vessel on the billows of our own thoughts. Through the bright heavens, and through the abysses of the night, I have sought for thee; I have found thee; thou wert not far from me; truth of the gospel, I clasp thee to my heart!

Whilst I, with my thoughts and my prayers, followed the Captain, the diligence entered with great clatter into the old town of Bâle.

This time we saw none of its curiosities. We left the Palace of Justice, and its red sculptures, in peace, and the stork with her traditional nest on the roof of the church.

The hotel of *The Three Kings* was full of families from Baden, taking shelter from the political storm. We consulted our host in some alarm. "Oh, it is nothing at all!" said our contented Boniface. "There are no *refolutions*," he assured us in his Swiss accent "The Governments are in flight—*foilà tout!* But order is not disturbed."

"But the King of Bavaria?"

"Fled—*il s'est saufé!*"

"And the Grand-Duke of Baden?"

"*Saufé*—il s'est *saufé!*"

"And the King of Prussia?"

"Il n'est pas encore *saufé*—Ah, bah! it is nothing!"

All this he said with the most paternal air in the world, which made us smile, if it did not completely reassure us.

However, we resolve to continue our journey. We had cogent reasons for so doing. On the morrow we set forth again.

There was revolution apparent everywhere. The train which took us, brought to the German frontier some body of volunteers, with the scarlet plume in their hats. They were exiles returning to their country,—young men, ardent, inflamed, shouting hurrahs of victory.

In the boat that carried us down the Rhine nobody at all. Not a single passenger. Yes, there were two Jews, whom *business* could induce to run whatever risk there was. They took possession of the vacant saloon, and as it happened to be their Sabbath-day, they recited their prayers —the prayer especially called the *Assault*—with linen bands rolled round the arm, and a veil thrown over the head, and with alternate rhythmical sentences, like a piece of counterpoint.

As we approached the insurgent towns, loud cries were heard, and the report of fire-arms, explosions of triumph which were either to welcome or defy us. At Mannheim, a drunken soldier, the republican cockade in his shako, came, escorted by a band armed with scythes, to deliver to us, on the landing-place, a discourse on the rights of humanity; uproarious clamours from the quay supported him.

In Prussia nothing stirred. It was a calm too complete not to be factitious; a calm under which one felt as it were the ebullition of the rising storm.

The only external symptom we met with of social disorder, promenaded itself in the little town we inhabited, under the form of *Burschen*, displaying a wondrous quantity of hair, more than the sacred race of long-haired kings ever boasted. They passed and re-passed under our windows, arm in arm, clothed in short frock-coats of apple green, of celestial blue, the boldest of them having the red cap on their heads. The triangle, emblem of equality, the level or the axe, a sort of jewellery in fine steel, glittered on the front of it; some even displayed a miniature guillotine. Under the cap escaped silken fleece for hair, light or dark or tawny; and they sang to the cadenced step, with flashing eyes, and defiant countenance.

This exhibition did not last long. Three or four regiments took up their quarters in the little town, then some squadrons of cavalry, then some artillery, then some dragoons, till a *corps-d'armée* had formed itself. Farewell to our students, farewell to our fantastic perukes, all has disappeared in the twinkling of an eye.

I shall never forget those beautiful evenings—melancholy nevertheless, for civil war muttered on the horizon—when, under the acacias in blossom, we listened to the military music,—that admirable metallic music, so correct, so disciplined, under which throbs a spirit all the more ardent, because it is well restrained. I shall never forget that overture to *Tannhaüser*, which was to me the revelation of a new world of harmony, with its introduction, reminding me of the gigantic architecture of Egypt, and those ironical phrases insinuating themselves into the melody like an infernal laugh; while the whole rose, like a rising tide, in one swelling chant of all mingled emotions, sadness and agony, and heroism and worship.

At these times, I know not why, the memory of my Hegelian captain returned to me. Before these troops which were about to enter Bavaria and besiege Radstadt, I could only feel compassion for him.

Sometimes this metallic orchestra gave out a patriotic song, then, suddenly pausing, the sonorous voices of the soldiers took up the melody, repeating the refrain; and there was, in the contrast between the metallic sound of the band and the flexible sweetness of the human voice, something unusual, something unexpected, that touched the heart, like the contrasts one meets with in the moral world.

One fair morning all this military array departed. The sun rose, and there was nothing but the scattered hay in the market-place. Our birds sang with the greater courage,—the thrush in the meadows, the nightingale in the grove.

Some way out of the town the several regiments halted to receive the Prince of Prussia, who commanded the expedition. They halted at a spot I knew well,—under the cherry-trees, and where the grass had been lately mown. How they laughed, how joyous they were, as on some green and shady slope they threw their knapsack on the ground, and the shako from their head! All on a sudden an electric shock ran through the ranks: "To your arms! the Prince! the Prince!"

In an instant all were on their feet. The Prince of Prussia galloped along the battalions, sword drawn, with lofty mien. Stopping before each regiment, he pronounced some words with rapid utterance: *Hilf Gott—Gott mit uns!* Salvos of cannon and musketry responded.

He placed himself at their head, with his staff and his group of young aides-de-camp: *Vorwärts!* and the army put itself in motion, the several corps one after the other; the artillery, with its cannon, making the earth tremble; the hussars, clad in their sombre colours; the lancers, with their crimson pennons; the dragoons, with their golden helmets; the solid infantry, advancing with well-timed step. As each corps moved on, it raised its song of war.

It was a grand, a royal spectacle; one of those pictures which twenty years of tears and joys cannot efface from the memory. The fresh and fragrant breeze played over the landscape, and unrolled the military standards; never was a sky more radiant, never was an army more elated: all care seemed swept from their brow. Nevertheless, to me the glorious spectacle brought with it one thought of mortal sadness: it was no foreign invader that these troops marched to encounter, but children of the same soil, speaking the same language,—Germans like themselves.

This is what I could not make an old general, a friend of ours, comprehend, who had been left behind to guard the position.

Ten days had not passed before there arrived amongst us messengers swelling with their great tidings: the Duchy of Baden had submitted, Bavaria had been reconquered, governments, kings, grand dukes, all had been restored.

Radstadt held out a little longer. Then commenced reprisals which were severe, and martial law, terribly expeditious.

"*Fisulliés!*" cried the general, who had long ago ceased his attempts to bring into order the rebellious vowels of the French alphabet. "*Fisulliés* the chiefs! *Fisulliés* the soldiers! *Fisulliés* the blockheads who let them do it." If I named this one or that one, the general answered by an expressive gesture, took aim with his walking stick, pulled an imaginary trigger, and uttered with a laugh his absurd *fisullié!*

This is all I have been ever able to learn of the Hegelian

THE SPRINGS.

THIS is the name given to a small enclosure of the mountain, situated about a third of the way up. The firs, which grow very high, and are very thick there, suddenly open out, and leave a free space; an orchard, planted with apple, pear, and half-wild plum-trees, with a strip or two of field full of potatoes and lucerne. These rise steeply to the forest. Beyond, on the very edge of the wood, stands a rustic dwelling, with a fountain before it! Four springs incessantly flowing into an old wooden trough, carved long ago, and embroidered with mosses, some velvet-like in texture, adhering to the bark which still covers the trough; others floating in long green filaments that for ever wave in the water as it escapes. The situation is solitary. The inhabitants seldom go down to the plain; this enclosure affords them occupation enough, and the people from the plain still more seldom come up to the Springs. It is not a *châlet;* there is only one cow, not any butter to sell, nor provisions to take to the fruiterers.

On Sunday, the mother or the daughters, the son or the father, make themselves smart, and go by turns to a preaching about three miles off.

In summer, some child, gathering raspberries amidst the labyrinth of brushwood, branches of broken fir-trees, fallen trunks, and brambles spreading in all directions, comes sometimes with its basket to drink at the Springs, and to sit in the deep shade that, at five o'clock in the evening, the pines cast over the fields.

There is a moment of positive transfiguration for this small domain. This is in the month of May, when the orchard, enclosed by its dark frame, blossoms like a bridal nosegay. Will it be believed, this spotless white rather saddens me? I prefer the enclosure in the midst of summer, when each separate vegetation colours the ground with its own particular tint; or still more, in autumn, when the wild pears grow golden, the crab-apples crimson, and the crops are heaped up under the granary pent-house. At such times, a smoke may be seen rising from a sheltered spot near the house; a bright fire is burning under a shed hung round with trusses of hemp. There sit mother and daughter, noisily beating out the sheaves. This sound is almost the only one you hear; the folks at the Springs are not great talkers, nor great singers either.

During the dull November mornings, when it is very cold on the top of the mountain, and the ground is strewn with wild fruit not worth the gathering, the enclosure sometimes receives a visit from a stranger—the bear—the great brown bear—the harmless bear of our Jura, strays down in the fog, and before the inhabitants have opened their door, comes and stuffs himself with crab-apples. He would willingly enjoy a little honey too, but the row of hives leans up against the house; and besides, they are but poor ones; the young July swarms, which would die in the plains for want of flowers, being sent here, where they can still get at some late clover; to be taken back in September, only two being left, closed up during the winter with little fir-branches.

When Master Bear has feasted sufficiently, he trots off again into the wood. Never has he allowed himself the least impropriety, such as carrying away the goat, the heifer, or some stray child. He is indeed a most saintly character this bear: he lives upon little; abstains from flesh; the most he permits himself is to crop the young barley in June, when about the length of his tongue. The people at the Springs once saw him; if not the father, the grandfather did; at all events, they firmly believe in him, and on December nights, when the south wind howls in gusts through the forest, bending the firs, and making them groan again, the frightened children think they hear Bruin growling in distress in the depths of the wood.

In winter all is white, the branches bend under the snow; great drifts block up the path, and flakes fall silently; you only hear the crystalline voice of the Springs; the flail of the father busy in the barn with his son; and in the house, the little monotonous murmur of the spinning-wheels. But when one of those fine January days comes, when the sky is blue throughout, and the sun marches on royally crowned with beams, and not a breath is stirring,—there is in this sparkling enclosure, in these firs rearing their jagged pyramids—each spike of which is turned to a diamond, in these rocks that look through them, in the pure atmosphere and the great calm,—there is something at once very striking, solemn, and splendid.

In May, the firs are in flower; the orchard has not yet opened out its blossoms, which at present show in abundance, as little red balls at the edge of the dark-green of the wood. You would say that summer in her haste had overturned a basket of cherries there.

When I went up thither, however, it was neither the season of snow nor of fruit, it was on a beautiful Easter Sunday.

"The girl at the Springs wants you," one of the women in the village had said to me; "you'll just have to go at once there."

"What does she want?"

"Who can say? She has been too much at her books."

I smiled, and took the way through the meadows. There were no leaves on the trees, none on the bushes and yet it was the flowery Easter tide.

The black thorn projected its stiff boughs, covered with white buds and open blossoms, proclaiming the spring from every hedge. Tufts of violets spotted the brown grass of winter with their blue; green blades piercing through it too here and there. The air was filled with a thousand discreet murmurs from insects returning to life, newly-wakened flies flew hither and thither, long black lines of ants crossed the pathway. You could see the sap rising in the still leafless branches,—some were scarlet, some darker red, some yellow as rods of gold.

The country was bare. A pretty keen north wind careered over its hollows, the trees had no young twigs, no nests, no secrets, the glance that wandered to the distance came back disappointed, and yet April reigned. At ts bidding, spring scents rose from the earth. The tiny guitars, the unpretending Jews'-harps of instrumentalists, concealed in cups of flowers, celebrated the return of the leafy season. April laughed in the air; you felt that warm showers were on the way, leaf-bringing showers which would cover the hedges with a green mantle. The earth had not yet donned her variegated garments, but she had unstiffened; she was getting warm.

When I drew near the mountain, and plunged into the forest, the face of things changed. The pines, always green, wrapped me in their shade. Underneath them there is neither spring nor summer; you only feel the influence of their unchangeableness; always a soft arborescent moss covering the shady spots with a carpet that absorbs the light; always the smooth ground spreading away under the colonnade of trees; always an equably lighted atmosphere; always this profound peace; always this air playing freshly round the smooth, straight trunks that rise in the immense forest nave.

As I ascended, as the plain sunk, my eye travelled to greater and greater depths. Through openings in the trees I could see very far below me in the distance, the old town with its old Burgundian towers; further still, at the extreme horizon, the white Alps ranging themselves tier above tier, with the giant Mont Blanc calmly throned upon their heads.

The wood was impregnated with a freshness unknown to the plain; one inhaled there a keen aromatic air, which would have felt almost raw, had it not been tempered by some sunbeams falling on all open places, lighting up the raspberry bushes and brambles that grew there.

As I went along, I thought of the family at the Springs. Worthy people, though rather odd. Father, mother, sons, all hard workers, not mixing much with their neighbours, taciturn, dull-eyed, and absent; very intelligent as to what concerned their own affairs; but half afraid of their neighbours, and keeping them at a distance.

Margaret, the eldest daughter, had done the same till the age of twenty. Then she suddenly took to leaving her solitude; every Sunday she went down through the wood, accompanied the other young people to the villages round, and came back late.

Her father and mother did not object to this; on the contrary, solitary themselves in their ways, they were glad to push their children a little into the world. The sons did not venture out; they were awkward, and they knew it, were not up, as they said, to *talking to the girls.* But Margaret, with only her twenty summers over her head, her tall figure, and her lofty air, was not so easily abashed.

All at once, without any apparent reason, she left off going out. Her mother wished to talk to her about the dances down in the valley; she only wept. Her father tried might and main to send her off there again; she locked herself up in her attic.

One evening that her young companions came to look for her, she went so high up into the wood, she knew all its hiding-places so well, that not a youth among them, looking ever so cleverly, was able to find her out. That night, at eleven o'clock, she returned home.

Gradually she grew sadder and sadder, and shut herself up more. She would sit spinning at the window without even looking out: spring came, she went on spinning; she no longer worked in the garden, she who used to be so fond of it. But she read a great deal, especially in the large Bible.

"That's what has done it!" said her father, and he took her books away. Margaret said nothing; for a moment her spirits seemed to return, but it was a mere flash. She got gloomier than ever, spun more diligently, then left off spinning altogether, or very nearly so; sat pensive in the corner of the window; refused to eat, and took to her bed.

Twelve was striking when I got to the Springs. A few bees humming round the hives, which stood on a plank before the window, were trying their wings in an April sunbeam. The water gushed and danced with a fresh warbling sound. In the stable, the prolonged lowing of the cow was heard, she was conscious that, out of door, the grass was growing green. A handsome black tom-cat, with gentle, limped eyes, had settled himself on the threshold of the barn, enjoying the sun in supreme idleness. A pleasant smell of good rustic soup spread all round the farmhouse. Everywhere reigned perfect order and deep silence, suggesting thoughts of a simple life, which opened out upon the soul like sudden peeps into an unknown land, very beautiful and very good, that we have been skirting unconsciously.

The noise made by my entrance brought the mother out of the adjoining room; she looked at me without saying a word, half surprised, half pleased, but surprise prevailed, and she remained motionless and embarrassed. We exchanged preliminary civilities.

"Your daughter is ill?"

The mother's face fell. "She has been too much at her books."

"She sent for me?"

Without further answer, the mother stood on one side to let me enter, and then followed me in.

The room was low but cheerful, and wainscoated with deal. There were two spinning-wheels in the two windows, a table, walnut-wood chairs well polished, a clock in a wooden case, with a glazed opening, through which one saw the oscillations of the pendulum. In the corner stood a curtainless bed; on that bed lay Margaret.

"I brought her down here," the mother said to me; "up-stairs she would be too lonely."

You heard nothing but the monotonous sound of the pendulum, and a sort of cracking noise before the stroke, each time the needle reached the quarters.

Margaret was dressed in a brown woollen petticoat, the wool of their own sheep, and homespun. A blue handkerchief, with white bunches of flowers, was crossed over her breast. The only unusual thing was, that instead of wearing a black cap trimmed with lace, her hair floated at random round her face. And then the apron was wanting —a decided sign of moral perturbation; and her shoes too, strong leather shoes, strongly soled, which I saw standing against the wall.

Margaret was lying on her back, pale, her marked features standing out from the wainscot, her eyes fixed on the ceiling, her hands clenched. There was about this calm of hers a certain character of determination, defiance,—I might almost say, despair.

I drew near.

"You are ill, Margaret?"

Margaret did not answer.

"She has not eaten anything for the last three days," broke in the mother. "We could hardly get her to take a drop of cold water to wet her lips and her forehead."

I remarked a sort of dampness on the young girl's forehead, and saw that the hair on her temples was wet. I tried to take her hand, but her fingers contracted.

"You are dressed; you have been up a little, then, Margaret?"

Not a word.

"It is in your mind you are suffering, Margaret?"

She turned her large eyes, the rest of her face remaining rigid, and fixed them on me.

"You wished to see me?"

With a sudden energetic motion she rose, threw her feet out of the bed, and sat on the edge of it.

"You had something to say to me?"

Margaret looked full at me. "I am lost!" she said, in a firm, rather choked voice, but without any violent outburst. She had measured her strength against this thought; she had lived in the contemplation of it. It was one of which she knew the length and breadth and height.

A strange feeling came over me, almost of joy. This young girl occupied with the care of her soul at an age when, bewildered with pleasure, few inquire whether indeed they have one or not; this young girl seemed to me rather saved than lost; consequently in a voice vibrating with cheerful hope—

"You think yourself lost?" I replied. "It is a good sign, Margaret. You will not remain where you are; you will seek, you will find"——

She shook her head; then in a monotonous tone, as if speaking to herself, her eyes fixed on I know not what vague something where nothing was,—

"It is all over!" she said. "I went back to the world; I did so though I was well warned; I did so in spite of God; *I have committed the unpardonable sin;* there is no more forgiveness!"

"What are you saying, Margaret? Are you to limit the powers of God! What creature dares to utter such impious words as these,—no more forgiveness!"

"Another sin! another sin!" cried the young girl, clasping her hands above her head.

I went on to say, very calmly indeed, "No doubt another sin; and as long as we speak we shall go on sinning."

She remained in the same desolate attitude. I gently unclasped her hands, and succeeded in taking one which she left in my grasp.

"Margaret, do you not know that God loves you?"

"He used to love me; I turned my back upon Him."

"You believe in Him?"

"As the devils do."

"You are sorry to have offended Him?"

She did not answer, but tore away her hand and rung it.

"Do the devils mourn their sins, Margaret?"

"Yesterday!" cried the young girl, following her own train of thought without being arrested by mine; "*yesterday*, I might have been forgiven."

She rose distractedly, her head thrown back, and began to walk up and down the room with tottering steps, I following her. She continued saying in the same monotonous voice, broken every now and then by a wild cry—

"*Yesterday*, I might have been saved. I did not choose."

"Do you choose now, Margaret?"

"Too late! too late!"

"Margaret, in God's name! Yes, you are lost if you will; you have not chosen; be it so; but is there not a Saviour in heaven, Margaret?"

"Too late! too late!" repeated she, setting the words to the sound made by her uneven steps.

"It is not then Easter Sunday to-day? Those who rejoice on earth, those who sing up there in heaven, are mad then? The dead Christ has remained dead; is it not so, Margaret?"

She continued her cadenced walk, repeating all the while, in a low voice—"Too late! too late!"

She was fearfully beautiful; drawn up to her full height, tottering, her hands sometimes thrown out before her with a tragic gesture, sometimes clasped; her pale face subjugated by the despotism of despair.

Then a terrible thought crossed my mind, but I would not admit it. I pressed Margaret hard; I drove her from one entrenchment to another; I shewed her the cross of Jesus; I repeated to her the self-complaints of St Paul, and his cry of triumph. I was indignant; I was overcome; I wept. Margaret did not listen; at last she fell upon the edge of the bed, and remained there speechless.

I fell there beside her; the day was getting on; all was indeed over. Margaret was mad, with that appalling madness which reasons, argues—is armed on every side with logic—finds a fearful satisfaction in the depths of its own despair.

While I was silent, my soul lost in the contemplation of this abyss, Margaret raised her head, then bent towards me gracefully, as if to listen. Her forehead cleared, her eyes swam in light, a heavenly smile parted her lips; joining her raised hands in ecstasy—

"Thanks!" she cried, in a voice that might have thrilled the angels. "Thanks! I have got peace! Thanks! I am saved. I shall see my God! Jesus has spoken to me. I belong to Him, to Jesus." She wiped her dripping temples. "Can this indeed be me? Yes it is; saved, saved!" She threw a wondering glance around, and saw me. "I believe! You have done me good. I have faith. I have it here." And she pressed both her hands to her heart.

I know not why, but this burst of happiness did not expand mine. However:

"God be praised!" I said. "And now that you are more calm"—Margaret's brow contracted a little—"leave off this train of thought; you are ill." She shook her head. "Try to sleep."

I went on saying kind words to her,—gentle, caressing words, such as one would whisper in the ear of a feverish child. Putting aside all idea of uncertainty, all that could shake the electrical moral atmosphere, I tried to confirm her in her happiness as in a permanent state out of which she was never more to be disturbed.

I was still speaking when her face changed; she stretched out her hand to silence me. I stopped; she remained still for a moment; then, with a cry, the vehemence and desolation of which I shall never forget—"He is there!" she said, pointing to the corner of the room. She rose up erect, her hair standing on end, made a step forward, with a fixed eye, and hand still extended.

"He is there!"

"Who?"

"He who has lost me!"

"You are saved, Margaret, you are saved!"

I had seized hold of her arm; I shook her as though to waken her out of her delusion. She did not even look at me.

Her mother sat there silent and stupified.

"I was saved; I listened to him; I am lost!"

"It is not true!" I cried vehemently. Margaret raised her finger.

"Hush, God is speaking to me!" . . . . Then, in a very low, sweet voice, "My daughter, thou hast doubted! I had forgiven thee, my daughter; . . . . my child, why hast thou done so?"

"This is madness, Margaret, it is a delusion of the wicked one."

Margaret again began the same wild, uneven walk as before; only now I had to support her, and she no longer reasoned. At one moment, she listened to the hissing whispers of Satan the accuser; at another, to that counterfeit voice of God, those tenderly inexorable accents which sealed her doom. Her screams were sometimes maniacal; then came tears and tenderness, which melted my heart; then fits of silence more fearful still.

As for me, I could not speak. I could only look up to

heaven with that ardent look, almost indeed audacious, but glowing with so much pity, such strength of love and faith, and such humility beneath the boldness, that it goes straight to the throne, to claim the tenderest mercies of God.

And then, in a rapid revulsion of feeling, I asked myself whether indeed this mad woman might not be the only wise one. On which side really was the insanity; on hers, heart-broken, her eyes drowned in tears, her breast beaten by her hands; or on ours, frivolous, forgetful; on ours, the pious, the redeemed, indulgent to ourselves, and lulling our souls with the repeated cry, Peace! Peace!

No, my Saviour, Thou art not a God of despair; Thou art a God of joy, because Thou art a God of pardon.

And yet something like a shiver ran through my veins. This lasted all the day. This poor maniac who saw Satan, who heard the Lord, who weighed in the balance of the last day each word that had escaped her lips, each thought that had risen to her heart; this mourner who took in earnest the terrible realities of the Bible, forgetting only Jesus; this poor woman, deranged, sick, whom I wished to console; I in my sound senses, I firm in my faith; she shook me to the most secret centre of my soul.

When the day got low, Margaret, exhausted, sunk on her bed. Her father and brothers had returned.

"You must go back," said the mother; "we are much obliged, but you do no good."

"Shall I send for a doctor?"

"No. Her father was right about it. *She has been too much at her books.*"

I was disturbing the family; there was nothing indeed to be done, or rather the only thing to be done was what I could do anywhere. The God of the forests, of the mountain and the valley, the God of sorrowing hearts, is everywhere present. I walked very quickly under the fir-trees; I wanted rapid exercise. For a moment stopping at the lower border of the wood on the first open ground commanding the glaciers and the lakes, I inhaled the free air; I gazed upon the wide expanse before me; I dazzled myself with light; drank in the ineffable calm of the fields, and then I took my way along the meadows, and through the corn-fields.

Below me, beside the brook, on a wild pear-tree, and perched on its highest branch, looking steadily at the sun which was setting in his purple, or rather in that blended glory of scarlet and orange which overflowed the West, sat a redbreast, with throat distended and quivering wings. The sound of my steps had not disturbed him. He was revelling in all this magnificence; he was chanting his evening chant; a chant of adoration, love, and hope; a trusting, happy song, an humble ditty, sparkling all over with little cries of joy—a glorious hymn; it was one and all of these. The flood of light inundated him; he was lost in it quite; he sang as long as the radiance of the horizon lasted; then, when the sun had left our hemisphere, when the pomp of his setting rays was over, the redbreast, flapping his little wings, went to shelter under the nearest bush.

I do not know how it came about, but peace had returned to my heart.

A POOR BOY.

POOR, and, moreover, ugly to a degree hardly permissible, except to very clever people indeed, and he was half-witted.

He was the son of a shrewd countryman, a shoemaker by trade. His father, a great talker, musical too, in his leisure hours, had gray, wandering eyes, a countenance very difficult exactly to decipher, with something about it changing, slippery, and evasive, reminding one of a serpent under dry leaves. Added to which, he had an abrupt voice; and was hard to live with at home.

On wet Sundays our shoemaker would study an old book of the year 1600, full of formulas, semi-magical, semi-medical. Albertus Magnus had contributed more to it than Esculapius. Spectacles on nose, he would rapidly turn it over, then meditate in a way that brought him the reputation of *mège*.* One day this neighbour, to-morrow that, would come at nightfall, to ask for some specific, now for the cow, now for the wife; the usual fee being a sausage, or, better still, a bottle of wine drunk at the village tavern.

You should have heard the marvellous stories our man made them swallow. Of young fellows well thrashed, rifle-shots, broken teeth, balls in the very centre of the white—it was all one to him! Then came mysterious stories of cattle bewitched, girls who had drunk love-potions,

* Something less than magician and more than doctor.

while the peasants gazed at him open-mouthed. "Eh, he's a wise one, he is!" and they nodded significantly.

It must be owned that if our friend was not exactly a sorcerer, he had at least a singular aptitude for work of various kinds; farmer, carpenter, blacksmith, rifleman—at need he was one and all of these. "He has some charm," his neighbours would say.

The shoemaker let them say on, and laughed a silent sort of laugh, which did not brighten his impenetrable face.

He made a great deal of money; yet had nothing, or next to nothing laid by, for it was spent as fast as it came in. This, he averred, was all his wife's fault. No order, no comfort, no foresight—a gawky slattern! He did not scruple to tell her this, and the poor, weak creature, sure to excite her master's anger every time he chanced to see her, had, over and above an indisputable natural gift of stupidity, all the awkwardness that arises from constant fault-finding.

She lived in a hostile atmosphere, her husband ridiculing whenever he did not revile her. Her gait was uncertain, she was incoherent, her mind always clouded by the fear of doing wrong; her hands often trembling, though she was in the prime of life; her glance vacillating, too, but it was only constant fear which prevented it being straightforward.

Her home—had she indeed a home? She had never in her life said, *my* kitchen, *my* bed! Her house was always dirty and disorderly; not that she did not sweep and brush, especially in the first years of her married life, but she had no *faculty*, none of that calm necessary to systematic working. Her thoughts, all incomplete, whirled round in her head as if driven by the wind. As years increased, her activity grew less; not because she was gaining habits of reflection, but becoming more and more dispirited.

Without having thought the matter out, she had a vague sense that the less her husband saw her, the more peace she had; so she bestirred herself as little as she possibly could.

In the morning, she would drag herself to the well in an old cap, an old jacket, an old petticoat; having drawn up her bucket full, she would languidly wash her potatoes, go in again, put the dinner on the fire, and, with inefficient hand, brush the kitchen a little.

As soon as she heard the master's voice, she spilled the water, let fall the broom, and the moment her work was over, would sit squatting on the hearthstone, and remain there, in the darkest corner, for hours together.

In the adjoining room sat the master amidst his hides, drawing thread after thread, and, under his spectacles, casting an evil eye at her if she ever ventured across the threshold. She did so as little as possible. Such was their domestic life.

A son was growing up in this house.

The father, a great reader, pedantic, and pretentious, had chosen to call him Ulysses. Never was hapless new-comer on our earth saddled with a more palpable misnomer.

The shoemaker, disappointed in his wife, built great hopes upon his son; he would be this, that, and the other; he would make a gentleman of him! The mother, for her part, made him in her own likeness.

As a mere urchin, he had a dishevelled head, with two round prominent eyes, wandering, colourless, scared like his mother's, dubious like his father's. Beneath was the most inconceivably twisted nose ever seen, a mouth from ear to ear, the whole mounted upon two interminable bow-legs, a badly-made body, and arms whose dexterity might alone have excused their length; but had they been short as puffin's wings, they could not have been more awkward.

Only, whether he inherited it of his father, or owed it to a certain inherent innocence, Ulysses did everything with an imperturbable assurance. True, he did everything ill, but he did it with good heart. If he took up a mug, twice out of five times he would break it; if he moved a chair, he let it fall; if he lit the fire, he blew the cinders into the porridge-pot; if he tried to feed the cow, he would infallibly have put out her eye with his fork, but that the worthy animal, who knew him from a child, always turned away at once. Nothing daunted him, however, and when his father, who hesitated to acknowledge inherent inveterate awkwardness in his son, would storm and discharge, out of his workshop, double and triple volleys of epithets by no means select, Ulysses would look at him in amazement, shuffle his feet, shrug his shoulders, in a way all his own, and break out into an imbecile horse-laugh.

At school he fared no better. "*Il se cotte*," said the master, from the verb *cotter*, to shut, which is used in our district. Ulysses, whose mind remained almost impervious to the letters of the alphabet, was more than ever *shut up* when it came to syllables; while between syllables and words yawned a quite impassable abyss.

It was all the same with arithmetic. Ulysses knew, indeed, that, in point of fact, one apple and two apples make three apples; that when the innkeeper's son took two, he had only one left; but this transaction translated into figures left him stunned and stupified. He would contemplate with his unquiet eyes the white symbols on the black board, crush the chalk between his fingers, and then pass them over his face, till the whole school burst out laughing, and the master put him behind the door, and made him kneel there.

His best Sundays were spent in the wood-hole. For as to the Catechism, as to those dry and exceedingly abstract answers that have to be gone through without a single stumble, Ulysses never got beyond the first half of the first sentence. It is but just, however, to state, that he repeated it five times, ten times, that he would have repeated it twenty or thirty irremissibly chained to the same place, if the master had not administered a *back-hander* that broke the spell.

His father would say, "It will all come right by and by; he's not stupid, take my word for it."

What with the great ruler of the schoolmaster, a square ruler falling sometimes on the fingers, sometimes on the back; and what with the cuffs, varied with kicks, bestowed on him by his father, Ulysses grew indeed,—but it did not come right.

He remained where he was, *borné*,—knowing, parrot-fashion, the little he did know, not malignant, self-complacent, trusting, turning up his twisted nose with the air of a youth who, if he would, could afford to make fun of all the rest of the world.

A horrible suspicion now began to dawn upon his father's mind, that of his son being a simpleton. He resisted it, however, at first through pride, then through a species of instinctive affection little higher than that of the animals. He knew himself, knew that from the very moment when he lost all hopes of Ulysses, he should begin to hate him. This thought was painful; he clung might and main to his illusion; only he began to look more than ever askance at his wife.

The poor mother for her part would gladly have loved her son. Alas! the proper spring was broken; when he was beaten, she only suffered with a passive suffering which never led her to take his part,—that was all. While his father was still in doubt upon the subject, the stupidity of Ulysses was a settled point with his little playfellows. They made fun of him; they turned him round their fingers, without, however, teasing him too much, because he gave in to all so good naturedly. The more they bantered him, the better he was pleased; he believed everything with marvellous credulity; always good-humoured; laughing with those who laughed at him. As to ill-luck, he took it as it came, and good luck too. There was no thorough holiday without Ulysses. He was summoned and put at the head of the troop, supported by two sharp urchins, who played him fine tricks. He was overwhelmed with delight; he thought himself the sharpest, the most dexterous of the whole party; thought himself handsome, smart,—whatever they chose. There was nothing hostile about his vanity. It did not spring from self-love, but from unlimited trust, unfathomable innocence, innate ingenuousness, proof against the most sobering experiences. Tricked yesterday, Ulysses bore no malice; he was ready to be tricked again to-morrow.

And what tricks the boys and girls used to play him in the court-yard of the old manor! How they used to laugh at him! Happy days, proud days for Ulysses. It was a sight to see him when he came in perched on those long stilts of his, making a leg, and returning an imbecile laugh to the hoots and roars that welcomed him.

"Come here and try, Ulysses; come and try; we want you!"

Ulysses came forward.

"You are the only one to do this well."

They were playing at *the pyramid.* Ulysses was hoisted upon the shoulders of two vagabonds,—rocked, shaken by them, while they called out, "Take care! stand steady!" till, after incredible efforts to maintain his equilibrium, he fell like a lump of lead, rubbed his knees and elbows, then looked at the rogues, who were in convulsions of laughter, and only said, "Ah, very well, if I had liked!"

Or else a piece of money was thrown into a bucket of water: "Pick it up, Ulysses; you are the one to do it; we can't, any of us. Look, that's the way, with the teeth —so—open your eyes, shut your nose and ears."

Ulysses would plunge boldly, then, somewhat dashed by the cold water, he would jump about, sneezing, shaking his head, wetting all the curious standers-by, but quite ready to return to the charge a hundred times if they liked.

Or else it was the race. He who never saw Ulysses run on those great dislocated legs of his, with neck outstretched and paddling arms, may be said to have seen nothing!

Then they called out to him, "Ulysses, go and kiss the prettiest girl." Straightway Ulysses went; a general flight, a very hail of scratches! Ulysses was persevering; he did not mind jeers, he was used to them; he would have run on for three hours—feeling sure to succeed at last, if some one had not stopped him.

There was mischief enough among these village lads, but no malignity. Ulysses was not any one's friend, indeed, but no one would deliberately have hurt him. He got plenty of cuffs, it is true, and they risked his bones without much scruple; but he himself did not take much care of them. Indeed, but for a certain obtuseness which rendered him half-witted, Ulysses had in him the making of a hero,—indifference to pain perfect self-reliance, indefatigable perseverance; that simple resolution which marches straight forward through fire and water to its goal.

Poor Ulysses! he was very happy on these fine Sundays, these gay days of childhood, in that fine court-yard; always a prominent person, and even if not, leaping, playing away, animated by the same spirit as all the rest.

Sometimes in July there would come from the mountain a burst of the wind we call "Joran," sweeping the ground, making the leaves waltz wildly, twisting the trees in the orchard, strewing the fields with green apples. What spoils, what plunder! And while one gathered and munched, and exulted with flying hair in the violence of the storm—in anything out of the common way, the hurricane bent the immense branches of the planes, which shewed the white lining of their leaves as they flung themselves about; and the court resounded with wild clamours.

In June again, when the cows were leaving for the mountain, there was a very different scene.

One heard the cattle from a great distance; heard them coming along the paths and roads all round the enclosure. The ringing of the *toupins*,* with their solemn tones; the silver bells, the loud *yolées* of the shepherd; their prolonged cries spread through the air, drawing nearer and nearer still. The little boys rush to the entrance of the village, group themselves around the public-house, where the drovers halt to drink a drop or two, and get up their

* A large bell of the shape of a reversed tulip. There are about ten of them for every herd of one hundred cows. They are hung to their necks, both in ascending and descending the mountain; then taken off, and arranged along one of the beams of the "*châlet*." If some foolish practical joker sets them ringing, all the herd take their way again to the plain.

strength, for night is coming on, and it is no joke to climb the mountain at midnight with from sixty to a hundred cows at one's heels.

While the drovers drink, the lads take charge of the herd: "Ulysses, the great whip is for you; you shall hold the bull."

And Ulysses went to do so without the least fear.

Here they come! here they come! the handsomest cow first, with her large nosegay on her head, her bell round her neck, suspended to the leathern collar, with antique embroidery, and the escutcheon of the Canton: *Liberté! patrie!* She would die, the beautiful cow—this has happened before now—she would die if the drovers were to take away her nosegay and her necklace to give them to any other! Just look at her, how she advances, proud and stately, with heavy measured steps.

Here are the drovers, grave, fine-looking fellows. They have left the valley, left their homes; they pined for the mountains, the upper pastures, the long twilights, the wide view over the low country and the Alps; they languished for the free life, the long distances, the cheeses, and things in general up there.

There are the scanty household goods in a cart, a caldron in the middle. All the cattle follow,—white, black, red, brindled. As for the goats, they went first; they have been for some days on the mountain.

The boys cluster round with knowing countenance, and, while the drovers refresh themselves at the tavern, they *yole* in their turn, tutor, worry the cattle, till one or the other of the cowherds standing at the door, roars out—"Will you leave them alone, then? Do you want me down upon you?" Ulysses did not escape a few pushes and pokes, but that was nothing; he returned proud and happy, turning up his nose with a victorious air.

His father, seeing him in this mood, took courage again.

And then autumn! true season of junketing! no school! fruit everywhere!

There are in September golden days such as no other month brings. The sun is pale; heavy morning dews have made the grass green again; it is newly mown. There are hardly any flowers left, except the pale crocus, but you can walk freely through the fields in every direction. No standing crops, no hemp, hay, or lucerne; the eye glides over the green expanse, can take in all the country. The air is subtle; amber rays shine through the boughs; the foliage, not yet tinged with red, has something more delicate about it; less density; one would say that all nature was idealised. A few gnats, born yesterday, to die to-morrow, are executing in the ethereal atmosphere a dance, the undulations of which are full of mystery. At the foot of the apple and the pear-trees are heaps of red and white apples, and pears of golden hue.

Then it was that Ulysses feasted. His father had neither fields nor orchard; but his companions were there; they reached him apples,—a little worm-eaten, perhaps, but he did not look too closely.

Then came October. The cows descended in the order they had gone up. The warm nights during which they had climbed the mountain, when the moon shone bright, when the cytisus, together with roses and tulips, blossomed on their horned heads; when one heard, winding at various distances through the gloom, the sound of bells, *toupins,* and *yolées,*—these are past. Of late, especially these last few days, the cows have been cold up there, and summer being over, have had but scanty fare; and now they spread over the fields, twisting off great mouthfuls of grass, and sniffing with their cool muzzles at all tempting plants; and as they move along from one to the other, rubbing against the old trees, and pensively standing still to look over the hedge, then returning to graze with steady step, the little bells sound and re-sound. The great *toupins* have been taken off, they are hung up till next season. From one horizon to the other, the country echoes with this rustic music; the valley answers the hill; in the best concealed nooks between the rocks, at the edge of the wood, this ringing is heard, giving birth to wild fragments of melody, all their discords dying away in the misty air; drowned in a great universal harmony.

It is then that *boebes* * are in request. Each of them for a five-franc piece, and the addition of a pair of shoes, if the master is generous, may take the cattle to feed during the short season of autumn. One constantly meets in all the roads around, a cow, two or three cows, a few sheep behind them, and behind the sheep, a lad, fair-haired, chubby, bare-headed, with a brother or sister, younger than himself, running after him.

In the fields, a fire is made; a beautiful bright fire which crackles, smokes, and flames. Some underground hiding-place is made into which to stuff the yellow carrots left in the field, till they can be carried off on the morrow. On the very tip-top of a tree, on its highest branch, a pear is descried, juicy, melting, one can see that from here.

"Ulysses! Ulysses! this is the very thing for you. Up you go, my boy!" Ulysses never in his life tried to climb anything whatsoever without falling flat, more or less bruised; but never mind, he will go all the same. "Are you afraid?"

Ulysses shrugs his shoulders, makes a spring; they support him, squeeze him against the tree, lift him, push, pro-

* A little boy, from the German *Bube*.

pel: "Courage, my fine fellow; there you are!" Then they let him go; he is on his back on the ground, his great arms and great legs telegraphing like those of a field-spider. The rest are rolling in the grass in fits of laughter.

But for all this, these were Ulysses' good days. He too, like others, had a joyous childhood, thickly sown with pleasant memories. For him, as for the rest, there had been sunshine, apples, merry Sundays, a few more hard knocks, and all the rest. As for ridicule, he did not see his own infirmity, he did not feel it; as for his father's brutalities, he had never known him different; as for the suffering apathy of his mother, he was not aware of it. As he grew up, as she got weaker, he did what he could for her; he carried water, split wood. She used to say to him, "You are a pretty fellow, you are." He believed her: this went on for some years.

With his fifteenth year there came an increase of awkwardness; his whole life took a new turn. His ugliness grew with his growth. Ulysses became preternaturally tall, clumsy, and backward.

His companions, having grown older, were naughtier than they were, and dragged him into worse scrapes. The schoolmaster had given him up long ago. His mother got thinner and a greater nonentity day by day. His father was more irritable, more hard, a savage expression sometimes passed over his face; never a word of affection, never even one of indifference; he was either silent or storming. The mother had not sufficiently the habit of taking the initiative to dream of consoling her son; if she had so dreamed, she lacked the energy to carry it out, but the very idea never occurred to her.

The father in his workshop, the mother in the kitchen, the son driven from pillar to post by great volleys of oaths—bullied for what he did, because he did it ill; bullied for what he did not do, because he left it undone, —such was their domestic life.

Generally, Ulysses crouched at the corner of the hearth, near his mother, his knees pushed up above his ears, his hands groping for some brand among the cinders.

At last the father understood clearly that he had for his son a half-witted creature, below the average standard, below the inferior; a son who knew nothing, who would know nothing, who was good for nothing; a lad that others laughed at, and had a right to laugh at; a booby, the standing joke of the village,—his son, his!

All this was abrupt, clear, decisive. The thing once proved, the blow once fallen, with a change of feeling inexorable as a fact, the father began to detest his son. There was neither remorse nor reaction. As he was the master, he tyrannised over him. Henceforth, the only portion of Ulysses was work beyond his strength, poor and scanty food, and rude blows from a heavy hand upon every occasion. All this without premeditation, quite naturally and spontaneously.

Ill received, ill treated, rebuffed by all, except such comrades as made him subservient to their sports, Ulysses lost much of his innocent confidence. But if they took pains about it, the village lads were still able to waken in him some sparks of his former love of adventure. Then there were exploits that served for the diversion of long winter evenings.

Sometimes they would take him to the public-house, make him tipsy, then egg him on to attack some good boxer, who left him half-dead; sometimes they persuaded him to go by night and sing under the window of the richest girl in the place; the father of the lady, who was not to be trifled with, would throw a log at him, the brothers would sally forth—Ulysses came back with his head laid open. At other times they would get him into some scrapes with the *messeliers** and the municipals; and, when the mine was sprung, would make their escape, leaving him in their hands. The official wrath fell heavy on his luckless head, fine after fine was imposed, the shoemaker wielded his terrible cudgel, the frightened lad would go and hide behind the faggots in the shed, and it was much if his mother dared to keep back a little cold soup for him.

Then, suddenly as the truth had broken on his father's mind, there dawned a ray of light on that of the son. A vague consciousness of inferiority came over him, nothing very positive, indeed, but a species of self-dissatisfaction, a kind of apprehension of others. A confused sense of his own ugliness awoke, then grew, till the moment when he fully comprehended to what a degree he was misshapen, grotesque, ugly, with an inexorable, absurd, crushing, hopeless ugliness.

That was the first step, others soon followed. He saw himself awkward, stupid, more stupid even than he was. It seemed that sorrow developed his mind, that a soul was given him to suffer with. He saw himself repulsive, despicable; all his life passed before him like a bad farce, of which he had been the clown.

He did not lose himself in analysis; but the tide of sadness went on rising, and submerged him.

He became gloomy, unsociable; he would glide along the houses, escape from his former companions; and, his task done, climb to his garret, throw himself on his pallet, swallowed up in the contemplation of his misery.

No more smiles, no more confidence; an immeasurable

* Rural police.

wretchedness paralysed him. He had no anger, no hatred against any one, only he deeply abhorred himself.

It is a great misfortune to discern that one is imprisoned in ugliness and stupidity; to feel that one is an object of disgust to others, and that they are right. It is a suffering akin to egotism, and often leading to it. Despised by others, one takes to idolising self; in default of noble emotions, one falls back on gross pleasures.

It was not so, however, with Ulysses.

When he had once fully understood that he was an utter failure, that no one loved him, that all ridiculed him, that there was no help for it; when he had ascertained his limitations on every side, supremely disgusted with himself, he began to droop, as his mother had done, but with fuller consciousness of what he was and how he suffered. His sun had set with his illusions. A cold autumn fog had risen; he was, as it were, frozen up.

Formerly, after the paternal storms, he would shake himself, run off to the village, come in for fresh blows there, and return amused. Now, there was no more elasticity, no incidents; everything had foundered. His solitary days succeeded each other all equally unhappy. He did not give himself up to despair indeed; that would have implied some energy, but atrophy set in, and he rapidly declined.

His father was only irritated by his growing uselessness. Weakened as he was, Ulysses became still more awkward. The axe and the hoe, put into his hands by his father, were sure to slip out of his weak grasp. The shoemaker's bursts of rage, which used to glide harmlessly over his son's inert organism, his abusive language and rough treatment, now told indelibly on mind and body alike. He did not ask affection from any one; he felt no claim upon any kindness whatsoever; it never entered his head to bespeak his father's compassion; but he was dying from a dearth of all these.

Sometimes, when the anguish was too great, when he could not make head against it, he would look at his mother. It seemed as though help ought to come from her; not that he had courage enough to speak openly to her; not even to give her a caress,—that silent language of those whose lips are closed; but still a secret instinct told him to look for comfort there.

His mother, on her part, looked at him with surprise. She plainly saw that there was something wrong; that Ulysses got silent; that sometimes tears gathered in his eyes; that he was very pale, and could hardly walk; that his father's rages terrified him, him who used to mind them so little; but she could analyse nothing: she would glance at her husband, shrink into herself, retreat instinctively, and murmur, "Must have patience, my lad; must have patience."

The disease increased. His father's brutalities, insufficient food, heart-sorrow, soon undermined the poor body which had never had any overplus of vitality. At night, fever consumed him; in the morning, he was cold as death: there was never a drop of wine to revive him. Neither mother nor son could have had courage to reach a hand at meals towards the shoemaker's bottle. Extensive sores, that livery of extreme destitution, came to finish what atrophy had begun. He had to give up all work. His father said nothing; he saw that his son was ill, and got so much the harder.

Ulysses, idle through necessity, hardly dared to creep down twice a day from his garret, and take his place at meals. After getting a little unstiffened in the darkest corner near the hearth, he would drag himself up again. He passed whole hours motionless, without amusement, without consolation; repelled from the past by bitter memories, from the future by vague terrors; weak, languid, without a murmur or a complaint; gazing, lost in an undefinable reverie, at the dull daylight which shone through his dirty window, or at the bare walls of his wretched attic. No one in the village perceived that Ulysses was failing. He had gradually separated himself from all the young people; they got into the habit of leaving him alone; then, when he was no more seen about, he was forgotten.

He had done as the wild beasts do,—he had gone apart to die. His mother watched with a stupid eye the progress of his disease. One day, when his father was out working, she went up to Ulysses, and asked him in a whisper what ailed him.

"I suffer," he replied, in a listless voice.

She grew uneasy, drew nearer; her son's emaciation frightened her. She pushed his coarse shirt aside, saw his chest, saw the ravages the sores had made, gave a kind of suppressed moan; then went down, brought up some rags and some vinegar, and proceeded to dress them. Every day she secretly did this, choosing the time when his father was at the public-house. Her hands were clumsy, her treatment was wretched enough; but what good it did Ulysses! how he used to listen for her furtive step upon the wooden stair!

About the same time the pastor and the family at the manor chanced to inquire where Ulysses was, and why he was never to be met with about. As soon as he was known to be ill, he was visited; not with much hope, however, of giving him any pleasure, of getting anything out of him, or conveying anything to him,—his was such a dense nature! Still he was ill, he must be attended to; he had a soul, it might need consolation. His neglected condition, his disease appalled his visitors. All manner of help arrived. Ulysses used to thank, but he was stupified and reserved. There was no getting at him; he was conscious of the compassion felt, but that did not reconcile him to his own repulsive individuality. On the contrary, unconsciously it only depressed him the more. Then he was spoken to of God, of the Saviour. Ulysses listened very seriously with a pensive air, as if amazed at these new tidings; but he said nothing. Only, when those who spoke thus to him knocked at his garret, he used to rise with a spring beyond his strength, and to open the door for them.

This went on some time. Then, a little from weariness of talking, as it were, to the air, a little from a sense of human helplessness, recourse was had to God's own Book. Without well knowing what he could make out of it, they tried to read him some chapters in the Gospels, some Psalms, the history of the patriarchs; above all, the life of the Lord Jesus. They did not comment much; just two or three short, simple words; more would have been thrown away. Insensibly the expression of Ulysses lit up; his eyes brightened, his countenance awoke; I know not what intimate content,—not the stupid satisfaction of yore; no, but something humble, reticent, noble, ay, noble,—was shed over his pale face. Once or twice, in a quiet voice neither bold nor timid, he put some questions which amazed his visitors.

This went on progressing like the dawning light of day; with steady, royal step,—as God works when He does work. No clouds rose; this sun never stood still. No doubt, no fear, very little difficulty. The gospel in its fulness penetrated at once with all it beauty, its power, its tenderness, into this heart, disinherited heretofore of happiness. This heart grew radiant.

Jesus had met this fainting spirit in the desert; He had raised this poor child from the earth, and taken him into His arms. Jesus was the first who ever loved him. Accordingly, how well Ulysses distinguished His voice from all others! It entered his inmost soul, and he followed Jesus. To dispute, to doubt? Ulysses could no more do so than could Moses, when, standing on the holy mountain. God made His goodness to pass before him.

Ulysses had listened, believed with all his might, with his whole being. He loved unboundedly that Jesus who had called him by his name,—by his much-ridiculed name,—and had said to him, "My son, give me thy heart." There was about his faith a certain spring-tide innocence. One saw revive and blossom, but blossom as they do under the Lord's touch only, those natural gifts of trust and simplicity which formerly cast an unsteady light over his incomplete nature.

Jesus was not for him that abstraction, that great prophet that God dying for us on the horizon of remotest ages inhabiting eternity; nor was He that philosopher, tha legislator which many of our wisest only know Him as unconscious that they do not know Him at all.

Jesus was his Creator, Jesus was his Saviour. He died yesterday upon the cross in horrible suffering for him—him, a *scoundrel,* as he would cry out in his strong emotion.

And this Jesus, victorious, sympathising, his friend, would come and spend long hours at his side in his garret. He hardly dared to say anything, or said very little to other men, but to Jesus! The others were compassionate, were kind, worthy people; Ulysses was not worth the pains they took about him; but Jesus! Jesus who had hungered, who had been cold; Jesus whom they insulted throughout one dark night about Easter time; Jesus who touched the leper with His own hand; Jesus was his brother at the same time that He was his God; he was quite at home with Him.

Ulysses had never complained much; now he did not complain at all. One could hardly get him to say a word about his sufferings. He had received the Bible promises with the trust of a child who hears his father speak. He realised them all. To hope, to enter the paradise of light, to see his God, quench his thirst, possess inexpressible bliss from eternity to eternity, this was all one and the same thing to him,—simple, and easy, and, as it were, already done.

As long as he could hold up, he would drag about his garret, peaceful and pensive, his glance fixed elsewhere. "I am soon going," he would say, and then he would sit upon his poor pallet, while so much joy lit up his face, the few words he spoke vibrated so strongly, he possessed his Saviour in such royal guise, that one felt overcome in the presence of this poor, weak creature; overcome and humbled, adoring God because His hand was there.

Ulysses was in great haste to go, but he was not impatient: "When He sees it fit, He will come," he was wont to say; or else in village parlance, "He is certain sure to come."

His father never saw him now; Ulysses could not go down-stairs, his father did not come up. Some people, those who had courage enough, would turn in to the shoemaker in leaving the garret. "Your son is very ill." No answer. "He is very patient!" Nothing. "If you were to"—— A cold, dry look cut the speaker short.

The poor mother had taken to loving her son with all the little strength she had left. She did not well understand what had taken place in him; but she felt a craving to see and to hear him. When he spoke of God, she listened with a great effort to understand; when he prayed, she knelt down beside him. She crept quietly into the illuminated hemisphere where her son abode. She received a transmitted joy; a second-hand happiness; reflected, indeed, like the light of the moon, but yet coming to her from God. She found that it was good to be there; she felt herself more at ease; she would have liked things to have gone on always thus. But the poor lad had suffered enough.

One night he cheerfully embraced his mother, and said —"Mother, you want *us* to be together with the Lord; you must believe Him."

"Yes," answered she, looking much impressed.

"Tell the father to come up."

"The father!" she repeated in horror.

"Go and call him, mother."

Ulysses had never spoken so before. She went away trembling; clung to the bannister in going down-stairs; opened the door of the kitchen, then that of the next room, and remained on the threshold. She stood there some moments, not daring to stir. The shoemaker turned round.

"What's the row now?" he thundered out.

"The boy—Ulysses"——

"What about him?"

"He is asking for you, father."

An almost imperceptible shudder shook the father's hand.

"I have no time."

His wife, scared, turned away. While she was closing the door,

"To-morrow," he added, in a rough voice.

The mother went up again quite pleased.

"Well, mother?"

"He has said To-morrow."

"*To-morrow!*" repeated the young man, with a singular smile.

They were a long time together after that. Ulysses spoke more to his mother about the Lord Jesus than he had yet done; then, when it got late, said, "You must go down now, mother; father will scold."

His mother had not a quick intuition, but something weighed upon her heart; she would have wished to remain; but her husband was beginning to walk up and down in the room below.

"Go, mother," said Ulysses in the same grave tone. He turned to the wall; she looked long at him, left the room, listened to his breathing, she did not know why, then went down-stairs.

That night the angels of God came for Lazarus. He went away noiselessly, humbly. In what a rapture of bliss, Eternity will tell us.

In the morning, his mother went up anxiously to his attic. She was surprised to see him lie so still; she was surprised at the great stillness; herself, she could not speak. She touched him with her finger; then, with a shriek and beside herself, she rushed down-stairs into her husband's room, and standing erect before him for the first time in her life, with uplifted voice, and a gesture of desolation almost appalling—"*He is dead!*" she cried.

The shoemaker grew pale, then coughed, then looked at her with his dull, vacillating, merciless eye; looked at her till she bent again; till she shrunk within herself; till, with drooping head, and unsteady steps, drawing further and further back, she returned to the kitchen, to the corner of the hearth, to crouch there as she did yesterday, as she did a year ago, as she will to-morrow, as she will ten years to come, as she will so long as she lives.

THE GALLEY-SLAVE.

DO not know why this particular figure should haunt me so, but it is one which constantly recurs. I will sketch it here, with a few rapid touches.

I only saw the man twice.

The first time was at the house of a young invalid girl. She lived with an old lady who filled, I think, the post of inspector at the *Halle aux Blés*.* The two women, who were in no way related, but had a strong bond of union, in their mutual poverty, occupied a very humble apartment, in the vicinity of the Halle. Their rooms were on the fourth floor of a very small and crowded house. The elder of the two had to be at her post from an early hour of the morning. Euphemia, the younger—*Phemie*, as she called herself—always stayed at home. From the first day of her taking up her abode there, she had never gone down the stair. She was not able to do so; her limbs, paralysed in consequence of a long and dreadful illness, refused to support her. Her frame was worn, almost distorted by suffering, but her face was still young and fresh. One hardly noticed its insignificant features; the expression was all. It was gentle, intelligent, refined, and she had a gracefulness of diction, a charming voice, a glance so innocent, and yet so bright,—a *tout ensemble*, in short, which made the hours fly while one listened to her talk.

She spent her long days alone. By way of solace, she

* The corn market.

had always some embroidery on hand, which she executed rapidly and well; and for company, she had two canaries, who sung cheerily in their cage behind a trellis overgrown with nasturtiums, very green in July, very bare in late autumn, when Phemie would take the cage in and garnish it well with chickweed.

Her wants were few; in the morning she had breakfast with her companion, and took nothing till evening, except a glass of cold water, which she went to the kitchen to get, dragging herself thither with some difficulty on her crutches. That used to occupy a full quarter of an hour, and was as good as a walk, she used to say.

The room she occupied was light, pretty, exquisitely neat and clean, with its bits of old china and old glass on the chest of drawers; its white curtains, its little tokens of an elegant poverty, revealing spirits stronger than the pressure of circumstance.

Euphemia loved God. She would have liked to work actively for Him. He only permitted her to suffer and to pray; she took life accordingly, as He gave it her. Only, whenever a corn-porter came up to the little room on business, Phemie very courageously, with that delicate tact that she had, that simplicity enlightened by natural intelligence, entered at once upon serious subjects, and would hardly let him leave without speaking a few good words to him.

Many listened to her silently, not caring to prolong the conversation; while others spoke freely, nay, would even discuss the subject with her; but no one felt himself jarred,—no one laughed, and some of them returned.

I happened to know Euphemia. That day, when I went up to her room, I did not find her alone. She was sitting near the window, its light being softened by the nasturtiums in full flower. She was embroidering in her quiet way, with a cheerful look on her face. She greeted me with a bend of the head and a smile, with that modest ease free from familiarity as from awkwardness, which certain natures bring with them at their birth, under the thatched roof as well as under the gilded.

This is not a thing to be acquired: one has it or has it not. If one has it not, one never will have it. Now, Euphemia had it; she was a poor girl and a perfect lady, but her manners accorded admirably with her slender means. Everything was in excellent keeping; she was the right person in the right place.

There are some people whose every look and word raise legions of incongruities, which attend the whole course of their life. Euphemia, on the contrary, was one of those harmoniously gifted spirits, on whom peace ever waits,—peace, propriety, ease, and fitness. The little that she did was well, because spontaneously, done. She was graceful in appearance and manner; never embarrassed, because simple and self-forgetful. Infirm as she was, she had a thousand little methods of being independent of help; all so unobtrusive, one hardly noticed them,—they seemed in the natural course of things.

That morning we were talking of this, that, and the other, when a slight sound made me turn my head. Then I saw, at the other end of the room, a tall figure, which surprised me a good deal. I looked at Phemie; she was calm as usual. The man, very tall, as I have said, was seated on a bench. I could not distinguish his features; my eyes were dazzled with the light; and, besides, he was sitting in a dark part of the room; but he was in a sort of *Dantesque* position, which struck me, with his knees raised, his elbows on his knees, his face resting upon his clenched fists, and a fixed look which one rather felt than saw. He did not speak, did not stir; he was absorbed, either listening or dreaming, one knew not which.

Euphemia did not seem to be noticing him. I did as she did, or, at all events, I tried; but in my own despite, that man's presence, which she hardly seemed aware of, disquieted me. I kept thinking of him, and casting from time to time a furtive glance in his direction. There he still was, always in exactly the same position. I felt ill at ease; my voice shook a little, Euphemia's not at all. She went on embroidering, relating some incident or other of her own short past history.

"Must needs tell you!" she cried, with an animated gesture. She had that easy diction of the Parisians,—those familiar elisions which give language wings.

"Must tell you what happened to me one Sunday when I had legs of my own. I was agile then, a good walker. We lived at Auteuil,—not rich, you know. When we had to go to Paris, we walked. That Sunday, then, a fine summer Sunday, the nightingales were singing, I had been working till midnight. Never mind, I wanted to go to church to hear something about God. I look at the sun, —nine o'clock; I am late. I dress, make all the haste I can, run rather than walk. I get there! They are singing the hymn; I seat myself on the first empty corner I find, close to the door, and—only think! The singing, the cool air, the shady corner, fatigue, all together,—I fall asleep, fast asleep, and sleep as I had not done for a whole week before!

"That was wrong, that was," resumed Euphemia, shaking her head when she saw me smile.

"I slept half an hour, I slept an hour, I slept two hours, —the whole time the service lasted. I was wakened by a great noise; I saw every one standing up; they were just about to leave. I jumped up too, confused, blushing for shame, ready to cry,—I was so vexed!

"Then there was a pause; and then came the minister's voice, gravely pronouncing the final blessing: '*Go in peace! and the grace of our Lord Jesus Christ, the love of God, and the fellowship of the Holy Spirit, be with you and your families!*'

"There was my sermon, and a beautiful one it was! And so I felt my heart leap with joy, and went back with these words, which lasted me the whole week through. Dear me! the compassion the good Lord has for His poor children!"

A deep sigh, almost like a hiss, interrupted Euphemia. I started, and turned abruptly towards the bench. The man had not stirred, only more of his face was hidden by his hands.

Euphemia looked at him with her mild glance.

"One must have trust, Monsieur Victor," she said.

There was a short pause; then she began to talk again, just as her canaries sang, with an outburst of youth and happiness; a freedom from any anxious thought for the morrow, of which we lose the sweet secret after our twentieth summer.

While she was speaking, the man, without saying a word, rose and left the room.

Euphemia's countenance changed at once, and she grew very grave.

"He is one of our porters," she said. Then seeing that this short explanation did not satisfy me, that my glance was still a questioning one, she went on with some little constraint.

"He is very unhappy." Then in a low voice, as if what

she was going to say rather distressed her on his account, "He has been at the galleys!"

I shuddered involuntarily.

"If you knew all he suffers! Ill; no peace; a wild beast's nature; fits of fury which rise like flames,—less now than formerly, though! Then the strength of a bull; iron hands! Ill as he is, he can still bend a sovereign with his fingers! He was young, he was jealous; there was a woman that he loved. In one of his mad rages he bit her breast so ferociously, that she died of it. He was ten years down there; now he is weary of life. He does not want for work; he is steady, but he is consumed with remorse and shame;—he is afraid of God. Yet he comes here; I speak a little to him; he never answers, or hardly,—he is so timid! but he always comes back."

That was my first meeting with this man.

My second was at his own house.

His illness had rapidly increased; he could no longer work. Euphemia sent to tell me so.

He lived not far from the Halle, in a very mean-looking dwelling. I went up; I knocked. A hoarse voice bid me enter; the voice was his mother's!

The room was large, high, but squalid; with bare walls, their plaster very much stained, dripping with damp, and falling off here and there. No furniture, no chest of drawers, no wardrobe; only three nearly bottomless chairs, on one of which sat the mother, sewing a canvas sack, near the window; on the other lay the clothes of the sick man in the bed; the third was unoccupied, and placed beside him: it was there that I seated myself.

The window, very large, filled with little greenish panes of glass, darkened by the exhalations from within and the cold without, admitted an opaque light,—no blue sky; very sad to see. A bit of looking-glass, covered with black spots, was fixed to the wall. The mother, a large, bony-faced woman, went on with her sewing without looking towards me. She did not utter a word, did not make any gesture; but I felt that she was hostile to me. She reminded me of a she-wolf surprised in her lair.

Her son was lying on his pallet. It was then I saw his face, that face that I cannot forget. It was a long face, with hair cut very short; a high forehead, cheeks closely shaven; a straight nose, thin lips,—the upper lip very long; an uncertain glance, with something about it eminently hard, and at the same time scared; savage and irresolute; energetic, nay, passionate, and yet almost gentle.

But what pervaded and prevailed over all was the impress of an intense woe; a mixture of defiance and despair; a barren suffering; sorrow without tenderness; that sinister impress which seems to belong to the brow of fallen angels. He looked straight before him, neither at his mother nor me, nor the wall, nor the dust-laden atmosphere, nor at anything in sight. His feverish hands, still strong despite disease, kept throwing off the bed-clothes with a monotonous gesture. He was gasping for breath. His mother drew her needle in and out, (one heard the coarse thread pass through the canvas,) and turned her back to us.

A woman like that might indeed love,—did love, no doubt; but with a savage kind of undemonstrative love, —the love of a lioness, which crushed, not comforted.

He was going down alone,—going down gloomy and despairing, into the abyss. To annihilation? to judgment? He did not know.

I felt a boundless pity. Strange to say, I felt a sense of humiliation sink into the very depths of my being. This man had almost murdered; even in dying he inspired terror; yet, if I had dared, I could have taken him into my arms, and poured out all my heart towards him.

I did so to God. As to what I said, I really do not know. My heart spoke, my tears flowed; I implored him to let himself be saved.

He went on, looking fixedly away in silence. At last his lips quivered a little, a slight flush passed over his face, and when I rose, he reached out his hand to me.

"For the love of Jesus, believe!" It was a cry of anguish. Following an irresistible impulse, I fell on my knees: I prayed! Did he pray too? I believe he did.

The mother said nothing, but she had left off working; and when at a later hour, when it had grown dark, I left her son asleep, and passed her on my way out of the room, she rose, still sullen, but less hostile, and opened the door for me.

I never saw the galley-slave again.

THE DOVECOT.

IT is not what you think. I have no other dovecot to tell of than a poor room; no other doves than an old man and his wife.

I was reading in my drawing-room, in Paris, one snowy evening in the month of March, when the door opened, and a letter was handed in to me. Before I took it I knew what it was—a begging letter! They are all alike; the same paper, the same handwriting, the same smell of poverty, if it is not that of tobacco or of brandy!

Are we, then, indeed, such slaves of circumstance, that indigence effaces our individual characteristics? You have been rich, you have been fastidious, you have had your humours, your tastes, your originalities; you become poor, they all get faded, flattened; and if ever you are compelled to implore the charity of others, you too will dip your pen in the same pale ink. Your thoughts will follow this beaten track, you will fold your missive into the same humble shape; poor, you too will write a poor man's letter.

The letter I held in my hand smelt neither of wine nor of cigars. But my heart seemed withered; weary of the woes of others,—I had seen so much of them all the winter through; and much imposition, many tricks played upon me, gave me a right, so I thought at least, to take refuge now in selfish repose.

For a moment I had an impulse to leave the letter unopened, to send it back still sealed, to turn round and go to sleep again. I did not do so, however: perhaps because I was ashamed of myself, perhaps because the servant, who was standing by the door waiting my answer, mumbled something that sounded like "*They are there.*"

I signified to him that I wished to be alone; then tore open the envelope and read.

The envelope contained two letters. One, the begging letter itself, neatly written, like many others I had received, with certain words, *God, your charity, despair*, &c., in capital letters, with many flourishes, denoting a decided talent for caligraphy. There was nothing else to distinguish it from the rest of its class. It described extreme destitution; seemed, indeed, to have an impress of sincerity, some words that sounded like the soul's genuine cry; expressions of faith which denoted a Christian spirit; but I had seen so much of this carefully calculated simplicity, my ears were so weary of all this cold fervour, that positively I could no longer distinguish the ring of the true metal from that of the false.

And this is one of the trials of our vocation, we who seek to do a little good in the world.

The other letter was of quite a different stamp. It was a letter of recommendation, written in an off-hand style, by a wealthy inhabitant of Lyons, whom I knew, and who introduced an unfortunate pair to my notice—upholsterers, once well off, people of long-standing character, who had been ruined by a bad investment. Their misfortunes had brought them into contact with him, and, while assisting them in other ways as much as he could, he had imparted to them his own best wealth—Christian faith, in all its simplicity and power. This poor pair believed the Bible, they loved each other, but they felt it intolerable to live upon charity. There was no opening for them at

Lyons; a vision of Paris had risen before their imagination; from that moment there was no keeping them back. The wife would, indeed, have remained quiet, she retained fewer illusions; not so the husband. Paris, so especially the town of beautiful furniture, rich hangings! and then he, whose taste was so correct, whose hand so skilful! Why, had he not, some twenty years ago, furnished, from cellar to roof, the archiepiscopal palace of the second town in France? Paris! why, he should have nothing to do but to show himself there; workshops would open at once, work would abound. The only drawback would be that he should have to engage twenty workmen at least; he was sorry for that, his wife might find them troublesome. Nothing could stop him, neither arguments nor facts; they set off to Paris. This letter of recommendation to me was dated three months back. Three months! of work or penury—who knew?

I rushed to the door, opened it, and knew at once. There they both were, seated on a bench, dressed in old black garments, two pale, meagre figures, the very sight of them struck to one's heart with something of remorse. The husband was sixty years old, the wife fifty, but she looked more. She had a very sweet face, shaded by nearly gray hair, clear eyes, the only remnant of youth, a contented mouth, a resigned, thoroughly calm and good expression, with all the courage of perfect openness. But gentleness and modesty were the prevailing characteristics. She drew a little back, with an air of suffering, slightly embarrassed, but by no means awkwardly shy.

The old upholsterer, her husband, resembled her in nothing. He was a little man, with keen, feverish eyes, agitated rather than active, getting up, sitting down, with a sort of distracted air, looking every moment at his wife, lovingly, but with an anxious love. His forehead was low, a bush of white hair, a narrow head, gave him an appearance of flightiness—and he was flighty, a very few moments shewed it plainly enough.

Misfortune had assigned to each of them the same outward life; but peace reigned in the woman's sweet nature, while the poor man was devoured by anxiety. She knew the Lord, and rested upon Him; he knew Jesus too, and kept looking in every other possible direction for aid.

She waited patiently; he exhausted himself in barren efforts; she let the past be past, he was constantly reverting to it with a bitterness that undermined his strength; she loved tenderly, and this love was her best delight; he loved passionately, and this love was his worst suffering.

Such they were. For three whole months they had had disappointment after disappointment; no work anywhere.

"They say I am too old," cried the poor man. "They shut the door upon me; not a chair to stuff, not a curtain to hang! and I, who furnished Monseigneur's archiepiscopal palace!" and he shook his head. "Look at my arms, do you call those weak arms—those?" He turned up his threadbare sleeve. "Have I not got my ten fingers still? Beg! beg! beg!—There is no help for it, we are without bread in the house!"

He sank down again upon the bench. His wife fixed her beautiful quiet eyes on me, a tear rising in them the while. She placed her hand upon her husband's. "God will not forsake us," she said, and these few simple words, spoken in a very grave and very gentle voice, made me involuntarily think of that meek and quiet spirit which is in the sight of God of great price.

The old upholsterer grew calm as if by magic.

"It's very true, though," he said, "we are still happy."

When they went away, the husband, contrary to custom, instinctively took his wife's arm, and leant upon it. It was evidently a habit of years of which she was not aware. Never had that humble heart, that innocent nature, suspected the weakness of her companion; never had she found out that she was superior to him in every respect—had the idea ever crossed her, she would have detested it, but it never did so. Hers was not that modest manner which covers a haughty mind, that submission in words and gestures, united to an inflexible will which will creep towards its goal, if it cannot walk thither upright. She never said, "It is my husband that wishes!" Whatever he did wish, she was at once honestly ready to do. If the plan seemed to her a bad one, she said so openly and gently, for she had an opinion of her own, but she never insisted, she knew when to stop; and the mischief once done, she would instinctively and unconsciously set about repairing it. She cherished her husband with all the strength of her soul, she respected, admired him. As for him, narrow-minded, but upright in heart, impetuous, ardently industrious, indefatigable, self-denying, he saw life, other people and himself, everything, indeed, but his wife, invariably on the dark side.

People are soon lost sight of in Paris. Our worthy pair having been relieved, helped on as far as I could; others came. After seeing a good deal of them, I saw them less; two months passed, they never applied to me. I forgot them, then all at once they recurred to my mind, and I set off to look after them.

The husband was the only one at home.

One glance round the room told me how they had suffered.

It had nothing left but what was quite indispensable;

an iron stove on which their slender meal was cooking; little white curtains to the window, none to the bed; no old cracked cups, nor old gilded glasses, nor framed lithographs; everything had found its way to the pawnbroker's.

Only the cleanliness, the neatness, the pieces of old cloth laid down at the side of the bed, upon the cold brick floor, revealed a woman's presence.

The upholsterer was seated; he was writing, so intent, so absorbed, that at first he did not hear me. The next moment he raised his eyes. He jumped up, made me sit down; took his head in his hands—it was his habitual gesture—then said, in an agitated voice—

"Worse still! worse and worse! Not any work! not any! She is killing herself!"

He took up his wife's sewing, and let it fall again.

"As for me, I am idle; she feeds me, she does. I don't know which way to turn. Ask, ask, ask, always asking!" This with a gesture of impatience not unmixed with bitterness;—plainly the archiepiscopal hangings recurred to his mind:

"And, by way of finishing stroke, I tease her; yes, I tease her! I ought to encourage her, I discourage; I ought to strengthen her, I weaken; I ought to let myself be consoled, I get irritable. She has faith, she has; well I play the part of the devil! I try to deprive her of it. When she says *hope*, I reply, What's the use of hoping? I am a wicked, useless man; fit for nothing, but to kill her!"

He threw himself back in his chair, then went on: "At this moment, where do you suppose she is? at the pawnbroker's. She has taken her watch there, the watch I gave her on our wedding-day, thirty years ago. Do you know what I went and did? I said no end of hard things to her, that I did. She looked at me, she embraced me, and sat down again. I said to her, *Go!* like a brute that I was; and she went."

When he had recovered a little—

"And so!" and at once his voice took almost a cheerful tone, "Look here." He took up the sheet of paper he had been writing on when I came in. "Look here! I do myself justice at least." And he pointed out the words with an intense satisfaction, "That will please her, will that."

I read, "*My dear wife, I am a wretch; my dear wife, I am a wretch,*" and so on in text-hand, down to the bottom of the page.

"If I know anything about her, I do not think that will please her," I simply replied. He looked at me with his small, eagre eye.

"Tell her you love her; that's better."

"Love her, indeed!" cried the old upholsterer, in great excitement. "That woman! that wife of mine, is an angel! She is my life, is my wife. I am very unlucky; we are cold here." His glance flitted round the poor bare room. "Sometimes we are hungry, but for all that there are moments, ay, there are hours when we are as happy as kings. At night, we go to bed when it gets dark. Candles come expensive; there," and he pointed to the alcove, and the curtainless bed; "there, when we kneel down together; there, when she rests her head on my shoulder; there, look you, I am so happy sometimes I think my heart will burst. Oh, if I could only die so!"

"And your wife?"

He uttered a cry, "There it is, there it is; selfish, always selfish!" He clasped, or rather he wrung the hands he raised to heaven.

I could have fancied I heard that groan from the heart

of St Paul: that desolate sigh which rises out of the deep places of every human soul, "O wretched man that I am! who shall deliver me from the body of this death?"

At that moment the door opened; it was the wife returning. She saw at a glance the look of distress in her husband's face, and ran to him.

"Forgive me," she said, "I have given you pain. We shall get it back; you shall hang it round my neck again!" She clasped him to her heart. "I have got bread, got all we want; let us trust in God, in Jesus; was He not hungry once?"

A movement on my part announced my presence; she stopped, a little confused, then curtsied to me, remained standing, and thanked me for my visit.

The old upholsterer who had but few ideas of his own, held those few fast. At the first pause, he took up his sheet of paper, and eyes sparkling with delight, handed it over to his wife. She read, blushed deeply, went to the table, wrote a few rapid words, placed the page under her husband's eyes, then, with animated gesture, tore the paper into fragments. Later I knew what those words had been, words never effaced from the old man's heart. They were these: "My husband, I am thy most happy wife and thy humble servant."

All the charity in the world never yet made up for work. More than bread, more than help of any kind, the old upholsterer craved for occupation, craved to work at his trade.

"I have at home an arm-chair which wants covering, a very handsome one. Could you repair it for me?" The old man's eyes sparkled.

"Will you come?"

"When?" he asked with a trembling voice.

"Why, to-morrow; the first fine day; whenever it suits you."

"And I—I may bring my wife?"

"I should think so indeed."

"Because, you see, she is a better hand still than I am."

"Oh!" put in the wife, with a sweet smile.

The old upholsterer's face lit up: in two seconds he grew ten years younger; his forehead lost its wrinkles; he drew himself up; his chest expanded; he rubbed his hands; what the sympathy of the wife, the charity of the benevolent, never could have done, work—*his work* did. His status returned; his youth, his vigour, his prospects.

He ran to the press, opened a drawer, examined his tools one by one, taking up this, throwing aside that, without being any longer aware of my presence. His wife's expression was quite heavenly; she clasped her hands tight, and looked at me without saying a word.

The morrow was a splendid day in June.

Paris has not many rural retreats, but I may venture to say that, on that particular morning, my drawing-room, opening out on my garden, about sixty feet long by eighteen, had something so springlike, fresh, and balmy, that it made one dream Idyls.

A bit of blue sky, a bit of green grass-plot; glycine entangled in the trellis that covered the wall, that wall very low, with other gardens all around, beautiful rose-trees in flower, stands of geraniums which the bees were pillaging with busy murmurs, an awning that softened the light, rustic chairs, a table, and over it an acacia in full flower, from which each breeze that blew stole white perfumed petals to scatter them on the grass. Such was my garden, such my drawing-room. A poor reminiscence of nature, of those mighty joys which expand your heart when you walk in the country; God's great works around you, full of life and health, in sunshine and in liberty.

Happy he whose eye may, from dawn to twilight, wander at will to distant horizons! Happy he who sees the meadows grow green in April, who gathers the violet in the valley, who, with his own hands, alike plants and reaps! Happy he who breathes the free fresh air of the country; to whom the breeze brings in through the open window the scent of the lucerne in flower! Happy he who works at some healthy out-door work, whose faculties, continually reinvigorated, apply themselves fully, yet not feverishly, to the task God has assigned them, and who, when evening is come, returns not to the conventional duties of conventional life, but to the sacred pleasures of hearth and home.

At seven o'clock in the morning, there was a ring at my bell. The old couple entered. They had made themselves smart; their worn, thread-bare garments had a sort of holiday air; they were both radiant. The worthy man could hardly eat his breakfast, he was in such a hurry. That over, he set to work, his face beaming. He had on his green baize apron; his mouth was full of pins, and then came such cutting, measuring, pulling, fitting; for he was hard to please, and began again twenty times, and yet he was so alert and rapid, had such a correct eye and expert hand, that the work got on as if by magic.

His wife sewed, attentive to his directions, silent, her breast swelling with joy.

My great anxiety was to get them to eat and to walk about; their anxiety, that of the upholsterer especially—his wife understood me perfectly—was to work; to work on, to shew his skill, to shew he had not forgotten his calling, and that he could execute a masterpiece, and that he had a pair of hands of his own capable of maintaining his wife without any need to beg.

It was all I could do to get him away from that unlucky arm-chair, and to make him take an hour's rest in the garden in the middle of the day. But the sun flooded the room with light, the bees would sometimes wander about it, puffs of fragrance came wafting in. Then the upholsterer would raise his head, inhale the air, say, "It smells sweet here;" and set to work harder than ever.

That did not matter; he was happy in his own way, profoundly happy. He exchanged little playful words with his wife; I heard them laugh, he with an abrupt chuckle, she with a clear, fresh laugh.

The good times were come back again, he was making money, he should make more. God had granted his wife's request; he, too, prayed with his whole heart, but as for his own prayers, he held them cheap. The prayers of his wife, oh, these would mount straight to heaven!

When evening came, I was called in. The arm-chair was finished; it was perfection! I told him so; his hands trembled with delight; he was a different man. He examined his work, rather proud, not too much so, for he was accustomed to work well; he looked well to do, hopeful, he was calm and composed for the first time. His wife contemplated him, then the arm-chair, then me; one could see that she was returning thanks to God. It was she who was overcome now; happiness moved her more than sorrow had done.

When they went away, the husband, with an easy gesture, offered her his arm; it was he who protected her.

Would that I could stop here, stop at this fine summer's day. Alas! this time I have to go on to the end.

The old upholsterer was not deceived; work did come in. Not very abundantly, but steadily; enough to keep the house, enough to make him happy.

When I left Paris in July, the room had been modestly refurnished; there was a pot of mignonette in the window, two canaries singing in a cage, the watch, the wedding gift, hung at the worthy woman's waist. It was a home, an affection that might well inspire envy; it was the *Dovecot.*

There are people who laugh at these ancient loves. Not so I. I pity those who believe that there blooms one short season for youthful tenderness, and that, this season over, the time to love is past, the heart withered, and nothing left but to lead a prosaic life, without fervour, sunshine, shade, or mystery.

We were two lovers, a man, a woman; we had a thousand delicacies of feeling in our soul; all the shyness, all the fascination, all the secret ardour, even the little sorrows and the beautiful tears of a strong affection. Age comes; we become mere companions. Two boon comrades, good fellows, heart in hand, easy tempered through indifference, equally amused, equally wearied with what remains of life, having nothing more to ask, not much to give, without hope, without regret, waiting for the time of separation, and when it comes, quitting each other with great composure; we, who had loved one another with so great a love.

Some find this very natural and supremely wise; for my part, I find it revolting, and the dreariest folly.

I left Paris. That year the cholera ravaged it cruelly.

When I returned, the frozen breath of December was blowing through the streets, my apartments were cold, uncomfortable; I had a good deal to do in my home.

One evening, it was New Year's Eve, my door-bell rang, the old upholsterer was asking for me. Could it indeed be he that I saw there seated on the bench, in the same spot as last year—alone, bent, with haggard eye? He looked at me fixedly.

"I am hungry," he said, in a hollow voice. "That's why I am come to trouble you."

My mind at once foreboded some terrible misfortune that I did not dare to verify. He looked at me again; saw that I knew nothing. Then, with a fearful outburst—

"I have lost my wife!" he cried. "I have lost her, lost her, lost her!" and he buried his head in his hands.

Then, in a melancholy voice, he began to repeat, as if to himself, the tragic story.

It was very simple. In the thick of the cholera, the poor woman had gone out to make a few purchases; on returning, cholera had seized her, torn her to pieces in the course of four hours, during which she had not been able to say anything more to her husband than a 'Good-bye!' murmured out through her tortures. Her hands had been constantly clasped, her smile in dying that of an angel.

"I have been alone!—for three months! I have nothing, I am nothing, and yet I live!—God Almighty has not yet had the charity to take me!"

I gently placed my hand on his arm, as his wife was wont to do; he shuddered; and while he went on talking, in broken sentences, I was able to take in, one by one, the ravages his immense sorrow had made in this poor creature, weak in body, weak in mind.

He was ragged, unshaven, untidy, almost dirty,—he who used to be so rigidly clean, to have his old clothes so neatly put on. His cheeks were thin and hanging, his eye burning, his frame shaken by a constant and almost convulsive shiver. He spoke much and fast, hardly seemed to hear himself, could not listen to me at all; went on with his wail like the wave of the sea, which beats again and again on the same portion of the shore. If I struck strongly a religious chord, it would, indeed, give back a feeble sound; but this rather from force of habit than its own proper vibration; despair had swallowed up all.

"I don't do any more work; I have no head for it," he said. "I keep going, I walk, I go errands when I get them, I am a gone man!—*and I can't die!*" he cried vehemently, starting up. "*I eat,* could you believe that *I eat?*—Yes, I am mean enough to eat because I am hungry. I am devoured with hunger."

I had some food, some broth brought in; he would not touch them, his throat was closed; he said it did him good to talk, good to weep, that was enough for him.

Man feels his littleness before the sea in storm. The consciousness of his own impotence overwhelms him. He can but contemplate the everlasting surge, the boundless horizon, and lend a meditative ear to that mighty voice marching on the waters. There is another ocean which makes him feel his limitations more keenly still—the infinite of woe! some one of those fathomless sorrows, with no earthly hope, which feed upon themselves; some Promotheus on his rock, with vitals constantly gnawed; some abyss where every consolation, every aid, is swallowed up at once and disappears.

I did not tell this man that he had made himself an idol, and that God had broken it; I did not tell him that his wife was a creature, and that our hearts must not attach themselves to creatures; I did not tell him that the Christian is to rejoice when God has made him weep. I have found consolations of this kind in the books of men; I have never seen such in the book of God.

Only, in a voice that I tried hard to render calm, I gently asked him whether he would, at this very hour, recall her from the heaven where she was, to the earth where he suffered.

That idea struck him. "No, no!" he answered, with a burst of tenderness and tears.

"Would you have her in your place, you in hers?"

"No, no!" he said, in almost a joyous tone.

"The Lord loved her much."

He repeated '*loved her much*' several times; he hugged the words to his heart; it was his first ray of light: *He loved her much!*—that reconciled him to the sovereign decree of his God: *He loved her much!*—that idea worked its royal luminous way through his soul. *Loved her much —much!* The poor man went away repeating those words.

That evening he could take no other food.

The following day I went to his house. Over the door one saw a little black plate with white letters, "Here lies Bénard, *widower!*" That was his name,—*widower* was written in immense letters.

My heart was wrung. Suffering had been stronger than this man's reason.

On entering, I stood still on the threshold. Bénard was sitting motionless before the alcove, which he looked at fixedly. The bed had disappeared; it had been dragged into a corner of the room. It was unmade, disorderly. In the alcove rose a sort of catafalque, extremely finished in all its details.

I approached. Bénard sprang towards me, took me by the hand, and led me to the alcove.

"This is what I have been doing!" he said, in a tone

that revealed a species of satisfaction through all its sorrow. "See!" and his voice shook more and more, his gestures became febrile. "See! here is her table, covered with black cloth; here is the cage, the canaries are dead,—in my agony I forgot them: she would not have done so; *she* would not! Here are white flowers,—whatever I gain, I put it all here; all that is given me—all! Here is her watch, the watch that"—— Tears choked him. "It has never gone since that day; here is her wedding-ring; here is her shawl,—her poor shawl."

He fell on his knees, hid his face in the shawl, buried his head there. I heard him sob: I remembered the silence of the friends of Job. Then from beneath the folds—

"She was my faith," he began again, in a despairing voice; "she taught me to love Jesus, to support affliction; she has taken away everything with her—everything! I do not pray any more; I do not know whether I believe! Will God have anything to do with me?"

At this fearful thought, this thunderbolt hurled by Satan's deadly hand, he tore away the shawl in which he had wound himself, and shewed me a face so distorted, that it made me shudder. Without knowing well what I was doing,—with one of those dumb cries which the Lord hears, I snatched at a book, which I recognised as it lay on a chair, and I placed it open upon the catafalque. Bénard saw it, rose, bent over the pages without touching them, with an eager eye, like one dying in the desert over living water.

"Death shall be no more," he began tremblingly to read. "There shall be no more sorrow,—nor crying,—nor pain; —for the former things have passed away."

The almost frantic man grew gentle as a child.

He took up the book reverently, kissed it, and put it back where I had placed it.

"It is her book,—her New Testament; and I who had forgotten it! Yes, there! it is well placed there! Her beautiful book, in which she read every morning; which we read together every evening! It is thy answer to me, my beloved! It is thy message; thou givest it to me; yes, thou biddest me from God to have hope. Yes, yes; I will read, I will pray, I will submit,—that I will: He will have pity on me; we shall be together."

From that moment the old upholsterer was more calm; with relapses into desolation, almost rebellion, he still progressed in his obedience. Sometimes he believed strongly enough to be happy; sometimes he doubted, and was lost in misery; sometimes he would be overwhelmed with remorse; at others, he would lay hold on the forgiveness of Jesus.

His was a weak, worn-out head; one of those natures that the wise willingly reprimand, because they are fatiguing, full of incoherence, full of contradictions; because in dealing with them, one has always to begin anew, and one likes to see an end to every undertaking, even the best. His was one of those poor hearts: mighty to suffer, unfitted for daily life; violent, earnest, impossible to divert, humble, broken always, for which the Lord has ineffable tendernesses.

He worked no more; his pride in his calling, his trade, his skill,—all that was over. He wandered about, picking up odd jobs as a porter. But in the alcove his former self returned. There the upholsterer revived; the old, ardent, exact upholsterer devoted to his business; every penny that he earned, every alms he received, went there. There he fitted on different stuffs, decorated continually, invented new devices. Half famished, ill-clothed, ill-kept, he still possessed in the matter of his catafalque all his former enthusiasm and most minute exactness. People said, "You should clothe him: it is no use to give him money; it all goes in knick-knacks and nonsense; it only feeds his folly." But his folly was one of those which will be fed. If you cut off their allowance, they devour the heart.

One day the old upholsterer came to me almost radiant. "I have an idea!" he said. "It may take me years to carry out. But, never mind; I shall do so in the end." He lowered his voice: "I mean to hang my room with black, with white cords and white drops. When this is finished, I have a notion that Jesus will take me."

He shewed me the box in which his treasures were accumulating,—a five-franc piece, some smaller money, his daily bread, his daily toil.

Before it was finished, Jesus took him.

MARIETTA.

"SO you will not come and see Marietta? She understands French, and then you would be giving her so much pleasure!"

Thus spoke Master Schimp. Master Schimp was a shoemaker, settled in the little German town held in charge by the old General, where I had gone with the Baroness.

Master Schimp had brought home my shoes. He sometimes made shoes for me; and when finished he brought them home, and when he brought them, he sat down, and when he sat down, he never knew when to get up again!

He was a hale, thick-set man of seventy, as wrinkled as an ancient banner, with a tangled shock of hair, small, clear gray eyes, a flexible mouth, a comfortable opinion of himself, and the best heart in the world.

He talked well, and he talked a great deal in French, and almost without accent; in a neat, precise fashion, allowing himself full leisure to seek for the fit expression, which being once found, he proceeded at a steady pace, even and monotonous as the drip of water.

Steadying his green bag between his legs, he would dive from time to time into the capacious depths of his pocket for his snuff-box, and giving it three short, sharp taps upon the lid, would say to me, while he helped himself to a large and liberal pinch—

"You do not take snuff?" then, shaking the box, he would give his shirt-front a side sweep of the hand, and resume the thread of his discourse.

Have you ever known what it is to sit in the very fever-heat of impatience, upright and smiling, with now and then a gentle inclination of the head, a *yes* and *no* repeated at fitting intervals; while in your heart, far below this surface affability, a voice went on exclaiming, "Provoking unconscionable creature, do you never mean to go away at all? You have been here at least an hour! and no doubt will sit there for another! Oh that somebody else would want me! would come to fetch me away!"

Then conscience murmurs, "Selfish being! are sixty tedious minutes so very unendurable! And is not this my neighbour, my brother, worth far more, it may be, than myself? If it was money he wanted, it would be given him, —it is so easy to be bountiful; but the bounty of a little kindness is not so readily bestowed."

The mind takes this into account, and says, "Let patience have its work; little annoyances pave the way to great obediences. Bend to this one with a good will. It is now and then that we meet with a lion on the path; but ants will run across it every day."

"True," replies the first voice; "but, on the whole, I should prefer a lion."

So proceeds this confidential discussion, and with it, Master Schimp at full length. He holds forth; he goes back to his youthful days; upon reminiscences he engrafts anecdotes, in no way remarkable for point or purpose; he branches off towards religion, he branches off towards philosophy. The unfortunate man, it seems, has been a reader; has picked up everywhere the odds and ends of all things, and has forgotten nothing! We pass, by an easy transition, from philosophy to politics, from politics to France, and from France to Paris, his favourite place of residence; he lived there ten years in the days of the great Napoleon. Napoleon sets him *en croupe*, and carries him to Germany; the Allies bring him back to Paris,—to the streets as they were then, and to the streets as they are now; their original names, and those they are now known by!

And the sun is sinking, the fresh, cool evening stealing on; is it all to be absorbed in this way? A studied silence, a slight fit of coughing, a fidgety rearrangement of the chairs, but nothing will do.

Till at last he began to talk about Marietta.

And who was Marietta? An invalid cousin, whom, with her sister, he had taken to live with him.

And Marietta, be she who or what she might be, saved me. I blessed her, and putting on my bonnet, drew a long, relieved breath, and said, "We will go."

Even Master Schimp, who was not easily impressed, seemed struck with this sudden energy. A few steps brought us to his small neat dwelling, coloured with the peculiar spinach-green the Germans are so fond of. Its windows shone and sparkled with cleanliness; on one side of the door was the shop where he kept his men at work, reserving for himself (as we have seen) the task of carrying his goods to their destination.

A pleasant-looking middle-aged woman, Marietta's sister, who was standing on the door-step, moved aside to let us pass. Master Schimp went into the shop, put down his parcel, and taking the leg of a boot out of the hands of one of his men, he addressed him at some length in German, which address, or one of similar weight and emphasis, he appeared to repeat to another of them, while carefully examining an upper leather; he then looked at me with a smile which seemed to say, "You have perhaps understood a little," to which I replied by a lowly gesture of deprecation, when he smiled again, and, replacing his hat by a green shade, put on his spectacles, and with another dive for his snuff-box, another pinch, preceded by the three sharp taps, he murmured an apology for passing before me, and led the way into a dark passage.

I followed him, and as we went he said, "So you do not know Marietta? Well, then, you have something curious to see!"

He opened the door, and as the light streamed into the passage, I saw indeed *something* which seemed rather to spring than rise out of a chair, and come forward to meet us. I stopped short, and but for one of Master Schimp's quick keen glances, I think I should have screamed. How shall I describe this something, this poor, strangely deformed creature, three feet at most in height, and with a head so out of all just proportion as to recall the paste board monstrosities that milliners sometimes use for blocks, her hands, in the absence of arms, sticking out of her shoulders, more like fins, it seemed to me, than hands; without legs, almost without feet—a *maillot*, set upright on the earth! And yet this lived; it spoke; it had a soul: even now it was colouring deeply.

Master Schimp, who had meant to produce a strong effect, looked just a little remorseful at the extent of his success. This passed, however, with the moment, and a few laughing words with Marietta set him at one with himself again.

"No fear, cousin; 'a friend,' as one says to the patrol. Come now, we are going to have a little French."

And Master Schimp began to exhibit his prodigy. While he recounted, without sparing me a single date or incident, how after having brought Marietta to live with him, he had first taught her to read and write in German, and then to read and write in French; how he had followed this up by arithmetic, the two grammars, geography, and history; and how Marietta had taught herself knitting, embroidering, and all varieties of needlework; while he shewed me her copy-books, and drew a crotchet collar out of the poor girl's work-basket, Marietta, who had been at first even painfully embarrassed, began to be more at her ease. She looked at her cousin with mild eyes so full of gratitude, of affection, of deep respect, of implied confidence, that they seemed able to take in no other object.

And I, too, had by this time regained my self-possession. I ventured to look again at Marietta, and again not without a shock; so pitiable, so appalling was this malformation, that the heart knew not what to make of it. It was a contradiction, an *impossibility*. One's innate sense of fitness seemed outraged by such a strange freak on the part of Nature, and when I remembered that Nature was but another word for the Creator, and that this deplorable travesty had been *permitted*, a *wherefore* of fearful import arose within my mind. It came there, however, and was gone like a flash; another look, and the dark surmise passed away for ever. This poor head could boast of its dark abundant hair, of fine eyes, and of regular features, but it was not in these that its charm was found, but in the tender, inexpressible charm of its expression; in the joy, the peace, the purity, that spoke there with such a pure, restrained simplicity—the soul looking forth so clearly, that one forgot whether the body was there or not.

But had this soul itself,—Marietta's, any thoughts about the singular setting in which it found itself? It might be so, but the consciousness was not apparent. After the first embarrassment of my introduction was over, Marietta talked to me without constraint; her voice had a youthful, touching tone in it that went very straight to the heart.

Master Schimp was called away and the expression of her eyes changed a little; they seemed to send forth a dimmer light, as a lamp does after it has been let down.

"My cousin is so kind," she exclaimed, with animation; "so very kind; he spoils me," she added, with a smile; "he thinks that I know everything, when I scarcely know anything at all. And everything is *his* doing; he has been both father and mother to me."

Her eyes filled, and I saw that her heart, too, was very full. After a short silence, she went on, as if in answer to my unspoken thought—

"I am happy; the Lord Jesus has loved me,—a poor little creature like me," (this was the only allusion she made to her infirmities.) "My cousin loves me, too; my sister, everybody; the day is not long, and in the evenings we read together, and are very happy."

"You go out sometimes?"

"Not now; my cousin had a little carriage made for me, which he used to draw, but since a very serious illness, I have not been able to bear the movement of the wheels."

"And you will sometimes wish for a sight of the country?"

Marietta coloured slightly. "Once I used," she said, "but not now. I look elsewhere." Then, after a short silence, and because she saw me look sorrowful, she added, "There are flowers in Paradise."

Yes, I thought,—and a glorified body; but this I did not say to her.

She had lived, it was evident, in an atmosphere of kindness, and having never been exposed to those collisions which wound the heart just when it is seeking to expand, she expressed her feelings artlessly, and just as they arose.

"My greatest sorrow is, that I am ungrateful. Yes," she continued, not quite understanding my look of surprise, "you would not have believed it of me, and yet it is so. There are times when I am so cast down; everything seems so dull, and my heart so heavy. Then I could gladly cry; but this never lasts long, and God forgives me for it. He has forgiven me all."

She then began to tell me how she spent her time.

Her cousin had so stored her mind with knowledge, had so built up her life in the strength of practical faith, that in neither was there room left for weariness or for despair; and this poor being, disinherited even of the outward semblance of humanity, had gone on her way unchallenged by any of those desolating problems which pierce through the very bones and marrow, and make the knees of the strong to bow under them.

Cousin Schimp did nothing, it was plain, by halves; he had finished off his work, just as he had finished off his sentences. It was impossible to look round the room without being struck with the exquisite keeping of its arrangements. Marietta's furniture, arm-chair, table, desk, even her vase of flowers, were all adapted to her height: everything was pretty, everything perfect in its way; little steps to enable her to reach the window, and the splendid stock which was now beginning to blossom. All this seemed quite fit and natural; the eye was not startled, but as it passed over the little interior picture, and took in all this watchful considerate detail, one felt something like a loving Presence there in the warm, wide bounty of a loving thought.

The door burst suddenly open. Six rosy, curly. little

girls, basket on arm, rushed in tumultuously, and flew to Marietta, almost overwhelming her with kisses. Now it was that her face lightened up in earnest, and her smile grew heavenly.

"I teach them," she said, "to read and work."

It was worth something to see the happy, self-important look of the little things as they placed themselves on each side of Marietta.

I left her, and as I went into the shop, met Master Schimp, green shade, spectacles, and snuff-box.

"Well?" he said.

I could not speak, but pressed his hands within my own.

"She is my child," he said, in a subdued tone.

Master Schimp, you are a great man; and Thou, my God, art the great God of earth and heaven!

THE SCULPTOR.

N a foggy day of December, I found myself in one of the oldest streets of the old city of Paris. I was seeking there, guided by the address of a letter received the evening before, the dwelling of a sculptor. It was no easy task. The street was composed of mud, of two walls, behind which was land to be sold, of piles of rubbish, and five or six miserable houses. All this was enveloped in a noisome fog. After going backwards and forwards many times, I discovered the number, half effaced, and half fallen down with the plaster.

The house fully responded to the street. The very walls spoke of poverty, stained as they were with that nauseous hue, the result of mud, of filth, and of rain, which is the general paint of the hovels of the poor. There was no porter; the foot slipped on the dark and slimy staircase; at each landing-place a faint ray of light struggled through a small window, which was soon lost again in the gloomy labyrinth. Here and there dilapidated doors opened on some miserable threshold. At length I found the one I sought; it stood half-opened; I pushed it and entered. To the right of me was a kind of studio or workshop, strewed with statuettes, and tools, and clay; at the bottom of this a larger chamber. It had lofty windows, but one half was paper, the other cobweb. It was a dim light that entered there. For the rest, it was a chaos! A mere confusion of casts and plaster, and more tools, and broken chairs, and cooking utensils, and an old petticoat, crusts of bread, and something left upon a plate, cold and disgusting.

Near the window were two children; one of twelve years, thin, with pale face, with large eyes of extreme sweetness, and long hair, soft and thick, which gave to his features an almost feminine delicacy. With his long thin fingers he was modelling, entirely absorbed in his work. I imagine that Raphael, when a child, had just that melancholy face.

His brother, a smaller child, with round, full features, but pale also and sickly, watched him at his work. When he walked, I saw that he was lame.

At the noise of my entrance both turned, then took to consider me with the same astonishment.

I asked for their father.

The elder one put aside his model, made some steps forward; the other followed, limping. I penetrated into the recess, they returned to the window.

It was so dark where I was, that for a moment I could distinguish nothing. The air, too, was stifling, a fit of coughing seized me, which was so far opportune that it relieved me from some embarrassment. A sonorous yet broken voice asked what and who it was. My name told him nothing; for a silence followed, in which I felt an air of constraint. There was nothing heard but that hissing respiration which marks the last stage of consumption.

It was the wife of the sculptor who had written to me; the husband, it was evident, knew nothing of it.

Feeling my way to a chair, I muttered something about art, about statuettes, awkwardly enough.

Meanwhile, my sight grew accustomed to the obscurity. I began to discern a bedstead, and a man sitting up in it, breathing hard, and looking at me in silence.

It was a noble countenance, one of those faces that

attract you at once by their sympathetic revelations; whilst there are others you may have seen twenty years, and may see twenty years more, which remain flat, and hard, and secret as a wall.

He had a piercing eye, dark hair thrown backwards, a forehead beautifully formed, a beard slightly touched with gray, mouth refined, candid, loyal, and an air of distinction which was felt even through his extreme pallor.

"Is it as artist—or amateur?"

"Both—a little. I have heard your works spoken of; you are suffering; I think that"——

The sculptor saw that I was embarrassed. Without stopping for explanation, with a charming smile, and the perfect air of high breeding that seeks to put at his ease some stranger fallen from the clouds, he called to his son—

"Francis, shew us the *Rachel, the Child with the Butterfly*, and the *Young Girl*."

Francis brought these little figures, and with them two or three of revolutionary subjects, which the father had not asked for. In the first there was great talent, and true feeling for the ideal, and a supreme elegance of form; the others were inferior; they were highly finished, but it was the tool of the workman more than the thought of the artist that you saw. In fact, it was trade and speculation; a bill drawn on the popular passions of the day. The sculptor at bay had asked for bread. Poverty, not art, had inspired them.

"Oh, these are nothing!" he said, pushing them aside; "the others, perhaps, have some merit."

The ice was now broken; he talked of sculpture, painting, music. On everything he spoke well; in simple unpedantic style; in the language of good society, as the highly-educated gentleman. One felt there was some terrible incongruity in his life, some degrading circumstance was tyrannising over him. The scene by which he was surrounded was not the only proof; certain intonations, certain gestures, involuntary habits of another life, struck me with pain; and he himself became conscious of them, for he suddenly paused.

"I have worked too much," he said; "during three months I have laboured night as well as day. It was for a physician,—he wanted some anatomical models: one must earn one's bread!"

His voice failed; but afterwards he resumed more gaily—

"This illness of mine is nothing,—some influenza. I am better; in a few days I shall be well. I have work enough to do."

The idea had crossed his mind that I had come on some charitable errand. It was but a momentary thought; but it knit his brow, gave a hard, dry tone to his speech, and threw over his whole demeanour an air almost of hauteur. By a brisk turn in the conversation, I dissipated this idea, and he again became natural and gracious in his manner.

I admired enthusiastically the *Child with the Butterfly* and the *Young Girl*. The eye of the sculptor kindled. Artist and man,—the artist, proud of his work; the man, proud of his unsubdued energy: both seemed to revive. He raised his head with easy complacent movement; life and almost gaiety was restored. I asked permission to carry away with me those little masterpieces.

"It is you who grant the favour by taking them!" And there was that air of the perfect gentleman as he said this, that positively I did not dare to ask the price of the little figures, nor to deposit it on the old chair that served us for table.

At this moment his wife entered: a woman of lofty

stature, thin, draped in a faded tartan. She had regular features, a majestic carriage, a tragic step. When she saw me, she concealed under the folds of her shawl the long carrots and the loaf of bread she had brought in her basket.

The sculptor turned his face to the wall, and was silent. It seemed to me that I comprehended something of the mystery of his destiny.

This woman deposited her basket; then, with a theatrical gesture, embraced her children, as Medea might have done her sons. She looked at me, saw who I was, and knowing the errand on which I had come, beckoned me out of the recess; then she extended her hand, received the sum I placed in it, spoke to me, with great emphasis of voice and manner, of her husband, of herself, of the expensive malady, of poetry and literature; and finally launched into abstruse regions, where she lost her footing, and I too. In everything, the tone rang false; she declaimed as on the stage; not that she was absolutely dissembling, but there are human instruments which, from the beginning to the end, have a false pitch. The worst is, that such instruments never cease; they clang through all, and put others to silence. There are people whose very nature is an extravagance; with whom simple truth would be an affectation; whose thoughts are always mounted upon stilts; who must talk through a speaking-trumpet. The wife of the sculptor was one of these creatures. Very stately, always inflated, constantly preoccupied with her own dignity, full of mystery, profoundly oracular, playing her comedy very seriously, as if queen of the theatre,—perhaps she had been.

The sculptor did not open his mouth. By his short, nervous cough I knew that he was impatient; I left.

I returned often; the sculptor grew worse and worse. He always said he was better; did he believe it?

By degrees he grew more sociable. When his wife was absent, he talked with perfect ease, with a perfect freedom of mind. There was rarely an allusion to other times, or it was so veiled, so covert, or so slight, that only a quick observer could have detected it. We talked of art; each time I carried away some statuette. One day—there remained very little else beside—I chose to covet a little Republican figure,—a Buonapartist, I know not exactly what. The artist looked at me with his keen, clear eye.

"You wish that?" he said, with a tone slightly contemptuous.

"Yes! it pleases me; it has energy."

He reflected for an instant: a tenderness stole over his countenance; he stretched out his hand—

"Thanks!" he said, then fell back upon the pillow.

This was the only occasion on which, upon that terrible question of money, he departed from his accustomed reserve, his proud rigidity of manner.

Between him and his wife there was a wall, a gulf,—I know not which to call it. She attended on him with a certain ostentatious respect; but without tact, or taste, or any anticipation of his wants. He, on his part, never addressed to her a single reproach; he never called her to his side. She declaimed about herself and her services as she did on all subjects. Meanwhile, she left him in that dark recess. He never asked to be drawn from it, and she never dreamt that he had need of fresher air. Around him no comfort, no little attentions; and in the chamber, no attempt at order or cleanliness. One might as well have expected a Clytemnestra to sweep out the kitchen.

With all the pretensions of the great lady, this woman

was mean to excess. This man, under his poverty, in his rags, on his pallet, in his silence, had an incomparable nobility.

More than once we conversed, or rather I spoke, of God and of the future; he listened to me, but did not answer.

She discoursed abundantly on Providence and the Supreme Being, and poured forth her pious insipidities. He coughed, looked towards me, then turned away. On those days I obtained not a word from him.

Soon, alas! there took place what in all such unions, at a given hour, is sure to follow. As the malady advanced, as his feebleness increased, he who was born to dominate, was subjected to the coarser will. This was brought about without a struggle, without noise, without premeditation. The woman was robust, powerful, could comprehend animal courage, and in proportion as the sculptor lost his strength, the fear that she had of displeasing him vanished from her mind. She did not attend to him less, if she could be said to have attended to him at all. At my suggestion, she even decided to draw his bed into the open chamber; but she put less restraint upon herself, she talked louder, she harangued more frequently, she took less pains to conceal from him the reception of pecuniary aid. Formerly, she used to accompany me to the door, leave her hand open, when I had deposited my offering in it, she would, with mute solemnity, point her finger to the skies! Now, she made constant open allusions to domestic wants. The sculptor frowned or sighed; then subduing himself by an effort of self-command, and casting, as it seemed to me, a retrospective glance over a past in which *all* had proved false or illusory, he shrugged his shoulders,—an ironical smile played upon his lips, the smile of the man of the world at the treacheries of fortune.

There had been some great blunder followed by its great penalty.

The disorder made frightful progress. The sculptor spoke no more of recovery; neither did he speak of dying; he kept silence.

I think he liked me; at least he saw me with pleasure. I belonged to his own class, and then I certainly did not harangue or perorate.

One day he said to me, with failing voice, "I know you will take a pleasure in rendering me a service. Ask of ——," he did not name her, "my last pledges, and go to the Mont-de-Piété, go yourself, and withdraw my set of napkins. I want," he said, looking round him with disgust, "something clean."

I pressed his hand.

Early on the morrow I was there with the packet of napkins. The bed, drawn out of the recess, stood close to the window; you saw distinctly the beautiful lines of his pallid face; the eyelids were half-closed, there was a smile upon his mouth. He raised his eyes, saw the packet, and, hardly observing me at the moment, began immediately, with trembling hands, to undo it.

"Ah, yes!" he said; "yes! I recognise them, my beautiful napkins. Yes! there is my number, 120; they are the same."

He took them, one after the other, and buried his face in the soft folds of the damask, revelling in the sweet odour of cleanliness. Closing his eyes, all his old luxury came in vision around him. Weakness fell on him—physical or moral, I know not. His grand head sunk in the pillow; the napkins fell from his hand. When his eyes next opened, he fixed them intently on the sky, which was now growing pale with the close of day.

Have you felt when death approaches a human soul, one of those noble souls that God endows with poetry and truth and power, and that the world has deceived, that it has perhaps spoilt—have you felt before that strength which is dying down, before those nameless miseries, before those poor failing limbs,—have you felt an immense pity rise into your heart,—have you felt a mute, ineffable tenderness penetrate into your very marrow,—have you felt, notwithstanding the ardour of your faith, that your mouth was frozen, and your throat closed, dried up? Without voice, without a word, have you fallen on your knees, conscious of your absolute incapacity, prostrated, exhausted, before the God who saves? If you have felt this, you know what I at this moment experienced.

The sculptor never turned his head, nor withdrew his gaze; he was absorbed in the contemplation of the darkening sky.

His wife did not venture to touch the napkins, thrown by hazard here and there upon the bed; the children stood by motionless. This state of things continued for some time.

The day following, at six o'clock in the morning, I received a letter with the deepest of black borders. The sculptor had died in the night; his wife prayed me to come to her.

I was very little disposed to do so, nevertheless I went. It lay there, that noble head, cold, and with an ideal beauty. It lay there, that poor body, extended, weak with the last utter weakness. The soul, in its departure, had left peace upon the brow; it was calm, clear, unwrinkled, and the lips had taken their first delicate contour.

At my entrance, the widow, raising herself to her full height, and standing with her two hands upon the heads of her two sons, one foot advanced—tragic attitude of the desolated mother—began to pour out her benediction upon these orphans, in a discourse swelling with redundant epithets. It was an actress, wanting only the passion of one.

Francis stood with eyes cast down, and tears running on his cheeks; a slight bending of his head, as if to withdraw it from the hand of his mother, betrayed an internal revolt; he was subjected, but he suffered.

The younger brother, utterly inattentive, looked here and there, kneading all the time a piece of clay in his fingers. He was accustomed to his mother's declamations; one more or less mattered little; when she had done, he would return to his playthings. And he did return to them.

Now there entered a working man, a moulder, a taker of casts; honest fellow enough, in rude health, red lip, black moustache, ignorant of suffering. "Ha!" he said; "seems that it is all over! Poor man!"

The widow resumed an attitude, and improvised expressly for him a new monologue, to which he listened with open mouth, and with some pleasure, as if all were passing at a theatre.

The grief of the widow was not certainly to the level of her demonstrations, yet there was some sincerity in her tears. She felt that the dead man extended there, had been the poetry, the ideal of her life. All *that* was gone, never to return. Besides, he had been kind to her. His own illusion and bitter disenchantment, she had hardly suspected. Whilst he could work at his art, he had concealed them from her; when ill, she accounted for his silence by his malady; she could see no further. Now that he was dead, she paid what respect she could. Here was the man with plaster to take a cast of her husband.

This was all in her part. And then he had a beautiful head, and then—the cast would sell.

When she had finished her discourse, the man took his plaster, and threw handfuls of it on the face of the dead. The younger boy approached the moulder, and followed his operations with a curious eye. The elder son concealed himself in the solitary workshop.

As to the widow, she had put on her shawl, and gone to seek something for the *pot au feu*.

THE ARBOUR.

ND now I return, to seat myself under the service-tree Arbour at the Old Manor-house in my father's garden.

This garden had broad walks, bordered with box; it was well walled in. The orchard trees looked over the wall, and above the orchard trees rose the misty mountain, in successive stages—some wooded, some bare, all with projecting-roofed cottages, perched on a peak, or hidden in a dell; the Jura, with its dark pines, and upper pastures, dotted here and there with *châlets*, dominating all.

In April, before the leaves are out, the service-tree arbour is starred with yellow flowers; bees swarm there, the buzzing is like that of a hive. Through the flowery branches, you see the sky, with light fleecy clouds, moving on gently before the softened breeze. Behind the arbour there is the stand of bee-hives—a beautiful stand, resting against the bakehouse, facing due east, and covered with wild vine; four rows of hives displaying themselves proudly in their smooth, polished deal case.

In May, when the apple-trees of the garden are in flower, you might take them for orange-trees; then it is that spring-tide scents and living murmur spread all round; the branches scatter a very rain of pink petals and golden pollen; the bees seem delirious with delight; bright-hued insects poise themselves over the fragrant tufts; there is an exuberant burst of blossom on all sides. The ground is still bare, except for the gay tulip beds, but the white silvery dome of the fruit-trees, with the blue sky above them, make the garden a gorgeous scene such as man could never have imagined, had not the country been strewn abundantly with such by God's bounteous hand.

On fine May Sunday evenings, when one is seated beneath the service-tree arbour, one can hear the village girls going round the large green enclosure in groups, hand clasped in hand, taking the road that winds through the meadows, with the Alps sparkling at the horizon. The girls, as they go keep singing plaintive songs, their voice dwelling chiefly on the high notes, and having a certain shrill and melancholy, wild and sylvan character, that recalls the fragrance of the lily of the valley. While the moon rises, they go on stringing couplet on couplet, sometimes nearer, sometimes further, always in one measure. Occasionally this mournful song is broken by bursts of laughter. This occurs when the young men, who follow at a distance, also in parties, and hand in hand, have stopped short to wait the return of the young girls, and stop their way. Then the song bursts out again, clear as crystal, full of wild modulations, fraught with an inexpressible poetry, only to be met with in the fields. Night falls, the stars light up; gradually, the singers return to the village, everything is silent except the frog, who croaks discreetly at the edge of the brook.

In June, the whole country is leafy; there are deep shadows, and places scorched with sunshine. The arbour is well shut in by its service-tree; you catch warblings, little cries, flutterings, flapping of wings; and, when evening comes, whole broods shelter amidst the branches. Through them we can just see the hives, from whence exhales a scent of virgin-wax; the bees hang on them in brown clusters; they keep returning with bundles of pollen round their legs, and such buzzing, and such frantic haste! At the mouth of each hive—on the stand which is gilded by the yellow dust dropping from the spoil—stand the sentinels, strongly entrenched, their head within, their body outside the hive, making the air vibrate with the rapid movement of their wings.

A clump of trees shelters the stand of hives from the north winds: nut-trees, elders, lilacs, privet, the chestnut with its fan-like leaves, and the maple; all these with their soft tones and infinite shades; their bright display; their cool depths of verdure. On the top of the wall, pinks blossom among the stones; and there are wild poppies there too; moss fading in the sunshine; lizards listening to the cricket in the hay-fields. Over the wall trails an entanglement of convolvulus, nasturtiums, and sweet-peas, luxuriantly falling over on the other side.

The little girls when they pass by look up; stand on tip-toe; catch a fragment of a petal, and go on their way delighted.

The fountain leaps in the sunshine; its jet cuts the Jura with a diamond line; the drops keep playing their clear uniform melody in the freshened air.

The mowers, the hay-makers, take a path that keeps close to the garden; children are fond of loitering there. They come at night to see the glow-worms shining on the wall, while the frogs repeat their mournful note. There it is that gossips are carried on, hurried good-byes, fresh laughter, quiet cogitations, scraps of talk, little nothings; all that makes up the nature, the village, the simple country life that one so passionately loves.

As soon as the sun is set, the massive Jura stands out against it, with outline admirably pure. The sky behind it then assumes that transparent, almost green tinge that one sees in Perugino's paintings. I do not know why that particular sky, that ethereal hue, that light without rays, that brightness almost polar in its severity, should attract my gaze, as if it were just there that we might look for the opening out of Paradise! That immutable fortress makes me muse. When my thoughts travel along unbroken horizons, they get fainter and fainter; melt away like mist before the breeze. When they meet that fortress, with battlements of pine; those slopes furrowed by steep paths; those openings in the forest; the perfect line of that far summit,—then my mind wakes; my life seems doubled. I do not indeed say that the ideas raised are always very definite; it is rather a healthy gust of liberty and energy that flows down from thence, and fills my heart.

How many sweet hours, how many blessed hours I have spent in this arbour I speak of! What raptures of sun and song and fresh breezes, what prayers in agony, what grateful hymns have been mine! And when my eyes, while reading the old Bible on my knee, wandered till they lost themselves in the distance, following the valley, taking in the indented ridge of the wood; then returning to those peaceful walks close by, which so many loved and lost ones have trodden; when my glance through my leafy nest pierced to deepest depths of intensest azure,—oh, how I have thanked God! oh, how warmly I have loved Him! how keenly felt that this was true life, healthy life! that it was a mercy beyond all others to be permitted to have one's dwelling-place here, in this full, free nature, from morning dawn to evening gloom!

There has been much singing along these old walks, much laughter, some weeping too. Many children's steps, many young girls' feet, have sounded on this gravel; many fair dreams, great projects, have been nursed there. When the village-bell strikes the hours, when at twelve it rings for dinner; in the evening, summons the labourers home; there will rise out of my past, as it were, swarms of loved faces I shall never see more.

My own young years rise too. See, they bring me back now two innocent faces; two old faces fresh as roses,—Nicholas and Marianne, the guardian spirits of the garden.

They had the management of the Manor; he of the cellar and the bee-hives, she of the garden. Nothing hardly to do, only to keep their eyes open.

They were good, plain, well-to-do villagers. He was a Bernese; she belonged to our part of the country. Their united ages amounted to at least a hundred and thirty years.

In the morning one used to see Nicholas, with a thick, short cap on his little round head; breeches of velvet, like those in the song; a great waistcoat down to his knees; always in shirt-sleeves, and these dazzlingly clean; hands resting on two sticks, and pipe in mouth, move very slowly along the orchard, along the Manor. He took his time; he was never in a hurry; but he got all the same to his journey's end. One never heard his voice except in a little, contented sort of grunt, or on days of great eloquence, in a certain "*See, see, see*," hummed inwardly. It was a way he had of consulting, haranguing, and approving himself.

In the spring, when the bees began to swarm, he would establish his wife—"*the* Marianne" under the Arbour.

She sat there, the charming old woman, a measure of dried vegetables in her apron; with quiet hand shelling the red, white, striped, and spotted kidney-beans; while with the corner of her eye she watched the hives. She would let us children sit round her, our hands buried in the pretty beans. She wore a white cap with old-fashioned lace, much starched, and falling stiffly down her face. What sort of eyes had she? I do not know. I only know that she was beautiful, with those red-rose tints, that fresh bow-shaped mouth you no longer see in town or country, and that mouth always smiling. She had, besides, two dimples in her cheeks, which smiled too. When we were seated on the gravel before her, we contemplated her, listened to her, and that was enough in itself to make us good.

She never scolded; all her moral teaching was contained in these few words, "You must be very obedient, and then —*pouis*, you must love the good God."

Her talk was of that peaceful kind that murmurs on like a brook; now flowing through fields, now over stones; kissing this flower, wetting that leaf; while the butterflies poise themselves over it, and look at their own reflection. She pointed out bird and bee: "Look here, see there;" or else some venturous insect climbing a blade of grass; and when some gayer bean than the others passed through her fingers, she would say, "Here, take it; it is the king of the company." And so she went on shelling, talking; the hours passed. It was all very pleasant; peace such as I have not since found.

All at once here are the bees in great agitation before the hive. "Go, call Nicholas; go quick; that's a good child now!" Oh, the delight of being useful, of carrying a message! Nicholas listened, took his pipe from his lips, tapped it on the seat to shake away the ashes. "See, see." Then, after a moment's reflection, "Go and get me the *casse;* that's a good child now!"

And slowly, on his stout sticks, Nicholas would cross the yard, and mount the garden steps one by one.

The *casse* is a shining copper basin, very red and bright, which floats in the bucket of cold water that always stands near the door in country kitchens; whoever is thirsty taking a draught therefrom.

"Here is the *casse;* is all right, Father Nicholas?"

Father Nicholas sometimes, arriving too late, would see the swarm all assembled in the air, set off like a flash of lightning for the mountain, under his very nose. For a moment he would remain motionless; then—it was one of those rare occasions on which he expressed his sentiments —"Go your ways, then," he would say to the bees. "The good God bless you. It is not I who am going to run after you."

Marianne would be much distressed. "Are they not *bold?*" she would say, in her peculiar diction; "are they not *infidels?*"

Nicholas would shake his head; that long sentence having been uttered, with a merry eye and placid mouth, he would leisurely retake the way he came, and reach the yard, the bench, the pipe. When he got there, he would give a grunt, *ouf!* let himself drop down all of a piece, half close his eyes, and inhale his tobacco smoke with a low murmur of comfort.

More often, however, the bees, who knew their man, would wait for him, agitated and quivering. Nicholas placed his two sticks against the stand; took the copper basin in one hand, an old, many-warded key in the other, and limping, whistling, tapping away, would move, followed by the swarm, to an apple-tree, where the bees clustered.

I hear it still that rustic sound, I hear those metallic notes, and that little blackbird chirp; I see the light cloud that hovers behind Nicholas!

And Marianne! In great haste she would bring a new

straw-hive, well rubbed with a bit of balm which she had just gathered. Nicholas would take the living bunch in his hands, and pour it into the hive. Calm, staid, deliberate always in the midst of the excited swarm.

"Is the queen there, Father Nicholas? Did you see her?"

"See, see, see."

The hive turned, Nicholas stooped heavily, slowly arranged it upon four props, then Marianne surrounded the bees with a large-patterned carpet. Was it not well to protect the new swarm from the fierce heat of the sun? In the evening it was carried to the stand, and throughout the rest of that day, and even all the next, the bees kept coming and going between the apple-tree and the hive.

When the month of August came, it was time to take the honey,—an exciting day for good Father Nicholas.

He covered his little head with an iron helmet, pointed, barred,—a genuine middle-age relic that he had found in some cellar or other of the manor-house.

Still whistling, he approached the hives, lifted them, methodically arranged the amber combs in red earthenware dishes. The bees raged—that is made believe—for they knew that there was nothing for it with Father Nicholas. Hive after hive had to submit; Nicholas, who was a just man, left them an ample provision for the winter. Poor Marianne used to be sadly frightened when he adventured himself thus in the midst of clouds of angry insects.

"Must take care, Nicholas, and then (*pouis*) pray God Almighty to have a care of you too."

But autumn has come. The trees have yielded up their fruit, the wild vine clothes the hive-stand with a drapery richer in purple and gold than any tissue woven in cities for monarchs' robes. The blue and silver aster-blossoms sway in the breeze; the redbreast tries to repeat his spring song—alas! he has left his best notes on the hawthorn bushes; he hops hither and thither in warm spots, whereon the November sun has power to chase the fog away. Brown butterflies display their velvet, purple-eyed wings on the year's last flowers; the bee comes there too, benumbed, melancholy. The red service-berries are fallen, the arbour has lost all its shade. In the field, behind the willows, smoke rises from the fire made by a *boëbe* herding cows. To-morrow they will be brought in; the white frosts wither the grass.

The vintage is over, the wine ferments in the cask. Walnuts are cracked during the long evenings at tables covered with cider, cheese, and apples. The hemp hangs in silken plaits from the ceiling, ready for the spinning-wheel and the winter nights. The shorn sheep gladly seek the warmth of the stable. A cold, north-east wind whistling, rushes by.

Adieu, my beautiful past! Adieu, my memories!

THE

HEAVENLY HORIZONS.

THE HEAVENLY HORIZONS.

WE who elbow each other aside in the crowd of the world, destined perhaps never to meet again; we, whom opposite positions, and often opposite characters, so widely separate, are, nevertheless, bound together, as in one sheaf, by the one fact—death.

Men die: we shall die; and it is not to teach you this that I open my lips; but all and each, we carry in the silence of our hearts the poignant remembrance of one loved and lost: it is there that I find a bond of union between you and me, such as, at any instant, may make the same tears start to our eyes, and blend together in one sentiment of grief, and also of profound love. our souls till then strangers to each other.

Who is it that has not wept? Who is it that has not sunk down before that couch, where reposes, without voice, without a look, one who loved him, and whom he loved? Where is the man who has not walked solitary after walking step with step, two together?

Alas! this terrible reality of grief! Some find it strange. To them the idea appears unusual, rare. To me it is the most actual and familiar of things; it would seem to me most strange to pass a day without thinking of it.

Besides, does any one restrain himself from loving? Can we say to the heart—Thou shalt not remember? Would we say it? And from that hour, when a cherished being who was ours, has quitted life, are there not certain questionings, consuming problems, which for ever rise before us?

These agitate the soul day and night. Unresolved, they make our torture. And woe to him who escapes by forgetting them; he escapes, but by a sort of moral forfeiture and degradation; he has committed treason against his soul. Better that they should live and torture us, than that we should purchase ease by their oblivion.

And now, tell me, does not a profound *ennui* of mortal life fall on you as you advance? Do you not feel yourself ill of this most fatal malady, the incapacity to be happy?

We are for the most part fatigued wrestlers, captives greedy of the open air, perturbed creatures, thirsting for peace.

In all this discontent there is, no doubt, some weakness or error to be combated. But I also find in it an ardent aspiration for the skies.

There are days which rise sadly, which proceed without the sun, which are extinguished without a glow. The trees are leafless; the fields have no verdure; clouds hang their dark-gray folds on every side of the horizon. And our life has these pallors, these glooms. A disgust of all things invades the soul; a disgust of ourselves, a hundred times greater than of others; the wretchedness of a combat where defeat has followed on defeat; secret shocks to our faith itself. Oh, in these moments, how we sigh for our deliverance; for the splendour of truth; for the hallelujah of the skies!

You have known these mortal languors; you have breathed these sighs; you have raised your hands to heaven, while the tears of an exile rolled down your cheek.

Well, these torturing questions, I attempt to answer

them; these tears, I come to take from them their bitterness.

Who am I that speak? It matters little. You know me not. Better thus; the false appearances we wear to each other hinders many a thought from reaching the heart.

I have loved; I love. I have suffered; I shall suffer. Many an object of my tenderness has passed behind the veil. I have known those nights peopled with phantoms which descend upon the soul of the mourner. Remorse that comes too late; cries uttered to an inexorable silence; anguish and doubts, revolt itself, and that prostration worse than death—I have known them all.

The consolations of friends might affect and move me, could not cure. They could not restore the dear face, the voice, the heart that wrapt me in its love. It was that I wanted; of what avail all else?

Or if some word uttered brought me hope, was that word a truth? Could I lean upon it, sure that it would not break and pierce the heart? Are there not beautiful errors more cruel than the harshest truth?

Then I sought honestly, passionately, for light. And light which descends from heaven has flooded me with happiness. As lips burning with thirst have hung over the fresh pure water flowing from the rock, so have I hung over the Scriptures of God; there, in long draughts I have quenched my thirst.

Do not be alarmed. I am no theologian. I do not undertake to teach you. Let me simply take your hand—that hand which trembles; which is still wet with the tears it has striven in vain to stop. Come, let us talk together of those who are gone. Come, we will together unfold our wings; we will together go into the land of life.

You demand them of the vast unknown regions of space. Oh, you will wander there for ever, cold at heart! Or, wearied, seized with terror, you will sit down immovable, your head covered with sackcloth and ashes, and remembering nothing but the days that were. I know where they are, our best beloved! I have seen them. This is no dream. Neither is it ecstasy, or the revelations of a seer that I have to offer; but the good promises of God.

On my part, nothing. I am nothing, can do nothing, possess nothing. But, on the part of my God, much: assurance of life, assurance of reunion, assurance of eternal love.

If this little book gives courage to some dejected pilgrim; if it brings under the sunbeam some countenance unaccustomed to the light; if it relieves by an infallible hope some heart in its affliction; if, like a fertilising dew, it should fall on some spirit hardened by distress,—my God, I shall thank Thee for one of the greatest happinesses of an existence in which Thou hast mingled much joy with many tears!

PART FIRST.

TO WHOM I SPEAK.

YOU know already, it is to those that weep.

But I must return to this.

One thing has always made me shudder: the rapidity of the last departure; the character of suddenness, joined with that of the irretrievable.

If there were no future life, such disruptions, violent, absolute, would be a fearful irony on the part of God, who would have united us intimately with other beings, to break us asunder at a moment, and plunge us and plunge them in an abyss of darkness and oblivion.

Do what we will, a day arrives when, without preparation, without adieus, your loved one is gone.

When he quitted you for a week, for a day, (if you loved much, for some hours,) what caresses were interchanged, what charges given, and how you kept in your memory his last precious words! And yet you had letters, those messengers which bring to us the thought, almost the look and voice of the absent. He now quits you never to return; he will speak no more; he will write no more. He whose heart vibrated to the least sigh of yours—oh, your most passionate appeals will not extract one word from him, not one! He has left you; his soul has escaped from you; his mouth and yours must be mute for evermore.

The exhaustion produced by grief, the fear of giving language to your sentiments—how shall I describe it?—the terror of finding yourself face to face with death,—everything had paralysed you. And then, when he was gone, who should have heard them, how the cries of the heart burst forth!—what ardent words; what embraces; what agony of supplication!

Even if you had talked together of the coming separation, if you had gathered as a treasure every broken phrase that fell from his dying lips, even thus prepared, you were not prepared. Death held its great surprise still in reserve. And when all was over, you stood astonished, smitten, dismayed, on a threshold you could not pass.

There is in death a sovereign dignity; the solemnity of a life concluded. The hour has struck; earthly activity has ceased,—the eternal, with the irrevocable, succeeds.

In one point of view, it is a simple and facile thing. Every day we see the light of a lamp extinguished. It was, and it is not; a breath of air sufficed. And so one dies. Pain and agony, these are not death. Death is one simple fact. A flame, as it seemed, hovered over the brow of the dying, and it disappeared; this is all. It might as easily return. But it does not return. Here is the sole horror of death.

I find in this last hour a strange sentiment of respect for the dead, mingled with grief; a reverence for one who has gone forth on this mysterious passage. Passage full of mysteries which we too, however, shall one day tread.

He who has gone forth could not be supported on his solitary path by any love of ours. A stronger arm was needful. He had our prayers, yes! and our last adieus. But there comes a moment when the eyes cease to see, and the ears to hear, when there is a silence and a halt between the two regions of life. It is a moment which God, in His compassion, has reserved for Himself. We, with our hearts racked with grief, stand watching the darkness of night as it descends upon him. We extend our arms, we cannot help it, as if to retain him; but He who wills to take, has taken.

Happy, a thousand times happy, those on whose pale brow has descended the peace of heaven!—God's pardon written in lines of light.

Now all is finished.

Where art thou? Thou whom I no longer possess; thou who liest *there*, inert, and near to me? Ah! what passes in thee when thine eyes are fixed and thy mouth closed, and there is the celestial smile illuminating the countenance? Let me follow; let me, too, pass behind the veil; some splendours escape from beneath it; my soul burns in me, for thou art there.

Patience! my child! Weep, remember, pray! Soon thy hour, too, will come.

At this time we rest in the presence of death, in one of its hideous aspects—destruction.

The delight of our eyes has become an object of terror; things inanimate retain their form, the body of our beloved falls into dissolution; and the world pursues its course, and the sun shines, and fields blossom, and friends themselves, saddened for a little time, link themselves afresh with the living; facts like these fall one after the other upon the heart.

There are men whom they revolt, there are men whom they crush; many forget, none are consoled.

Thank Heaven, there are some who do not wish to be thus consoled,—who do not wish to be pacified by the hard reasoning of egotism. They do not wish to bow before the inevitable fact simply because it is a fact and is inevitable. Neither do they wrap themselves in the indifference of mysticism. Their full and energetic hearts, retaining all their affections, love in death,—love, suffering, as before they loved, joyous, in life.

It is a hateful philosophy, this submission, without a faith, to the tyrannies of reality. Rather revolt, rather clamour for the lost, rather seek him madly under the skies; perhaps, in our desperation, we shall meet the Saviour Jesus, and He will restore him to us.

Terrible temptations await us—Christians as well as others—when we sit down on the borders of the tomb. It is there that the great enemy of our race, he who accuses us incessantly, is to be found; it is there that he calumniates God before our face.

In this consists the really *infernal* in his character, that pity cannot touch him. He sees us overwhelmed with grief, and, at one bound, he is on us, and fixes his talons in our throbbing breasts!

"You prayed—you implored God for his recovery—you had faith in Him. He has said, 'Ask and I will give.' What has He given you? Nature takes her undeviating course, all things in the world proceed according to their own laws, your prayer but breaks against an immutable fate. Your beloved one, will you ever see him? or with what form, and in what region? Will he love you there? And you, in ten years, in twenty, are you sure of loving him?"

Such thought is worse than death.

But I know a state of mind still more lamentable, that of utmost languor.

In despair there is life, activity; there is an infinite in an infinite sorrow; in despondency there is a sombre poetry on which the soul secretly feasts; this languor is near to annihilation.

Oh, well I have known her—this ghostly visitant with pallid face that comes and crouches near the cold hearth of the little chamber where a widow weeps. At her approach the last ember is extinguished, everything grows cold and dim—even memory. Then it seems that the soul, like a bird of night, traces the same circle again and again in a cavern where no light penetrates. Always the same questions, monotonous, incessantly repeated, without effort to seek, without hope to find an answer.

This is the hour for consolatory friends.

A poor heart in its grief resembles a wounded man stretched along the road, a prey to the charity of all passers. All wish him well; all do him ill. This turns him over, that raises him up; he moans, it matters not; we know better than he what he wants.

Into an afflicted soul the crowd thinks it has a right to enter; it is like a conquered city. The new comers overturn everything; carry off, bring in, derange, arrange;—protestations are of no avail; besides, they are so feeble, (mere sighs of pain,) that they are scarcely heard.

Health possesses a vital energy that repels all poisons; it will only assimilate what is suitable. The sick man yields to all, and suffers from all.

It is a grievous spectacle these barbarous invasions,—well intended, most of them; but very unseasonable, and very afflictive.

Each one is for shaping anew this poor soul, and casting it in its own mould. Light-hearted people speak of Time, and how it sweeps and effaces, with the folds of its robe, every mournful image. Kinder spirits speak of the virtues of the deceased, and pronounce him happy. Peace-loving men, whom long regrets fatigue, remark that he was well nursed, has been decorously mourned, that every propriety has been observed, and that now the living must be thought of. Prosaic, narrow-minded men, finding this soul prostrate on the earth, would rivet it there for ever,—would tear off its wings for fear it should escape from them. After having lost what he loved, the sufferer—last misery! —loses himself. He loses his liberty, his individuality; he no longer knows himself.

Of all distressful consolations, the worst are those which, coming truly from man, pretend to be derived from heaven.

The heart is open to receive these pious counsels; the sob is stifled, grief itself is silent; they speak, and they leave you more distracted, not less miserable.

For you had counted on God, on His sympathy, on His help, on some miracle of love He might still hold in reserve; and is it not the love of God that alone sheds a light on the mysteries of this world? And behold! they bring you a god of petty jealousies, or a god who demands joy of a heart transpierced, or a calculating god, who enjoins you to love none but him, because he alone dies not!

Oh, how often have I heard—dinned into the ears of some poor dejected creature, whose head is buried in his hands, who is incapable of resisting the aggressions of their falsehood—such words as these: "The Eternal commands that we love Him only; He must reign alone; He breaks all idols!"

The poor soul would answer that his father, that his child, was not an idol; that his love ascended in grateful prayers to Him who gave them; but he cannot speak. A fear has fallen upon him. Already his God turns on him a menacing aspect; his heart sinks within him.

In the war that you have kindled between God and his regret, which will be the conqueror? Whichever conquers, the soul will lose by the contest. If your God triumphs, it is because your soul, crushed by fear, has betrayed its love; if your regret, it is because you have measured yourself with God, and resisted Him.

See how careful we should be when we speak in the name of God!

God will not permit idols, but God permits strong affections. He has made our hearts for them; He has made them for the human heart. God wills that we love Him with all our energy, but to reign He has no need to create a void. If He afflicts, it is that affliction is good for us. The furnace is good, if the gold can be no otherwise purified.

Do not transfer our own little passions to God. In our happiness, such a God degrades us. We rather counterfeit a love for Him than feel it. In our misery, such a representation of the Divine Being revolts us or overwhelms us; in either case it separates us from the true God.

Others say to you, "Do not weep; God does not will that you should weep. Rejoice! He desires a glad heart."

Such men, in fact, are wearied with a prolonged sorrow. They cannot understand it; they have a certain vague terror of it. Therefore, be content. Your husband, it is true, is dead; but God does all for the best. Believe in Him, and sing a hymn of gratitude.

This is to kill the heart.

God wills that we should live! And for the very fulness of life He says, *weep!* Weep, but not as those who are without hope.

Our bereavements must be sorrows, if the gifts of God,

love and life, are joys. If God strikes us, it is that we should feel. Without doubt, even in the trial itself is found I know not what penetrating sweetness; I have felt it even at that moment when I sunk prostrate under the hand of God. But this is not a joy that bursts out in cries of victory and gladness. The joy I felt, poor vacillating light, sheltered itself in the recesses of my heart, and threw its pale glory before me as I knelt, and, with face hidden in my hands, wept on in silence.

I know a man who wept thus.

Job did not say that the gifts of the Eternal were a snare; he did not congratulate himself that his riches had been taken away, and his sons destroyed. The Eternal had *given!* it was gift. The Eternal had *taken away!* it was privation. Blessed be the name of the Lord!

Job cast himself upon the earth. Utmost suffering, utmost adoration.

Seeing him thus, the Eternal pointed him out to Satan, prostrate in sorrow, prostrate in obedience: "Hast thou considered my servant Job, who has not his equal upon the earth?"

What made Job to sin, you know it well, was not the malignant ulcer, the last of his calamities. Even then he uttered no word of reproach to God. What exasperated him were the bitter consolations, the inhuman counsels of his friends. Under this scourge, and bleeding from their hands, in the freshness of his wounds he raised himself, and was angry even with his God.

From want of reflection, from that idleness which goes on repeating pious phrases without considering their meaning, perhaps, too, from the influence of a certain mysticism, there are men who, in the most spiritual manner, preach the purest egotism.

Health does not last; to value it highly is to make a bad calculation. Riches depart; to cling to them is to make a bad calculation. Glory passes; to fix your heart upon it is to make a bad calculation. Science deceives; to devote yourself to it is to make a bad calculation. Husband, wife, children, often betray, and always die; to attach yourself to them is to make a bad calculation. In one word, he who loves the *creature* calculates ill. The good and infallible calculation is, to love God, and to love Him only. God does not die, God does not deceive. God, moreover, is master of us all. Look well at the balance; examine and decide. It is simple as the rule of three; peremptory as arithmetic.

I state bluntly what is expressed, perhaps, with more precaution.

Without pausing to contest an argument which seems to assimilate the immortal souls of others to perishable objects, without resting on that word *creature*, so disdainfully applied to all that is not *myself*—let me say at once, that I find in this motive to detach myself from man, and give myself to God, something so repulsive, that my whole moral nature rises up against it.

The more generous my heart, the more tenderly, the more closely shall I embrace a treasure of which you shew me the fragility.

What! because your affection may not be as constant as mine! What! because you will die, dear friend, shall I withdraw one particle of my love? No, a thousand times. My glory is to love more him who loves less; my consolation is to love beyond death itself.

Love is the destroyer of all egotisms—of the spiritual egotism as of others. He it is who enters into the last asylum, and breaks the last idol. And when the heart is thus sanctified, it becomes prepared for an eternal love.

My whole nature cries out against such reasoning. In the name of all moral dignity, I declare myself superior to your calculations. In the sublimity of moral freedom, I prefer misery with the integrity of my sentiments, to contentment with this mutilation; I seize my treasures, those treasures of the heart you would snatch from me, I embrace, I maintain, I vindicate them.

"Love thy father, and thy mother, and thy wife; love them with all thy strength, but love God more. He is thy God, He is their God; He loves them, He loves thee. Never in the utmost altitude of thy affections wilt thou rise to the height of that love!" Hold such language as this to me, and my heart feels that you speak truth; my soul obeys, and at the same time takes wider sweep. You have subdued me, but you have aggrandised; you have conquered by raising me to the skies.

Alas! many amongst us never raise their thoughts to the skies. Heaven would be strange to them; they rest on the earth, where they soon reconcile themselves. For one instant the traveller stops, looks about him, thinking on which side his companion has disappeared, then prepares himself for solitude, shoulders his pack again, and makes the best of it.

After all, there is very little need to teach men egotism; they have most of them taken their degree in that philosophy.

To gather myself together, and fall in the softest place, when a fall is inevitable; to throw the cargo into the sea if the winds are tempestuous, and to steer close to the land, —we are all more or less capable of this.

Oh, you, who after ten, after twenty years of absence,

weep with hope, and hope in weeping,—I respect you from the bottom of my soul. You are the true *lovers*, you are the truly happy.

One thing seems horrible to me in my sorrow: to think that it may have an end; that some commonplace well-being may replace it, that we may learn to dispense with what was once our life; that a little vulgar existence, with its repasts at stated hours, and its customary trivial pleasures, shall fill the void in the heart made by the loss of the dearest friend—so that if he returned we should not know where to place him. There is something in this which might well draw from Ecclesiastes, one of those cries he uttered when proclaiming the vanity of human life:—

Life is short, swift as a sunbeam; let us rejoice! The wind has swept away our tent; let us build again on the shifting sands!

Do not think I am an idolater of grief; I am not. Only I will not make a god of "happiness at all price." I know well that we must live upon the earth, and finish our career, but I choose to walk with the image of my absent friend: always we are two.

Our levity abashes me, mine more than yours; this incurable egotism, this aridity that I find in the most secret places of the heart. Even there a hard determination conceals itself to make the best of whatever happens.

God has overthrown me; I will rise again; we shall see who is the stronger. God has taken from me the child of my joy, or my father, or my wife; I will do without them. I will subdue my calamity, not by the power of a faith which, grasping the loved beings, constrains them to remain, not by the effort of a patience which has learned to wait, but by a careless, practical stoicism—by a secret defiance of the decrees of Providence.

I do not blame the man who has suffered much, because his heart lies open to new pleasures; because the opening flower, or the blue waters of the lake, or Spring, or Autumn, revive the smile upon his lips. Nothing in all this disturbs me. That tender thoughts, and other loves, should kindle in the solitary bosom, does not revolt me. What fills me with sadness is that condition of the soul in which the lost friend, gone joys and griefs of the past, have taken rank with things perfectly indifferent—in which if one should come to you and say, He is there! you would find yourself more embarrassed than delighted. The *comfortable* house built on the extinction of a great love—this I cannot see without a blush.

Grief is a flower as delicate and prompt to fade as happiness. Still it does not wholly die. Like the magic rose, dried, and unrecognisable, a warm air breathed on it will suffice to renew its bloom.

Often when the lips smile the heart is sad. Those who appear to forget sometimes remember better than ostentatious mourners.

In many of us there are two men. The one is active, rushes hither and thither upon his business, diverts himself gaily and noisily; the other, passive, dreaming, and depressed, turns to the hours that have fled. This last walks and weeps upon the old paths. He stops, he recalls a look, he pursues a phantom. Here we sat together, and her voice trembled; there, fatigued, she leant upon me; that evening she was sad, and we prayed God to leave us on the earth together; that other morning she was gay, and all the world was happy—Heaven seemed to have descended upon us.

Because you see in such a one the eyes reanimated, the mind resuming its old labours, life returning to the accustomed track, you say, What is finished is finished, and the dead are dead.

No.

After those first days when the separation rends the heart—word of terrible fidelity!—and when the torn heart cannot conceal its wounds, there comes a reaction. A strong desire for solitude possesses the soul; a bashfulness and jealousy fall upon it; intruders are repelled; the chamber of death is closed; one displays a stolid front that denies all,—tortures, memories. But within there are lights burning round the shrine; and a casual word makes the heart bleed, while the lips discourse of some indifferent matter, or are seen to smile.

There are secret communications with a departed loved one which the most compassionate listener would profane. At these times we are prodigal of expressions of tenderness, which we should have withheld, perhaps, in life. There is pardon asked, there are passionate avowals, utterances so thrilling and so sweet, that even the voice of a friend echoing them would jar upon us.

Oblivion! Oh, you deceive yourself! Not oblivion. but a sanctuary, a holy of holies, over which the wings are folded.

Even the light-hearted man remembers. A voice ascends from the past, low and soft; a word confided, the pressure of a hand in pain, some sudden recollection bids the tears to flow. His heart beats, he embraces in imagination the cherished image; she is his, she is not dead; the affections of the past still survive. It is good for him that he suffers thus.

Old men, chilled with age, who are said to be indifferent to the loss of friends,—do you believe that it is egotism, or some paralysis of heart, that keeps back their tears? I do not think so. The old man sheds few tears, afflicts himself little, because the old man knows that he has little time to regret the separation.

When young, our years are ages; in mature life they are each three hundred and sixty-five days; in old age, they have dwindled to a few weeks. Time is, indeed, the messenger with wings at his feet. Yesterday he took my wife, to-day my son, to-morrow he will take me.

No desert without limits extends before the old man. He walks beside a river whose banks are seen to approach; a diminishing stream separates them each day less and less; and on the opposite bank stand wife and son, with arms outstretched to meet him.

In fact, for the believer, at these last limits of existence, joy predominates over grief.

We who feel ourselves weak, and are humiliated at our own levity,—we who would prefer a thousand times to be faithful and broken-hearted than to be frivolous and happy,—we will not despair. The key of our treasures may be lost for an instant, it will be recovered. He who keeps our loved ones will restore them to us; not one will be missing Our heart on seeing them will resume all its pristine love.

It is but the silence of the dead which makes us faithless to their memory. The mind is weary with its flight through unknown regions, with following what can be never reached. It flies as a bird in the night over a land that has been inundated and become one watery waste.

Why is it that you see so distinctly this traveller who has quitted you, this son who sails in the Indian Ocean, this husband trafficking in the Far West? Why do they still seem near to you, their parting counsels still heard, and preparations made for a return, which yet is very distant? It is because you know where they are. You can follow the track of their vessel, or the course of their caravan; you can put your finger on the map and say, They are there! You trace them home, and forthwith you can make arrangements, even to the minutest detail, for a return so distinctly imagined.

Let us do the same for our dead; for indeed there is the same certainty of their return, and the same vivid recognition of their existence.

But those celestial regions, you say, are so vast, so vague! Speak to us of shores we know, and which they knew! And yet, if you speak of them, our hearts break, for our friends never will return. There is no hope. There is only a dream.

For me, I know no reality more true than this dream.

Dream! God prepares for you something far different. If He has not permitted between you and the dead that exchange of thoughts for which you sigh, it is because, if He had, death would not have *been* death. And then, we should have made idols of our loved ones.

I know a courier, swift and sure, who will carry us to the absent—Faith. He knows the road; have no fear, he will not stumble or stray.

For us, in our sorrow, there are promises, and glad intelligence of our dead. God has not shut them up in dark prison-houses. We can turn our eyes to the land they inhabit. No mirage, the country exists. No poet's rapture, the simplest see the clearest.

Gazing on that land, our affections will take new life, and the bitterness of despair will vanish; and when we return to earth, we shall bring back an imperishable joy in our hearts; we shall be faithful to the dead without a murmur of revolt against God; we shall be grateful without egotism—submissive, not oblivious.

OF WHOM I SPEAK.

THERE are two great truths under the sun,—God's pardon, and His justice.

There are two peoples on the earth: a people of men who speak different languages, and live in different climates, but who have all felt the horror of sin, and the need of a spiritual help, and have recognised, as accomplished in themselves, the work of the Holy Spirit; and another people very different, scoffers, obdurate, who reject all the appeals, open or mysterious, of the Divine grace. The prayer for mercy has never fallen from their lips; they laugh at the idea of pardon, they cast it from their minds. With this last people I do not occupy myself.

The future of rebellious spirits presents a prospect, the horror of which I would on no account diminish.

I was not made for such a subject.

I attach myself to the glorious phalanx of the redeemed. I turn towards the celestial horizon; I turn towards the light, to the infinite serenities, to the love without limit, to perfect joy. I would awaken joy. It is this we want.

By a redeemed soul, I understand the man who has felt himself guilty, felt himself weak,—who has, in utmost humility, thrown himself before the Eternal, murmuring, "Have mercy on me!"

But you who mourn departed friends, from whose mouth you have not received the full assurance of peace, do not you turn from me. If I cannot, with firm hand, point them out to you in glory, I can shew you something magnificent—a rainbow all radiant with hope—the love of our Saviour, the power of prayer, the free and royal gift of an omnipotent grace.

Love divine! It has depths we cannot follow. Even here below, has not the mother's heart felt that there was an inexhaustible tenderness which surpassed her own?

You who hang over the little cradle, when anxiety for the future seizes on you, and you grow pale before enemies who have not yet revealed themselves, is it not true that one single thought will at once calm you? God cherishes my child, and this my tenderness is as nothing compared to the love of God!

This husband or this mother whom I mourn, Jesus has loved them. Who shall unfold to me the mysteries of this love? who shall limit its action? He knows all, I nothing. When lost in grief, I can neither see nor comprehend; He sees, He loves, and He is the Saviour.

Permit me a reminiscence from my travels in the East, which will never be effaced from my mind.

We had passed Bethlehem, we had passed the Pool of Solomon; we had been traversing for a long time solitary hills, where some wild herb alone moved to the wind, when, on a sudden, a dark line cut the horizon. It enlarged, it approached, it defined itself in battlements; they were the walls of Jerusalem. Behind those walls I saw there,—with those eyes of the soul that look out beyond the present,—I saw the grand cross of Christ arise and dominate the city and dominate the world. My heart swelled, tears flowed down my cheek.

An immense love, an unmeasured pity and pardon descend from the cross upon the whole earth. Those who refuse it, destroy and limit it for themselves; those who hunger and thirst for it, find it always equal to their aspirations.

Whosoever calls upon God will be saved. Sublime words, which, descending from the throne of God, fall upon our lost world, and, in falling on it, spread a universal light!

I recognise no formula which has power to convert men; I adore a Holy Spirit which, under every sky, can tame the pride of man, and throw him repentant at the feet of his Creator.

Jesus died for all. All do not know the only name that saves. Knowledge must come from without; the sentiment of our guilt and misery springs from the heart. There is no heart beyond the circle of Divine action.

Every soul which in its famine cries to the Eternal, finds the Eternal. This ineffable cry, uttered in whatsoever zone or epoch, traverses infinite space, and sinks in the heart of Jesus.

Without doubt, where the atmosphere is thick, the light is feeble; without doubt, there are such clouds as can obscure the day—such ignorance and hardness of the conscience as reduce man to the condition of the beasts; but the power of God, but the love of God,—here are my two lamps for this labyrinth. I am ignorant of all, God knows all. I think I love, but I love nothing as He loves. My God, who has made the heart, can always touch the heart.

Come, contemplate with me this Divine love in its plenitude, as it acts upon some poor creature in the hour of death.

I would not encourage the idleness or the indecision of the soul. The man who has a long time refused to hear may lose the power of hearing. I know this well. But the moment also may come when the lost sheep, called in vain through all the fertile valley of the earth, may answer at length out of the sombre valley of death. It is thus God seeks his simple creatures engaged in the labours of life, weak, ill instructed, but with a heart still loyal and just.

In an instant the soul is transformed. It has comprehended, it has submitted, it has prostrated itself; God has raised it, it lives. A few days, a few hours suffice; God, in an instant, at one bound, can enable it to pass through the intermediate degrees. Frozen, it burns; lame, it runs; rebellious and pusillanimous, it is now accomplished in obedience and in courage. Leaving veteran Christians behind, it passes all, it has achieved all; and, nevertheless, it is itself, with its own individuality, but ripened by a single glance from the Divine love.

Jesus has done this.

What He said to the soul at that last hour I know not. What I have seen I believe. It is the work of God.

And what is ours?

An immense power is given us—a direct influence on the Governor of worlds—prayer.

Shall I recall the promises made to it? We have our ears filled with them, but what they announce so surpasses our hope that we do not believe in them.

Infinite goodness—poor fallen creatures that we are!—finds us more sceptical than infinite justice.

It matters not; prayer is a power; and if on earth it has a contested authority, it rules like a queen in heaven.

God dwells far off from us,—lost, so to speak, in the height of the empyrean. Prayer brings Him down amongst us, brings Him to our hearths, and links His power with our efforts.

The heart of this man repels me, but all his resistance

disappears before a Divine tenderness. My words irritated, this can move and assuage. I knew not how to constrain another soul; there is One who leads it by invisible cords Events defy me; there is One who can bend them to His purpose. He, God and Father, can unite in one focus so many scattered beams, that the darkest soul shall be suddenly inundated with light, and the coldest heart kindled with love.

I do not destroy the freedom of man.

Man can say Yes; man can say No.

To say *No*, knowing that it is the Eternal and His pardon that is refused—to scorn our own salvation, with eyes open and a sane mind—is perhaps that frightful sin of which it is written, Pray not for it.

But have I seen or known such culprits, or do they exist for me? God excepted, does any one know the hopeless? For me, I know my father, my mother, my friend, this or that man; God puts into my heart the cry of intercession; and if I hesitate, the same God says to me, Believe; all is possible to him who has faith.

In the time of Jesus there were paralytics and the dying. They could not of themselves go to Christ; their wasted limbs refused to carry them; they knew not that Jesus was near and wished to cure them. There were even the dead who could not stir. Who, then, interceded? who besought the Master? A father for his daughter, a centurion for his slave. And Jesus resuscitated the dead.

What we want is faith. The holiness of God dismays us, but his charity still more. We stand bewildered, fearful, and mute.

May I possess that sacred boldness which lies in true humility!

I will pray for you, dear friends, whom my own sins

and omissions have kept separated from the Saviour; I will pray for you whom my cowardice often, and sometimes a natural sentiment of bashfulness, have prevented me from addressing with words of serious import; I will pray for you whom all admire perhaps, and for whom none bends the knee. Grand and lofty minds, who traverse our sky, leaving trains of light behind—for you I pray!

Ah, we know not what surprises may be in reserve for us in the future life; how many we may meet there who knew us not, whose faces we had never seen, but whom our modest, ardent supplications had drawn softly towards Christ!

Have I said what I wished? Have I communicated hope? Have I made you feel the inexpressible love of our Saviour, the power of prayer, the sovereign, unlimited actions of God?—I know not. Perhaps emotion with me is stronger than argument.

Approach, then, the pages of Holy Writ. What figures, sublime in their simplicity, group themselves there! Contemplate them. Their aspect has more eloquence than these lips of mine.

Is it love you would be convinced of? See Jesus on the cross.

Is it the power of prayer? See women on their knees, and near them the dead who rise.

Is it the free action of the Holy Spirit? See the dying thief, and hear the murmur on his lips—Remember me.

THE AUTHORITY ON WHICH I REST.

REST on the authority of the Word of God.

Not that I am about to write a treatise on theology. I am incapable, and should have more repugnance to write than you to read it. But if we do not want theology, we want truth.

On our life to come, on our dead, I find truth only in the Word of God; no other book gives it me.

What is not true, however beautiful, cannot console us. At that moment of separation, when so many cherished realities sink into the dust, could we support the approaches of a consolatory illusion? Beaten by the billows of an unspeakable misery, I can find a footing only in the truth. Do not extend to me a rotten branch; in fact, I should not take it; the soul in its suffering has marvellous intuitions, unmasking men and things. I should prefer rather to sink at once, than, half saved, to fall back again into the depths of the sea.

One Book alone comes from God; one alone can reveal to us the secrets of God. It has its silences, its mysteries; it never deceives.

Eternal life shines forth from every page of the Bible. At first it is a serene, diffused light, strong enough to rejoice the eyes; not perhaps to define each detail of the immense prospect. Nevertheless, as at the dawn of a fine day, there are peaks touched with light. The brightness increases, the hills are gilded, the sun penetrates the valleys

Beautiful already, grand and peaceful in its veil of mist, the marvellous region grows more and more glorious with the growing day. Everywhere life eternal throbs and rises radiant around us. Promise after promise, fact after fact; at first immortality seems to hover over us, at last descends distinct and palpable. It is no longer a vague happiness; it is a positive felicity, and our hearts bound to meet it.

This will be admitted by all with reference to the New Testament. There are who contest it with reference to the Old, and especially some of its earlier books. These tell you that they seek for the immortality of the soul in the writings of Moses, and do not find it. They look for it in the desolations of Job, and meet only with a desponding Materialism. They ask it of the Psalms, and the Psalms answer by mournful elegies on the dead, who descend into the regions of oblivion. They expect it from Ecclesiastes, and the wise Ecclesiastes celebrates the pleasures of the world: for, after this life, what is there?

Before examining into this, I throw back my thoughts over the earlier pages of the Divine Word. Here I do not find myself oppressed by low and narrow skies; but on the contrary there is a feeling of the Infinite over all. The Eternal and the Immutable shine through the fleeting forms of this world. Man, whose feet are in the dust, lifts high his head, and breathes the air of eternity.

That time when God took Enoch and transplanted him to heaven, and no one was astonished; that time when Abraham spoke with God as a friend speaks to a friend; that time when the marvellous ladder was let down by the pillow of Jacob; that time when a poor woman wandering on the sand of the desert with her suffering child saw without surprise the angel of the Lord descend from heaven,—that time was not a time of Materialism; be very sure of that. Then the princes of the East followed their flocks in the valleys of Judea; then they pitched their tents on the borders of the desert, in regions whose solitude brought God more near. In these beautiful nights of Arabia, clear as our days, they stood at the door of their tents and prayed. They prayed under the oaks at Beersheba; they prayed on the summit of mountains. And constantly there was a voice near them that gave answer. Sometimes it was a celestial messenger, with light from heaven on his brow, who came to the patriarch as he sat before his tent in the evening, reflecting on the past years of his life, distinguished by so many communications with his God.

Think you it was necessary to teach these men that the soul does not die? Think you it was necessary to explain to these pilgrims, travelling incessantly to some land of promise, that their days were short, and that after their brief duration there would commence a time that had no end? Oh, with what a sublime smile would Abraham or Jacob have listened to such doctors! The soul never doubted; it believed as the body breathes; it had no need to discuss its faith, it held firm what it held.

Proofs are for sceptics.

Would you prove the magic of the night, the rich harvests, the flowering meadows, to a man who, from dawn to twilight, and often under the moon, traverses the fields, who draws his scythe through the grass glittering with dew, who returns in the evening by the side of rivers in which the stars are reflected? But what eloquence would be necessary, what power of description and of reasoning, to bring all this, living and real, to the child of a miner, some poor, dwarfed creature, who in the bowels of the earth, a smoking lamp fastened on his head, pushes his truck along a dark gallery.

To him who sees, belief is easy; the thing exists; I touch it; it is mine.

To him who sees not, you must bring faith; and he who names faith, names contest and conflict. Arguments are for the blind; the loud voice of reasoning for the deaf.

Do we resemble, then, the child of the miner? Perhaps. Most certainly our world has for ages resembled a city over which an eternal fog is hanging. To such a city give torches, give beacons, at full day. The sun advances and blazes over it; but the fog constantly interposes—nothing clear is seen. There, indeed, the lamp held by a hand that does not shake is most needful. Nothing of all this is wanted by him who walks abroad in the magnificence of a summer's day.

Those who study even those books of the Old Testament most charged with Materialism, find them, as it were, interpenetrated with eternal life—find the doctrine of immortality everywhere implied. It vibrates in their diction; constant allusions are made to it; no one dies, but he is *gathered to his fathers.* One feels it breathe through every dialogue; it is like a heavenly history running parallel with the earthly, written in indelible characters above, as the latter gradually unfolds amidst the hills and valleys of Palestine. God, who is educating man, is letting him draw his own inferences. This is a very striking feature of the first books of Moses, and agrees well with the positive intervention of God. Weaned from those direct relations, those familiar conversations, the patriarchs would have had greater need of written explanations and demonstrative reasoning. The hour came when God deprived man of

His presence; from that hour God bestowed on him prophets, into whose mouth He put a miraculous teaching.

And even granting that man in those remote ages had no positive information given him on subjects upon which he never doubted, still, from time to time, we find his assurance proclaimed in unpremeditated shouts of joy.

Moses, on the borders of the Red Sea, just when the arm of the Lord has divided the waters, and His people have passed over,—Moses, mentally transported to another passage, cries aloud, "Thou hast guided them in Thy strength unto Thy holy habitation. Thou shalt plant them in the place, O Lord, which Thou hast made for Thee to dwell in; in the sanctuary, O Lord, which Thy hands have established."

The dying Jacob, suddenly filled with joy, exclaims, "I have waited for Thy salvation, O Lord." Then he pours floods of blessings on Joseph kneeling by his bed-side: "*Blessings unto the bound of the everlasting hills.*"

And what are the words whispered by the wife of Elkanah in the temple at Shiloh, when, her prayer granted, her heart overflows in thanksgiving? "I rejoice in Thy salvation. The Lord killeth, and maketh alive; He bringeth down to the grave, and bringeth up. The Lord shall judge the ends of the earth."

And Balaam, constrained by conscience against his will, cries, "Let me die the death of the righteous, and let my last end be like his."

But I am not going to trench on theology; and, to be brief, I will simply take up the charge of Materialism as brought against the book of Job, of the Psalms, and of Ecclesiastes.

First of all, of Job.

Who is Job? The most afflicted and despairing character

in all the Bible; and his book is one where our heart in seasons of bitterness sees its every feaure faithfully reflected.

Job spoke of annihilation; nay, he did more, he invoked it with all his might: "I have said to corruption, Thou art my father; to the worm, Thou art my mother and my sister. And where is now my hope? As for my hope, who shall see it? They shall go down to the bars of the pit, when our rest together is in the dust."

Job, in his indignation, takes pleasure, as it were, in his Materialism, reverts to it continually, plunges deeper and deeper into it; and in one of those moods known only to passionate natures, revels in it, and would plunge deeper yet if he could.

That surprises you? Alas! that does not surprise me. I know the dread luxury there is in rebellion—know the overwhelming invasion of sorrow, the madness that courts worse suffering still.

"Ye call to me, ye depths! Thou hast forsaken me, my God! Thou who art strong and mighty, whose unchangeable bliss our cries do not disturb; Thou takest pleasure in discharging all the arrows of Thy wrath on me! Thy thunderbolts at a worm! Be it so, then; I too will be great. A giant in misfortune, infinite through desolation; I will go so far, I will fall so deep, that even Thine arm must grow greater still to strike me."

"Will it be to strike me only? will it not be to raise me up again? The excess of my grief, my very madness, the yawning abyss on the edge of which I walk, wilt Thou not have pity on me for the very sake of all these? For Thou art still my God; Thou didst love me once."

Yes, it is even so; the heart has these infernal joys, these touching reactions; it sees the abyss, flings itself into it; God, too, has a heart; God cannot leave me to perish there.

Or, to take a more familiar and milder image, have you never seen a little child, which its mother has for a moment left, burst out crying, knowing well that she is near, that she is listening attentively? have you never heard its screams, I might say its howls, of grief and rage? It knows that if it goes on crying thus, its mother may perhaps punish it, but will certainly return.

Thus it is that in the martyrdom of human tribulation, we, too, weep; thus at such and such an hour we are ready to become sceptics, materialists, what not? God comes, and God once come, what happens?

Let me bring you back to Job.

His friends have, one after another, told off the tale of their sententious harangues. Job has resisted them to the utmost; Job has, with his own hand, torn off the dressings which rude hands have sought to lay upon his wounds. He has arraigned the earth, arraigned mankind, nay, in his delirium, he has arraigned the eternal God. "Oh, that I might have my request, and that God would grant me the thing that I long for! Even that it would please God to destroy me, that He would let loose His hand, and cut me off!" And so his angry complaints go spreading on through burning page on page.

At last comes silence.

Then, from the midst of the whirlwind, "Who is this who darkens counsel by words without knowledge? Where wert thou when I laid the foundations of the earth? Who shut up the sea with doors? Hast thou commanded the morning since thy days? Have the gates of death been opened to thee? hast thou seen the doors of the shadow of death?"

Then Job, prostrate, ashamed, happy a thousandfold in the triumph of his God, exclaims, "Behold, I am vile. I have uttered that I understood not; therefore I abhor myself, and repent in dust and ashes."

Are you still amazed at Job's Materialism?

For my part, I thank God to have shewn me thus my own reflection. This is indeed myself as I am in my worst hours—rebellious, unbelieving, idolising my own despair; and yet raised up, yet forgiven, uttering from the very hottest of the furnace that cry of faith repeated from age to age, that glorious trumpet-burst sounded in defiance at each of death's apparent triumphs: "I know that my Redeemer liveth. . . . And though this body be destroyed, yet in my flesh I shall see God; whom I shall see for myself, and mine eyes shall behold, and not another."

Let us take the Psalms.

There is everything in the Psalms. They sing of eternal life in accents of ineffable sweetness; they speak of death as complete annihilation. Sustained by the mighty hand of God, the Psalmist enters triumphant into heavenly places; left to himself, a prey to his adversaries, he grovels in the grave, and remains motionless there.

Here again I recognise the deeply humane and sympathetic purpose which, in the Revelation of my God, shews me my image to attract and draw me on: I am that man. But I see another and an important fact, and it is perhaps because this has been too much neglected, that doubts that shake our faith have risen up between us and the full beauty of the Psalms.

This fact is as follows:

In the Psalms habitually, as occasionally in the writings of the Prophets, Death is looked at from a terrestrial point of view. The dead are considered with reference to this world which they have absolutely quitted. When David appears to speak the language of Materialism, he speaks as an observer of material facts only. Does this imply that he denies other facts? I do not think so.

In his hours of dejection, the very lugubrious character of Death, looked at in its external aspect, is the only one that fills the mind of the Prophet-King. He takes up his position in the realm of appearances, of our present realities; and he tells us what he descries there.

That what he tells us is unutterably sad, who can deny? But if we look only at what he is looking at, can we employ, even we, believers, any language but his?

The grave is the region of silence, shall the dead praise the Lord?—they are gone—the place that knew them shall know them no more. The living, the living, they shall praise Thee, shall celebrate Thy name! But the dead men, silent, senseless, soon to be turned to their dust!

Then again, all that is relatively true, when we consider the dead in connexion with earthly existence, is true with an absolute truth as regards the body, our own dead bodies.

Yes, absolutely true. Till the morning of the resurrection, our bodies will lie motionless. Never more shall our lips praise the Lord; never more shall our eyes laugh in the light of His sun. The actions of living men, their conflicts, joys, and sorrows, the clay above our heads shakes with these, and our bones feel no thrill.

It is this very prospect which is presented by the grave to our frightened glance; it is this fact which it includes, this hideousness, this gloom. If it were not so, if death had not this appalling aspect, where would be its horror?

Why do we weep, we Christians who see heaven opened? Why, when we are going down to those dark dwelling-places—we, whose eyes are lit with light from on high, we who know that it is to God our souls will rise,—why do we feel this shudder, this anxious amazement, this transient gloom?

Ah! the Psalmist was not wrong; our lifeless body remains lifeless, useless, indifferent to all that goes on beneath the sky. The prophet did not deceive us; on the side of earth, our side, all is over for the dead. But on the side of heaven, all is only about to begin, and he has proclaimed this glorious truth in hymns of incomparable beauty.

What words console the dying, what weapons do they seize in their trembling hands?—the Psalms: "Whither shall I go from Thy Spirit? If I climb up to heaven, Thou art there; if I make my bed in Hades, Thou art there also."

They drag themselves along the gloomy path alone, terrified: "Thou art with me; Thy rod and Thy staff they comfort me."

Their sins crowd round them numerous as the sand of the sea, and no more time is left: "As for our iniquities, Thou shalt purge them away."

The mystery of the last breath draws near: "Thou wilt not leave my soul in hell; God shall redeem my life from the power of the grave. He will receive me. I shall see the goodness of the Lord in the land of the living."

With the Psalms, martyrs have walked with unshaken spirit to meet a bloody death; with them, mothers, husbands, wives, have strengthened their heart for the inexorable parting; with them the widow, the father, the daughter bereaved, have been able to pursue their solitary way without repining. Poor souls, disinherited at birth of all earthly joy, have while repeating the Psalms felt unspeakable blessings descend from heaven, and bear them up, and transport them to the land of happiness.

I do not think that a Book which works such miracles as these can be a materialistic book.

And now for Ecclesiastes.

There is on earth a greater misfortune than to have to fight for one's life. There is a sadness more complete than that of bereavement, sickness, poverty, even pushed to their extremest limits; there is the bitterness of a soul which has exhausted, fathomed everything, and in all directions met with nothingness.

Then, if that soul does not—powerfully succoured from on high—return to Him who solves all doubts, to the throne whence flows the mighty river of truth, it goes wandering through the desert places of this world, alone in a crowd, a stranger alike to love and hate, disdaining all coarser pleasures, indifferent to highest joys, crying ever in one sardonic voice, "Vanity, vanity!"

The Preacher has traversed those desert places; he has lingered there; he has measured their empty immensity; their mirage has infatuated him: he has fingered the stunted thorns that shewed from afar like forests fresh and green; his lips have been glued to the arid sand, and when he chanced to find some drops of water there, lo, it was stagnant and impure. But, arrived on the utmost limits of this desert, he saw the borders of the promised land indent the sky with a line of palms; the scorching air grew softer; with his finger he pointed to the mountains, pointed to the green shadows, and then he was silent, for we understood him well.

The Preacher is an Oriental. The East, land of light, with its rarified atmosphere, does not need our compendious explanations. A gossamer thread floating in the air suffices to guide the Arab through the labyrinth of thought. An apologue, an enigma, are enough, let his mind have free scope; what he knows best is just what you have not told him.

Our logic seems coarse to the Oriental, our demonstrations cumbersome. The moral of the tale, he perceives it long before you do, and if you tell it him, he smiles, casts on you a long look, and murmurs within himself—O Frank, of the babbling lips, the sluggish mind, son of the fog and of nights of darkness!

The Preacher passes in review all systems, all philosophies, all pleasures, and selects, by preference, intellectual pride. We see him in turn sceptical, voluptuous, ascetic, in love with glory, devoted to science, then philanthropical, and keenly sympathizing with human misery, then an idolater of good, and bent upon attaining it in his own strength. He follows each wayward impulse of his heart; sinks to appalling depths, soars to sublime heights, always sincere, speaking with implacable precision; and, when he has tried all, out of the darkness of those lowest, and, as it were, lost depths of that land of infidelity into which he sought to annihilate himself, in one second, with one bound, he traverses space, and falls—earnest, a little sad, and yet with beaming brow—before the throne of God.

The book is full throughout of ironical sentences, which, one after the other, strike heavy blows at all the theories of human pride. Is it wisdom?—"What has the wise man more than the fool? Better is the sight of the eyes, than the wandering of the desire."

Is it noble deeds, courage, power?—"Better a living dog than a dead lion."

Is it sorrow for the dead? does the heart seek to take possession of the skies for them by vehemence of desire?—"I praised the dead which are already dead, more than the living which are yet alive. Yea, better is he than both they, which hath not yet been."

Is it happiness?—"All go unto one place."

Is it animal enjoyment?—"Take thine ease, eat, drink, and be merry, for a man hath no better thing under the sun; this is his portion all the days of his vanity."

Death still remains, a vague hope: "That which befalleth the sons of men befalleth beasts; even one thing befalleth them: as the one dieth, so dieth the other; yea, they have all one breath: man hath no pre-eminence over a beast: all is vanity."

The circle is closed, the soul in extremity has gone through it all, has possessed whatever science could give; has known whatever experience could reveal; the only result, a little dust soon scattered, nothing more.

Then comes the gist of the book, a book which, to be thoroughly understood, must not be read in fragments, but all through at once, as it was thought out; mounting the same rapid steed that bears the traveller along, and completing the cycle at the same pace.

The key to the enigma is given us in a few sober, simple words, clear as the sky of Judea: "Rejoice, O young man, in thy youth, and walk in the ways of thine heart, and in the sight of thine eyes: but know thou, that for all these things God will bring thee into judgment."

Then, in a tenderer voice: "Remember now thy Creator in the days of thy youth, while the evil days come not, nor the years draw nigh, when thou shalt say, I have no pleasure in them: or ever the silver cord be loosed, or the golden bowl be broken, or the pitcher be broken at the fountain, or the wheel broken at the cistern: then shall the dust return to the earth as it was; and the spirit shall return unto God who gave it."

Is there the shadow of a doubt still left?—"Let us hear the conclusion of the whole matter: Fear God, and keep his commandments: for this is the whole duty of man. For God shall bring every work into judgment, with every secret thing, whether it be good, or whether it be evil."

If there be hearts oppressed with grief who have blessed the Lord for the book of Job, if there be heart's buffeted by this world's storms who have blessed Him for the Psalms, I believe that there are reasoning, investigating minds, souls not to be taken in by appearances, weary of the emptiness that confronts them on all sides, more sick with nothingness than others are of a deadly wound; and I believe that it is for the book of Ecclesiastes that such will specially bless the Lord.

These momentous questions have detained us. I hasten on to the end of the journey.

The writings of the prophets, properly so called, are interpenetrated with the life to come; they are illuminated thereby, and if, like some shadow of a cloud, chased by the north-east wind in a serene sky, a discouraging thought ever crosses the revelations of a *seer*, instantly the cry of triumph bursts forth: "Thy dead men shall live, together with my dead body shall they revive. Awake and sing, ye inhabitants of the dust, for thy dew is as the dew of herbs, and the earth shall no more cover her slain."

Be it so! you say. Nevertheless death in the Old Testament, remains a somewhat gloomy fact. In the New Testament, on the contrary, it appears as a deliverance. There is no relapse into incredulity and alarm. Such a contrast as this weakens the authority of the Bible, by destroying its unity.

For my part, I discover no opposition between the teaching of the prophets and that of the apostles. I see different men, I see a growing light, I cannot see night on one side, day on the other, white here, black there.

Before Christ, the prophets saw afar off; their hearts were stirred with holy hope; at times they held it very fast. With Christ, and after Christ, the apostles possessed. The difference is great. What those foresaw, these touched. The truth that a lightning flash revealed to the former, the latter lived in close contact with; they were surrounded by it, could no more escape from it than we from the ambient air. The conqueror of death was their Master and their Brother. With their own eyes they had seen Him die on the cross, with their own eyes they had seen Him return into their midst, sit down at their table, walk with them by the Lake of Gennesareth; then, one April morning, from that very Mount of Olives they had so often ascended together, they saw Jesus, their Lord and their God, carried away on clouds to sit down in triumph at the Father's right hand. Tell me, is it not natural that their words should have other tones, their hearts possess a higher courage, and that death, death itself, should put on a harmlessness, nay, I may say an attractiveness for them, such as it never could have worn to those who saw these miraculous events loom indistinct through far-off future ages? Again, there is a melancholy but true remark that I desire to make here. Christian knowledge is not always accompanied with joy. Whether through ignorance or weakness of heart, or by one of those decrees of God of which eternity will reveal the blended wisdom and love, a singular sadness may, at the approach of death, take possession of a redeemed spirit.

To be a believer, to have clear views, to love God, to know one's-self accepted, is not enough to make one welcome with radiant smile the messenger of the livid wing

Many a strong man has felt his courage sink, many a bright flame has grown pale.

St Paul, he who used to say, "to die is gain;" St Paul in Asia, *despairing even of life*, and then saved, glorifies God who has delivered him from so *great a danger;* who delivers us, he adds, and in whom we trust that He will yet deliver.

In the fortress at Jerusalem, this same Paul, learning that the Jews are laying snares for him, has the governor apprised of it that he may watch over his safety. At Cæsarea, he takes the same precaution.

In the midst of the tempest, when the ship that carries the Apostle to Italy, dismasted, broken by the force of the waves, is about to fall to pieces, forsaken by its crew, Paul detains the sailors, "Except these remain in the ship, you cannot be saved."

At Rome, before Nero, on the occasion of his first trial, he writes, "And I was delivered from the mouth of the lion."

Is Paul afraid to die? Not so! But, thank God! Paul is a man. Paul has times when life seems to him sweet, his mission grand; Paul, too, has seasons when the gloomy aspect of death presents itself to his mind. Were it not so, he would no longer be one of us: we should not understand him.

There is another and greater than Paul, who is man also. He in the darkness of the garden, on the cold night prostrate on the ground, and that ground wet by blood, which flows drop by drop from His face; He cries in the anguish of His soul, His soul which is exceeding sorrowful even unto death, "Father, if thou wilt, remove this cup from me."

What doest Thou, Saviour of mankind? Redeeming

God, what is it Thou dost ask? For this hour Thou art come, for this agony, this cup; and Thou growest faint, Thou sayest, "*if Thou wilt.*"

Thus speaks the stoical exactingness of man, the coarse cruelty of his logic. Man looks only for the ideal in his fellow-man; no flesh, no fibre, only an iron bar, straight, unbending, which pierces or breaks. God will have a man, man above all; and thus He who is to conquer death will faint for a moment at its dread approach.

Oh, very precious to me the faintness of my God; the fears of His apostle, I bless them too.

The heavenly visage of a Stephen stoned to death, rouses my energy; what the Lord has done for him, He may do for me also. But if the hosts of the redeemed presented only such lofty shapes as these, not any pallor, not any shadow, I should feel myself, as it were, a stranger in so holy a company; a secret voice would whisper to me, "Art thou indeed one of them?"

Now, on the contrary, I know that one may die humbly, silently, perhaps timidly; may be more sorry for the sins committed than thankful for the pardon given, and nevertheless and certainly belong to Jesus. Not to all Christians are granted joyous and triumphant deaths. The most esteemed among them, those whose great deeds have been the most widely spread by fame, whose voice has made many hearts thrill, may depart obscurely, shuddering at the vanity of all terrestrial glory, holding indeed the hand of Jesus; but trembling the while. And at the same hour, some unknown woman, some little child who lends an innocent ear to the Divine promises, shall behold the heavens opened, soar away on unflagging wing, and greet their last day with hallelujahs.

There are many ways of dying for Christians; for all

there is the same eternal life. The departures differ; the goal is one. There may be more or less light; but it is always the same sun. Where we see contradictions, there exist only the opposite sides of the same object. Sometimes fully illumined, sometimes half in shade, it is still the same believing soul; and there is also the same revealing God. In the centuries anterior, as in those after Christ, the future life promised to believers always makes them glad. But the luminous hemispheres have their dark spots, the dark zones their bright ones; everywhere the Book proclaims aloud, that the soul does not die. The more busy the times, the harder of hearing the ears, the louder becomes the voice. It is to this voice I want to listen.

One last word.

I take the Book of God in its familiar sense. I leave allegories to sages, knotty points to theologians. As for us, very little, very simple as we are, we want simple words, and are fain to receive them just as our Father gives them us. In point of fact, it is for such as we that He has spoken.

The Bible contains mysteries; God forbid that I should seek to lift their veil. The Bible contains deep sayings; these belong to the discerning and the wise. The Bible uses transparent images, simple parables spoken to fishermen, to shepherds; these are for us. For us too the natural language, the positive meaning, the words taken for what they are worth. Ah! if the Jews had only received in their literal sense as they were presented to them, those revealing details, the poverty of Jesus, the thirty pieces of silver, the lots cast for the coat, the rich man's grave, and so many others!

Do not fear. We are not about to open subterranean

galleries, or devise audacious paths to inaccessible heights; we fit out no balloons for the air, no lofty ships for the wide sea. To sit beside a tomb, to listen to what our Father says; to receive it in silence, and strengthen our hearts thereby,—this is all, we propose nothing more.

THE PARADISE WE FEAR.

HAT we fear the last judgment is easily understood; that we should have a fear of Paradise seems unintelligible. Yet, if we look closely at the matter, nothing is more justifiable than such a fear.

There are two Paradises: that of God; that of men.

The one, perfect in its beauty, must have for us a sovereign attraction. But it is known to few, for few seek to know it in the pages of Holy Writ. The other, which men have fashioned as well as they were able, astonishes more than it delights. It is this which excites in the better order of minds a secret terror.

No, it has nothing distinctly evil, but its utter vagueness fills one with dread. Plunged in a luminous mist, I feel the terror of a drowning man. To be drowned in light, may seem very beautiful; it is still to be drowned.

Splendour! Immensity! Eternity! Grand words, grand things. A little definite happiness would be more to the purpose.

Shall I tell you what repels me from your Paradise? It is that I seek an object I cannot find there—*myself.*

I seek also what I cannot find there till I have found myself—a personal God.

This individuality, this *I myself*, that I know and feel, by which I am what I am, and not another, I demand it of your heavens; your heavens shew me spirits, intelligences, impalpable abstractions, indistinguishable from each other; I turn away saddened, confounded.

Fill the void with light, it is still a void. Where all personality has disappeared, where the individual life is extinguished or absorbed, I see nothing but an abyss. If from age to age, part of a column of light, I am to be ascending and descending this abyss, I am still lost in it.

God has made me a living unit; has made me *me*. Before all—there above, as here below—it is this *me* I want; without it, how can I remember, how can I see, how comprehend and love my God?

If the golden vapours of the morning can celebrate and adore their God, if the purple clouds of evening can indeed glow with love, then let us be mists and clouds, which the wind impels hither and thither. But if to know God, if to worship Him, I must be man; if to love Him I must have a living soul, I keep my humanity, I keep my individuality, I keep them there, and more ardently than ever —there beyond the skies.

At times, the Paradise which men have imagined emerges a little from its dazzling mist.

I see immense desert spaces of milder light, which sometimes remind me of those Elysian fields, whose sad inhabitants pass eternity in regretting the earth,—its cheerful sun, its combats, its hatreds, its errors, its tears; sometimes they call to mind that melancholy region where Dante encountered Virgil, which was bathed in a diffuse lustre, that knew neither morning, nor evening, nor mid-day; a region that was without grief or joy, which was traversed by the slow steps of pensive spirits, which strikes upon my heart colder than death.

The Paradise of man is not intended, however, for death. They have discovered a word to express it—a word which says all, and which says nothing—*repose.* Repose! Each one finds in it what he can.

One thing it certainly implies—immobility.

Repose is immobility. It would be silence, but that one accords to the blessed the privilege of singing without pause, in the same voice, the same hallelujah.

Repose is placid contemplation, fixed, congealed, so to speak, on one point, God.

Repose is absorption in a thought which is also a sentiment. A fixed star, planted in a sky of brass, would have as much of movement and of life.

Repose is the oblivion of the past, effacement of everything except one present ardour, changeless, eternal.

The creatures who repose like this are no longer men; they neither think nor remember; one eternal thought is tantamount to no thought at all; without change, no life. Emotion, activity, the aspirations of intelligence, character, all have disappeared.

Look at the Paradise of painters; for the Paradise of those ages which are especially called the ages of *faith,* may be seen in their pictures. The idea of the time is written there. What do we see? A blue fluid, or ether, illuminated more and more as you penetrate its depths. An immense circle, or interior of a vast cone, thickly covered over with human heads, beatific faces planted between a pair of little wings; the first row highly finished, the next more slightly treated, the third just indicated, the others growing fainter and smaller as far as the perspective is carried, till the winged head dwindles to a mere dot, a point upon a circumflex. The same expression upon all, the same smile, the same lips half opened by the same ecstasy; and at the bottom of our cone, in a focus of light, the triangle with the symbolic dove!

Such is the heaven which awaits us.

Tell me, you living, you thinking creatures, you who love with veritable emotion, are you ravished, are you melted with tenderness? This region—desert in its multitude—do you sigh for it, do you really desire, can you put up one passionate prayer for it? It chills you, it terrifies you, you turn trembling towards this earth of ours, and cling to it like idolaters.

Look at the heaven of Dante. If there has existed in the world an ardent spirit, a creative imagination, if a word of power has resounded in it, if, in short, there is a poetry you will find it under that pen which kindles into light whatever it touches.

Light, yes!—there is such an intensity of light shed around us, so energetic a feeling of some luminous vibrating atmosphere of bliss, that every verse seems to be on fire. There is ecstasy in the air we breathe. But these circles—these interminable circles! There, for ever, in immense orbits, revolve the beatific cohorts; love, which is their light, gives them also their movement; the more vivid their affection, the more intense is their brilliancy, and the more rapid their revolution. Wild tournaments of spirits, rushing through the skies, and glittering with the stars of heaven, which they sweep onwards in their mad rotation—such is the Paradise of the poet and theologian.

Volgeano a ruota. Hope not for other happiness. To sing three words through ages after ages; to shine, to whirl, lost in the intoxication of light and movement—these are the joys, the distant reflection of which is to dry all human tears.

In proportion as we rise from heaven to heaven, are the last vestiges of personality effaced; in proportion as our happiness augments, are the last human feelings lost in this celestial mechanism.

These souls in bliss arrange themselves in symbolic figures ; agglomerate into a cross, a ladder, an eagle. The best placed represent the eyes of the imperial bird, the dazzling pupils where *Trajan* throws his rays by the side of Hezekiah and Constantine the Great.

In a still higher and transcendent sphere there are immovable souls ranged—I was going to say *stuck*—in rows round an amphitheatre, who sit bathed in light. In the centre, God. Three circles of equal diameter, the Father, the Son, and the Holy Ghost.

The happiest of the happy fix their gaze for ever on this triple circle, whose brightness would extinguish the sun. An eternal hosanna fills the immensity with its one invariable note. This is the empyrean.

What do you feel? For me, I feel terror. I cannot be solaced, or deceived by the grandeur of styles ; and the tumultuous emotions which doubtless stirred the poet, in his poet's frenzy, do not reach me. This God is not a God, is not an angel, is not comparable to a man. Give me an avenging God, or give me blind Destiny itself. But this abstraction—but this infinite abyss—this hollow, bottomless cone, with its three immovable circles—my soul revolts—I fly from it with spread wings. I should fly even to the borders of Hell. And if your Paradise imprisons the soul in a wall of fire, I would take refuge in that heaven which is most remote from perfect bliss.

These unnatural beatitudes oppress the heart. In fact, some freezing air from a Pagan Paradise has passed over our heaven, has withered its flowers, congealed its life. We remain sad in the presence of such happiness. And with good reason.

A poor woman, eighty years old, pious, resigned, was approaching her heaven. Her time was come, she obeyed :

but she cast more than one wandering look on this side the grave, on a world where there was activity and affection. Even her poor old body, worn out and wrinkled, she seemed to quit with regret.

This Paradise, how do you represent it to yourself?

"Ah, well!" she answered in her simplicity; "I suppose that, like at church, there must be chairs put all along the sky; one sits there, and sings psalms throughout eternity!"

Ethereal abysses, winged heads piled up close together, Elysian fields, pews in a greater church,—always some monotony, always an obliteration of self, and an immeasurable *ennui*.

It is not thus with the true beatitudes, with that intense happiness, that life and warmth which fall upon us in the glowing promises of our Lord; it is not thus with our magnificent heritage of the earth; it is not thus with tears that are dried away by love, with the full feeling of satisfied justice, and clear recognition of the Divine government. Yes, we shall see God, and my soul leaps at the thought; yes, we shall taste of peace that here our agitated hearts can never know; yes, we shall sing marvellous hymns, and our bosoms palpitate with joy; yes, we shall adore, we shall glorify God; but contemplation, repose, celestial concerts, love and adoration, you shall be a life, not an absorption.

But let us not anticipate; let us return to our apocryphal Paradise,—Chinese screen, painted with strange figures, which hides from us the true country.

To lose one's-self in the ocean of life, and to be annihilated, are the same thing; to be absorbed in unity, and to vanish out of being, are to me the same thing.

To remain impassive, the whole of my faculties gathered up in one, in an adoration identical in us all; this is so opposed to everything I know, to everything I *am*, that my whole nature revolts from it.

Revolted, saddened, I nevertheless have submitted to this Paradise.

It is so. This Paradise of Hindoos and of some Pagan philosophers, is also the Paradise of many Christians. It is the heaven of very many, because they can imagine nothing better.

They do not love it, they do not desire it, they fear it; nevertheless, as the only alternative, they are reduced to hope it.

After having lived, to arrive at this new tribulation! to plunge into this western sea! to end in this cheerless joy, of which the individual has not even a distinct consciousness! to become a *number*, or something less,—for there must be difference where there is number,—one of the identities fixed in space! This is called *spiritual.* A heaven otherwise fashioned would be *material* to the refined intelligences of our age.

Blessed be God! He has otherwise ordained what shall be spiritual. His Paradise, I know the borders of it, and from these borders emerge so many genial rays of warmth as well as light, that my heart burns within me. In His Paradise I find myself perfected, sanctified, with all my soul, my affections, my memories. His Paradise, oh, it is simple as it is splendid; more grand, yet nearer to me; life in its personality, and personality in its perfect harmony with God. It is my native country, not a foreign land; it is the house of my Father, not the temple of an abstract divinity. I do not see an indistinguishable throng of phantoms; I meet brothers and dear friends. Such is the happiness my nature craves. To such country I desire to emigrate; the remotest view of it sustains my courage;

there I shall repose as one reposes in the house of a father. I should tremble to enter into your heaven; I should grieve if a friend entered it; I can find no consolation, for them or for me, for such a happiness!

Is there any other Paradise that men have created? Have I done justice to human inventions?

A vague idea of transmigration of souls may be detected, more often than one would expect, in our prosaic age. Dreams of the East wandering into our latitudes; I know not if they demand a notice,—they seem as distressful as they are insane.

That Paradise must indeed be disinherited of joy from which we are to escape by recommencing our lives. To possess a glorious eternity, and to abandon it! Strange idea. To grovel again upon the earth; to become a little child; to struggle through the ignorance and incapacity and unreasonable afflictions of youth; to engage again in the rude combats of maturity; to suffer its deceptions, to sink under its defects, to grow old again, and die,—and this to gain the harbour at last, to cast anchor at last? No, to resume the open seas! Do not tell me that such souls come from Paradise. If any such there be, they were enclosed in some subterranean abode, deprived of air and light; they fled from some desolate region; they had never known the Paradise of God.

Superstition (the guest of faithless as well as cowardly minds) creates also its Paradise, transporting there the vulgar passions of this earth. The legendary heaven is, on one side, a pale insipidity; on the other, a burlesque home. Ghosts shadowy as moonlight, or troubled as the poor mortals they terrify, glide through the night; representations of eternal felicity! Did ever ghost rejoice the heart! Have the inhabitants of heaven indeed this melancholy smile, this freezing look? Are they thus austere, or utterly impassive; or do they retain the rancours of the past?

Distressful creations of the imagination; tormenting and tormented, you come not from the Paradise of God. You know nothing of its inhabitants. Father, brother, husband, child, take here forms which inspire us with terror. Something most repulsive envelops them. It is more than a modification, it is an absolute change. If I go where such creatures inhabit, what reunion can there be? And I also, I am to become a ghost, whose approach congeals the blood in the veins! From a living man one is to become the impalpable light.

What are the agonies of separation itself compared to the lying joys of these figments of a Paradise? The bitterness of tears has reached its height when we lose for ever a redeemed soul that loved us. And if he is lost to me in the serene ether of your fictitious skies, I must still mourn him inconsolably. If you wish to raise my soul, tell me that he lives, he himself, and that I shall see him again, and shall love him with a love submissive to my God; tell me that my individuality will not die, nor my remembrance; tell me that life is life, and not a catalepsy, not annihilation.

Then my brow will be uplifted towards the skies, and with reinvigorated step I shall pursue my pilgrimage. But annihilated, but reduced to the state of a luminous point; if you tell me this, I sink overwhelmed.

Up, dear brother! Give me your hand. It is to God's own heaven we will walk together.

PART SECOND.

THE SUPREME TYPE: A RISEN SAVIOUR.

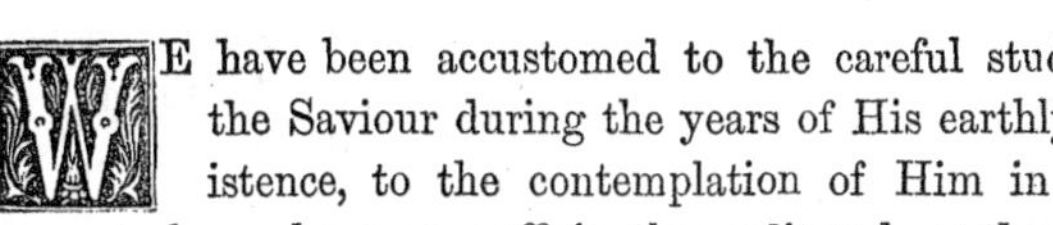

WE have been accustomed to the careful study of the Saviour during the years of His earthly existence, to the contemplation of Him in His present glory; have we sufficiently meditated on the risen Jesus, during those forty days of a life at once so mysterious and so simple,—led so near us, led with us, and yet as far removed from the conditions of our own as the heavens are from the earth?

For my own part, these few pages of Holy Writ have an ineffable charm for me; I feel that they contain the very substance of my dearest hopes; I am constantly reverting to them, and constantly discovering some detail which strengthens and comforts my heart.

Jesus is the Atoner, the Great Example, the King; but Jesus is also the Conqueror of Death, and this is the character which best dispels my fears.

He did not vanquish it from afar, like some god of the ancient Olympus; He did not strike down the foe by arrows shot from heights of the empyrean. No; He Himself came down, Himself wrestled with Death; for a moment its cold hand was laid upon His heart, and then He arose, felled it to the ground by His glance; and walked our earth, as He had done before.

Oh, how this comforts me! A triumph won with more display, if I may use such a word, might have dazzled me; I doubt whether it would have equally consoled. The very simplicity of the action brings it within my reach. The body had lain down, it rises up; no need for this of angels' trumpets or a convulsed world. The will of God effected this; God willed, life returned. The crucified, the dead Jesus, is the same who walks now along the shores of Gennesareth, up the Mount of Olives; He rises to his Father, He revisits His loved disciples; the earth does not quake, the slightness of the effort put forth speaks to me more emphatically of the power of my God than the most splendid display of His sovereign authority.

I dearly love them, these scenes of the Resurrection. How often I have bent over them, seeking to penetrate deeper into their meaning. The sleeping waters that mirror by night the star-filled sky, do not more faithfully reflect infinite depths than those few quiet, straightforward narratives, sublime through their very simplicity.

That which chiefly attracts me is doubtless the divine radiance shed around by the person of my Saviour. As I follow Him afar off, I seem to catch a celestial reflection; I breathe the air of Paradise; joy wraps me round like a garment of light; but would the picture move me so deeply if I only saw therein the victory of a God? It is that of a man, too, and therefore is my soul so stirred within me. I contemplate with moistened eye those three that are taking the road to Emmaus; my heart thrills at that one word, Mary! And when, at day's earliest dawn, the gloomy waters of the lake are tinged with red, I cleave the waves with Peter, I cry aloud with triumphant voice, It is the Lord!

Man has conquered. Jesus, made like to me in Death, shall make me like to Him in life.

Like! It is in this that all my happiness consists.

If He had restored to me life, life of any kind, my heart must needs have been grateful. But would it have bounded as it does now at the thought of the gift of a human resurrection, identical with the resurrection of the Lord?

There are some happinesses that crush us, as we know. But this, of which I have fathomed the nature, fills me with confidence as well as with wonder.

This risen one is not the Lord of I cannot-tell-what far sphere, lost in the bosom of the Infinite. He is my Saviour, I know Him. I see Him again as I saw Him before. He remembers me, He loves me; His face, those hands they pierced, I see them, they are the same—no apparition, no metamorphosis—only a return.

This is so sweet, that I need an absolute conviction of its truth.

And then, when I have certified myself, another doubt instantly rises,—Will it be the same in my own case?

Then I seek further, hard to satisfy, fearful of a too ready belief; and repeated assertions tell me again and again that I am not deceiving myself. Such as the Lord is, such shall His redeemed be; made like to Him (in all but His Divine attributes), bearing the image of His glorified humanity; very brothers to the Mighty One, who first shook off the grasp of death.

Are these vague, veiled promises? No, they are clear, definite, written in familiar words; their meaning easily apprehended, impossible to mistake.

Have we to seek them out from book to book? No,

each page presents them. This is the centre whence ray out all the promises; it is alike our starting-point and our goal; the whole edifice raised by the apostles rests on this unchangeable foundation; Jesus risen from the dead is the perfect type of risen man.

You understand now the stress I lay upon the contemplation of this central figure, and my ardour in keeping to it.

Jesus, Thou art indeed the same Jesus still. Ye who have watched Him walking through the corn-fields on a Sabbath day: one morning seated on the hillside, while the little waves beat upon the shore of Tiberias; another, climbing the grassy heights which divide Bethsaida from Nazareth; or again, not far from Cana, beneath the shade of oaks, whose branches bend beneath the honeysuckle in flower, in quiet retreats, where turtle-doves coo, and the tall hollyhock, with its brilliant clusters, blooms splendid but unseen; behold Him again, for it is indeed He!

How often His feet have trodden your paths! How often your hills and glades have heard His accents of incomparable meekness, when moving slowly on in the midst of publicans and sinners, a few women following, He would cry,—"He that believeth in me hath eternal life."

Do ye recognise Him, ye mountains, ye waters? There on the shore—alone there, while Peter and John, with their companions, are throwing their nets into the lake?

"Children!"—what a loving cry! Then comes that question, the very simplicity of which would offend many if they dared entertain the feeling, which on the contrary makes me thrill with gratitude, because I read in it a sign of my Saviour's permanent humanity,—"Have ye anything to eat?"

Then another miracle is wrought on those waters which

have witnessed so many. Another cry arises; a cry of tenderness and joy,—"It is the Lord!"

Next see them all reassembled around Jesus! Notice the fish counted, the familiar meal, the touching intimacy, the perfect freedom of their conversation!

What has passed since the last supper; for, in very deed, it was but yesterday that Jesus cut bread for them as He is doing now; that they questioned Him in like manner, that the fishermen divided the waves with the same steady oars, and that the Son of man wandered with His disciples on the self-same grass, which has not had time to wither.

Jesus has died; Jesus has risen again; and as He wore our likeness in His death, so we shall be made like unto Him in the life to come.

Jesus, come back to us from the unseen land, has forgotten nothing.

We will not quit these dear, familiar shores.

See, Jesus has taken Peter apart! The Lord's face is serious, not severe; His lips utter a question, repeat it again and again, a little sadly, but so tenderly that it melts the soul. Peter listens, his brow grows clouded, his bent head bends lower still; he is pale, overwhelmed with shame, till, by a supreme effort, and with an intense gaze fixed full upon the mild eye of his denied, his adored Master, he cries,—"Lord, thou knowest all things, thou knowest that I love thee."

This is how Jesus remembers.

He remembers when He waits for His disciples upon the borders of the lake; He remembers when He appoints them to meet Him on that Mount of Olives whither He so often led them; He remembers them when he fixes upon Bethany, where He loved Martha, and Mary, and Lazarus, as the spot whence He was to part from them, and to be carried up into glory.

What! Does Jesus, then, not retain the memory of the past! It were blasphemy to say so. He retains it faithfully, tenderly; as He has retained it, I too shall retain.

Jesus loves His own. He loved them in the agony of death. He loves them in the triumph of the resurrection.

The dawn whitens in the East; in the garden of Joseph of Arimathea it is still dark; a woman is standing there beside the sepulchre.

Some of the apostles have been there; they bent over it, saw that it was empty, and, true to their nature as men, logical, prompt in decision, the fact once proved, they have accepted it. But the woman remains there still. Why, she cannot tell you; only to weep, perhaps; to remember and to weep on.

Some one draws near, probably the gardener. "Woman whom seekest thou?"

"Sir," stammers out the poor woman through her tears, "if thou hast borne him hence, tell me where thou hast laid him." *Mary!—Master!*

How convey the full value of these two words! All of tenderness, all of respect, the past all recovered, the eternal future all possessed, love imperishable, victorious for ever and ever;—it is all this I find in them, and all this fraught with such ever-increasing freshness and pervading power, that night and day my thoughts might plunge and find unfathomed depths, that for a whole eternity I might feed my admiration thereon, and their immaculate beauty be in no way withered.

Again, Jesus is walking between the disciples on the way to Emmaus. The road is dusty, the hour late; the Saviour's countenance seems changed; something unfamiliar makes me for a moment hesitate, and yet, beneath this apparent reserve, I feel that love is vibrating.

"Why are ye sad?" A thrill passes through me. Sweet questioning of my Saviour, I recognise you. It is thus you gently press all bitterness out of the heart; to tell one's sorrows is to find a secret relief. Jesus interrogates His children; He makes them repeat what He already knows; then when the last sigh of dejection has been heaved, He in His turn speaks and consoles.

But there is another detail that touches me still more. Jesus "*made as though he would have gone farther.*" "Abide with us, for it is evening." And they *constrain him;* and Jesus suffers Himself to be constrained! Then their eyes are opened, then they utter a simultaneous cry —"Did not our hearts burn within us?"

My heart, too, is hot within me. Saviour, Thou hast loved! Jesus, risen from the grave, Thou hast felt for Thine own a love more merciful, more strong, more entirely, perhaps, imbued with tenderness and pity than in the days of Thy pilgrimage.

As Thou hast loved, my God, as Thou lovest, even so shall I too love!

Jesus rose from the tomb in His entirety. It was no spirit who appeared to the apostles when, gathered together in the evening, they discussed the *visions* of Mary, and refused them their belief. It was no phantom who walked in Galilee; it was His own body, crucified, dead, risen again.

This glorious fact offends the apostles. It confounds their preconceived ideas; comes, as it were, into collision with their habitual train of thought.

An immortal soul, we are ready, indeed, to admit that; we have not seen the soul crumble into dust. But the body? That ancient antipathy of ancient philosophy, that rag, that vile thing through which we are perishable, that coarse tyrant who subjects us to brutal appetites, that burden which our encumbered spirit can only free itself from by death; that only hindrance to our attainment of perfection, that animal part of our nature, mere dust and corruption! To revive that, to give it its share of eternity, more, its share of glory!

Such a subversion of human wisdom as this, such a complete overthrow of received notions, could not be adopted all at once. The apostles themselves, who admitted the resurrection, who had been present at the controversy with the Sadducees, and heard the reply of Christ, who had seen Lazarus come forth from the tomb, even they, believers, would not believe this. They conceive the idea, but the fact stupifies them. In presence of the Saviour's risen body, some are terrified and others doubt. Jesus must place their fingers on His wounds, must eat before them, must cry aloud, "Touch me, and see, for a spirit hath not flesh and bones, as ye see me have!" before, for very joy, blended with fear, His disciples could comprehend and believe.

There is an incredulity that arises from excess of happiness; there is a scepticism caused by the very magnificence of Divine transactions. Less grace would find an easier entrance into our narrow hearts. A God only half God, a limited power, a partial gift, would suit us better. But then this would be but a less gloomy night, it would not be day.

Jesus has risen again with His body. My dead body, too, shall live. My beloved ones, earth will restore your bodies to me.

Finally, Jesus made Himself known to His friends.

If the scarce-dispelled darkness, if the wonder of an unheard-of felicity, left Mary for a moment in suspense; if the eyes of the two disciples, journeying to Emmaus, were for a moment holden,—how short the doubts, how soon succeeded by perfect certainty!

The apostles could not be deceived; the evidence of their senses affords an irrefutable and enduring testimony to the resurrection of their Lord.

They doubted, indeed, the reality of the body of Jesus, but never His personal identity. That He was a spirit they did, indeed, at first imagine, but never that He was any other than Jesus. Whether assembled in an upper chamber, or alone; in the garden, or on the mountain side, it is always one and the same cry that bursts from their lips, "The Master!"

To have seen is enough, is all. They saw, they knew. They needed no other proof than just to look; that done, there was no more hesitation. For a moment two of His disciples failed to recognise Him, but only because their eyes were holden. When their eyes were opened, they knew Him at once; nothing more was wanted.

In proportion as these meetings with the Saviour were multiplied, their doubt, nay, even their surprise, vanished, so that, even after a night of watching on the Lake of Gennesareth, with heavy eyes and weary ears, a simple word is enough for them: "Children!" And John exclaims aloud, and Peter dashes in, and swims to shore. It is thus that I shall know again, shall be known again.

Nevertheless, there is a change, a difference.

Jesus, who before never left His disciples save for a night of solitary prayer, now leaves them often, for a long time, and no one knows where He is gone to. His absence used to be a rare occurrence, His presence has become so now. Formerly they had life in common, now only interviews. Doubtless, these were more numerous, more prolonged than we commonly suppose. A very marked allusion of St John's leads us to this conclusion; but the risen Saviour lives under new conditions; His body has faculties which excite our wonder as well as our admiration. The obstacles which once impeded, impede it no longer. He comes in and goes out, the doors being shut. He is here, then there, and no human eye has marked His passage from place to place. On the morning of the resurrection He says to Mary, "Touch me not, for I am not yet ascended to my Father." He ascends, He descends to earth again, and says to Thomas, "Reach hither thy hand, and put it into my side."

A deep mystery spreads its veil before our gaze.

Until the hour of His glorious reappearing, heaven is become the Saviour's domain. He traverses its immeasurable space, and, returning, seats Himself no longer—being weary—by Jacob's well.

What though He taste indeed a piece of honeycomb, those touching words, "He hungered," can never more be said of Him.

Still man, His humanity has put on glory, has put off infirmity. And thus is formed a grand, a beautiful personality, which we see indeed, but cannot fully comprehend.

Be it so. What matters comprehension when I have faith,—have the fact before me?

When the resurrection-day comes, there will be no more obscurity. Meanwhile, strengthen thyself, my heart.

Need we recapitulate? Are not the characteristics of Jesus awaked from death, self-evident, luminous, definite?

Man after it, as Thou wert man before; with Thy personal identity entire; with Thy memories, Thy affections unchanged, risen in a glorious body, recognised by Thy people,—such art Thou, my Saviour!

A light has burst forth; its radiance reveals the far perspective of the world to come. Rejoice, my soul, at a happiness within the reach of thy faculties. Do as did the Apostles: Look, and thou shalt see

THE SLEEPLESSNESS OF THE SOUL.

HE soul does not sleep, it lives; it is the body that lies low in the slumbers of the tomb.

Can you conceive a sleeping soul, a dreamless sleep? I find that such a state borders too closely upon annihilation, not to excite in man extreme repulsion. In fact, it is temporary annihilation.

To cease to exist during centuries, perhaps ages; to give up a life throbbing with the love of the Saviour; to be frozen up after the fashion of antediluvian mammoths; to exchange the activity of thought, the full employment of every faculty, for a suspension that amounts to total extinction,—to speak frankly, does this prospect fill your heart with joy? Mine remains aghast at it.

Nevertheless, if the Word of God declares this, we needs must submit to it. How many men, of high consideration, affirm that it does!

One word, one only, authorizes this opinion; a very strong word, it is true, and often repeated, the word *sleep*

Death is sleep; those who die *fall asleep.*

What remains to be said in reply?

Much; nay, all.

The word is there, no doubt. But as long as its meaning is undefined, the question remains open. In what sense are we to take this word "sleep?" How is it applied in the Scriptures? This is what it concerns us to know. This alone will solve the difficulty.

This word applies to the body, not in any sense to the soul.

It is the body that sleeps, absolutely unconcerned by all that goes on in this world or in the other. It sleeps heavily, no voice can rouse it, not even that dear voice whose lightest whisper sufficed to thrill it during the days of life on earth.

You know it but too well, that implacable sleep; you who have folded in a last embrace that poor body, indifferent now to every appeal of yours. An hour ago, it saw your tears, your pale face; it sees them no longer. All that the soul saw and heard, those angelic messengers that God often sends to light it on its passage; the body, if it saw them at all, sees and hears no longer. It has fallen down inert, it remains inert, and the immortal germ that God has placed within it, the spark which His breath will re-kindle, is so deeply buried in dust and ashes, that no human search can ever discover it.

Has the soul then succumbed? Is the spirit paralysed? Let us draw near, and examine more closely into this. This dreadful word "sleep," will—thanks to Jesus who applied it to Himself—at once assume its own proper and circumscribed meaning.

Here is the garden of Joseph; here is the sepulchre. The body of Jesus is resting there! What says Holy Writ?—Jesus sleeps.

He sleeps! This is the language employed by Scripture. When Scripture speaks of Jesus dying, they say, He fell asleep. When they speak of His resurrection, it is as of awaking out of sleep.

No distinction is here made between the body and the

soul of the Son of God. If we take the sleep of death in an absolute sense, the whole nature of Jesus was, for a season, subjugated by I know not what lethargy. For three days the spirit of Jesus, the Lord of Life, remained paralysed, benumbed. You might have traversed the whole earth, its height and depth; you might have sounded the immensity of heaven, nowhere would you have met with Jesus! For three whole days the Word—He who could say of Himself, *I am*—He, even He, *was not.*

Does not the shudder occasioned by such a thought as this at once convince you of its sacrilegious absurdity?

Well then, the whole of revelation declares of Jesus that He slept.

If it says this of Him, it may well say it of us. There is nothing in that which need terrify us any longer.

The Pharisees said it when they set a watch around His tomb—"We remember that that deceiver said, In three days I will awake, arise again."

The angels implied it when, seated by the sepulchre, they reassure the sorrowing women,—"Ye seek Jesus of Nazareth, who was crucified. He is not here, he is risen."

Jesus said, speaking of himself: "When I am risen I will go before you into Galilee."

The apostles repeat the phrase: "He rose again the third day." "God raised Him from the dead." Let us believe on Him who raised Him up.

Dust, thou shalt return to thy dust! I know thee, thou fearful sentence, thou art nothing new. Ever since the days of the Garden of Eden thou hast struck at our bodies; our souls disown and defy thee! The soul can no more sleep than it can die.

Have you still one lingering doubt? The last sigh of the Saviour will dispel it for you.

"Father, into thy hands I commend my spirit." Death takes his own portion, but the living spirit returns to the land of life. For three days the body shall remain laid in the tomb, treated as a holy thing, but still as a *thing;* it shall be wrapped in a shroud, heaped about with spices; sleep shall weigh the eyelids down, paralyse the limbs, but not the spirit. Death, thou canst not touch *that!* The spirit will patiently await in God's presence the hour when, returning into the very body it left, it will raise it up on its feet, soar with it to the Father, re-descend to earth, sit down in glory.

This is not yet all! Listen to a decisive sentence of the Saviour—

"I lay down my life to take it up again. I have power both to lay it down, and to take it up."

Who is this *I;* this victorious *I*, who is it? Who is the one who, being dead, commands life to return? It is the soul; the soul which can neither slumber nor sleep.

Be at ease; we shall sleep as Jesus slept. It is thus that sleep our loved ones. Their bodies, that is to say; never their souls.

This subject is one that must be thoroughly examined. When only indistinctly revealed, it saddens us; placed under a full, strong light, it causes our hearts to dance with joy.

Let us return in thought to days long past; remount the stream of time.

Here we meet with Abraham. In the midst of the terrors of night and darkness, he has been visited by a vision. The Lord has spoken to him, "Thou shalt be gathered to thy fathers." Do these words apply to the Patriarch's earthly remains? will his bones be carried to

Padan-Aram, from the land of Canaan to the country whence he originally came? Not so. Abraham having died in a strange country, is buried in the cave of Hebron: there rests his body; his dust will not be mingled with that of the plains of Mesopotamia. It is the soul that is spoken of; the soul is living still; the soul goes whither his fathers have gone.

Again, God meets Isaac in the valleys of Beersheba, and says, "I am the God of Abraham thy father." To Jacob he says, "I am the God of Isaac."

To the people of Israel, "I am the God of Jacob."

Magnificent name!—*His name throughout all ages!* "I AM!"—not *I was.* Jesus declares Him God of the living, not of the dead, not of the sleeping.

David cries aloud, "Thou wilt not leave my soul in Hades." Prophet, he announces the resurrection of Christ; believer, he expresses the fulness of his own conviction.

And Ecclesiastes responds to him, "Then shall the dust return to the earth as it was, and the spirit unto God who gave it."

Long before then, the Lord on Sinai came to hold con verse with Moses from the midst of ten thousand of his saints, living saints, not sleeping. Long after, the dry bones gathered themselves into battle array at Ezekiel's voice; but, lo! the *spirit* had not yet returned into them.

Who is that who rises down there on the plains of Endor, in presence of the pale and trembling king? A phantom? No; Samuel himself, the judge of Israel. "Why hast thou disquieted me? To-morrow thou shalt be *with me,* thou and thy sons."

Who are they who appear on the holy mountain, talking there with the transfigured Jesus? Two of the dead: Elijah, carried up body and soul to heaven; Moses, whose body is still hidden in some mountain-hollow on the other side of Jordan. Do they sleep? Have they slept? No; both have come from the land of life; both will return thither; their faces are lit with celestial glory.

What says Jesus to the little daughter of Jairus? "Maiden, arise!" The stiffened frame lifts itself up; the heart beats, the child walks,—and why? *Her spirit has returned into her.*

Behold a spectacle at once magnificent and terrible! A poor man, covered with sores, yields up his last suffering breath, and is borne by angels into Abraham's bosom. A rich man lives in splendour, dies, is buried, and then—I see him in a place of torment. This fate follows instantly upon his death; for amongst the inhabitants of earth are numbered the brothers of the man clothed in purple and fine linen.

A parable, you say.

I know it, and know that to draw too rigorous deductions from it, would be to pervert its meaning. Nevertheless, it has a meaning, else of what use would it be? When the Lord spoke it, He designed it to announce a truth, else He would not have done so. Was its only purport to teach the Jews that, after this life ended, there were felicities and torments both? The Jews knew that perfectly well What, then, did the parable teach? The striking fact, that the soul cannot sleep, that it merely passes through death, does not linger in it, that it is immediately happy or unhappy, one or the other, and that it can only be either through being a living soul.

Do you not at once see the moral influence of this fact? A thousand years of lethargy; that is a long period. A state of pain or a state of enjoyment divided from us by such an interval, does not affect me much with joy or fear

You will tell me that a thousand years are as one day! Yes, in the Lord's eyes they are so. But as for me, a finite creature, with my standard of time, I count the thousand years as they are here upon this earth where I am; in spite of myself, I see them in the light of a reprieve, and from that moment it is no longer my soul that sleeps, but my conscience.

My pen has stumbled upon that word catalepsy.

There are indeed cataleptics. There are people whose senses are all suspended, who cannot see, who are considered dead, who are dead in common parlance. Oh, but are they really so? Those motionless eyes follow your movements, those frozen ears catch all your broken words; each latent faculty, preternaturally excited by the con. straint laid on it, has acquired increased intensity; life is there, entire, vibrating, condensed. And when the blood begins again to circulate and the lips unclose, when that frightful torture of the living soul within the corpse is ended, it is found that never before did the heart feel so strongly, the mind think so intensely. And shall we still believe in the sleep of the soul!

But I return to the proofs afforded me by revelation.

Judas, who strangled himself, went, say the Scriptures, *to his own place.* You shudder. Sleep has no such terrors.

Paul calls us *fellow-citizens with the saints.* The city is alive, its citizens are awake, are stirring, acting; a city of sleepers would be rather a necropolis than a city; the fellow-citizens of saints are fellow-citizens of the living.

The same apostle exclaims: "Ye are not come unto Sinai, ye are come unto mount Zion, to the general assembly, . . . to *the spirits of just men made perfect.*"

These spirits are living at this present hour in the

presence of God; for *the body is dead, but the spirit is life.*

Do we need further argument?

Yes; there is still much to be said. A single word has given birth to the notion of the soul's temporary annihilation; another word refutes it—departure.

The soul *departs*, says the Bible. We depart from our homes. In order to depart, we must be alive. My home is not myself. My home without me remains a dead, deserted thing. Doors closed, windows closed, silence everywhere. Meanwhile I, this living I, am elsewhere, am animating some other dwelling with my presence.

Then, as for the desire to depart so often expressed by the apostles, how can we understand it if sleep follows upon death? Such a desire would be simply unreasonable. What! I want to quit this earth where I serve my God, where I feel, where I love; I want to quit it that I may sleep. Only a despairing lassitude can prompt such a wish as this; never will it be felt by a Christian in the full exercise of his faculties, his faith, and his affections. Such a one will never prefer lethargy to labour. Living, he may glorify his God; living, he may save souls; living, he may comfort the mourner; but paralysed, congealed, a thing and not a being, even the power to dream is not permitted him any longer.

Paul aspires after deliverance; he shall tell us why. "When at home in the body we are *absent from the Lord.* Therefore we desire to depart, that we may be *present with the Lord.*" Here is his motive. St Paul would fain depart, not to escape the sorrows of existence. A soldier does not shun the battle, that he may receive the prize. Besides, St Paul, in repeating it, further defines his thought. "We are willing rather to be *absent* from the body, that we may be present with the Lord." Absent from the body! What is it that is absent? My soul. Whither does it go? Into the presence of the Lord.

I fear to dwell too long upon the subject, to weary the reader; but I must needs recall that other expression of Paul's, when, his heart wrung with anxiety about the new converts whom he feared to leave, his soul possessed with the desire to behold Jesus, he wrote those lines so impressively true, so touchingly natural,—"I am in a strait betwixt two, having a desire to depart and to be *with Christ, which is far better;* nevertheless, to abide in the flesh is more needful for you."

One irrefragable testimony remains: I have kept it to the last.

Three crosses rise on Golgotha. On one of these, with arms outstretched, the royal title above His head, proclaiming to the universe how Israel treats the Son of God, see Jesus die. They ridicule Him. Insults are hurled at Him on all sides by the angry crowd, and fall blunted on that brow, which grows pale beneath the Divine wrath. Jews, Romans, all alike blaspheme. More bitter, more caustic still, fraught with more fearful irony, the sarcasm heard from the neighbouring cross,—"If thou be the Christ, save thyself and us."

Then, before any answer can be returned, a voice is lifted up, plaintive but firm, humble but vibrating with hope: "This man has done nothing amiss; we indeed suffer justly;" then that supreme prayer: "Remember me, when thou comest into thy kingdom."

Jesus answers: "*To-day*, verily I say unto thee, *to-day* thou shalt be with me in Paradise."

What a contrast! Have you seized its full power? It is as though Jesus said—

"You thought to fall asleep; you thought that ages after ages would heap their dust on your torpid spirit; to-day, as soon as the brutal club of the Roman soldiers shall have broken thy bones, to-day thou shalt be with me. For me, I do not sleep. My soul enters triumphantly into its kingdom; finds its ransomed ones there, other ransomed spirits coming, one after the other, to rejoin it; to-day, not later, Paradise will open for thee; and when, at the appointed day, I re-descend as Sovereign Judge, it is with my saints, the armies of my saints, my living not sleeping saints, that I shall return to earth."

No man can number these saints.

Do you see, too, in the pages of the Apocalypse—those souls hidden under the altar? Moved with holy impatience, they cry,—"How long, O Lord! how long!"

Do you mark the myriads clothed in symbolic white garments, come out of great tribulation, and glorifying the Lord, while the last scenes of our earth's history are being accomplished? These are the elect, happy *at this present hour*, but still aspiring, waiting for the redemption of the body.

And now if, by a singular reaction having been once offended by the idea of a glorified body, you are amazed at the idea of a soul deprived of its body and yet living, of a soul that perceives, feels, thinks, I have to ask you, whether you have never dreamed; if you do not know what it is to traverse earth and skies in the imaginations of your sleep; if it has never happened to you, as it were, to act, to speak, to live long years in one second of time; to be your own identical, complete self, the body only excepted.

And then I have to point you to St Paul caught up to the third heaven, whether in the body or out of the body he knows not. I point you to a Daniel, an Ezekiel, a St John; to all the prophets in their trances and their visions, and I say to you, Do not underrate any longer the power of God, the inalienable vitality of our own moral being.

We are convinced; we know now to a certainty that there is no state of torpor for our dead.

Their slumber weighed like lead upon our soul. It almost made us rebel against the decrees of the Most High, our bereavements became intolerable. How can we but regret life for those who sleep? The most laborious existence, the most troubled and tormented, is at least better than annihilation. The weary may at least love, the suffering may glorify God; but the unconscious tenants of the tomb have neither heart nor tongue with which to praise the Lord.

Would I wake you out of sleep, my beloved one? Yes. Must I needs rebel against the will which has snatched you out of existence, to cast you into a limbo, full of silence and of gloom? Yes. Do I find such a decree inexplicable, unjust, cruel? I do.

Would I recall you from Paradise, from the very fount of life; would I plunge you again into our darknesses, our sins; could I fail to bless through all my tears the merciful decree which has transported you to the seats of everlasting bliss? Never.

The way opens out before us. It does not lead down to the darksome bowels of the earth; it rises to the highest heavens.

Let us no longer look for the living amongst the dead.

PERSONAL IDENTITY

ITHOUT personal identity, I can comprehend neither heaven nor earth; we should fall into mere ciphers ranged in line with other ciphers. All relation between this life and the next would be done away; we should find ourselves in presence of two worlds entirely unlike, two races absolutely unknown to each other. Not a single link to bind the heavenly to the earthly; and as an inevitable consequence, divine justice giving way, and my interest in my own soul vanishing quite.

Justice is just only so long as it is applied to the very individual who has committed the good or the bad action. If you take away identity, you destroy the individual. His conduct is no longer part of himself. It may, indeed, be his arm which is raised to kill, his hand which is opened to give; but from the moment you do away with the individuality of the soul, you do away with all responsibility. The crimes or virtues of a being thus deprived of personality, you might as well reward or punish in his neighbour as in himself.

This is so incontestable, that the law does not punish the insane; merely shuts them up, to prevent their injuring society.

A crime committed in full possession of reason even, if it be followed by madness, does not draw down upon a man the sentence of the law We do not execute a madman;

we incarcerate him. If his reason returns, the law takes its course.

But in no case can it be put in force against the virtually absent.

So much for justice.

As for the interest I take in my own future, that noble sentiment which leads me to respect my own soul, to seek to perfect it, to desire its holiness and happiness; if I am myself no longer, I lose that sentiment altogether. In fact, the fate of a Chinese is much more important to me. I may know that Chinese, may meet him in the life to come, but, from the moment that I lose my identity, find myself, recognise myself no longer, I become self-indifferent.

Punishment! no doubt it will be distressing to that other individual to undergo it. Happiness! no doubt he will enjoy it if it be granted him; he has my best wishes, my charity reaches so far. But not farther; not to any effort, to any sacrifice for his sake. I repeat, I should exert myself more for a Chinaman.

So much for the moral aspect.

But there is more than this, the doctrine of impersonality which militates against our common sense, tears our heart as well.

I have seen a father depart: I shall meet again with a nameless being. All our life has been blended with the life of a friend; nothing will remain of our former attachment. A stranger myself, I shall take my place amongst strangers. We shall not even be able to speak of the earth, for I shall not know if there be an earth or not, the link between it and me will be broken.

What a heaven! one would be better off in a jail. There we might be uncomfortable, we should at least still be ourselves.

There is this to be said, however, it is not God who has broken the link we bewail. We find no trace in Scripture of a system, that by way of fitting man for everlasting life, begins by substracting from him his own self. No book respects individuality more than the Bible. There is even a marked contrast between the Divine wisdom and our own, in that God, who might absorb all, jealously preserves our moral personality; while our terrestrial philosophers, despising men in their zeal for man, willingly sacrifice the right of the individual to the good of the great whole.

The individual has a permanent existence in the sight of God; the individual is entirely lost sight of by the great majority of philosophers. They have invented a final absorption into the Divine essence; God has left His work as He originally conceived it—very simple, and answering to our common sense.

A common centre into which all are absorbed; such is the idea struck out by human wisdom. Each one answering for himself, there in heaven as on earth, such is the work of God.

Jesus knows His sheep by name. The very angels have their special characters and distinctive appellations. Gabriel is one, Michael another.

In the presence of God each individual has his proper life. One town, one people, is not confounded with a neighbouring town, a neighbouring people.

The word *each*, or equivalent expressions, so constantly applied to man when removed to his eternal abode, guards and maintains personality.

He that soweth sparingly shall reap sparingly. My reward is with me, to render to *every one* according to his work. *Every man's* work shall be manifest. He that overcometh shall be clothed in white raiment. I will not blot out *his name* from the Book of Life. *Each one* shall answer for himself.

I do not know how an inalienable individuality could have been more definitely expressed.

Identity! yes, we grant you that, some will reply. But memory!

Yes, there are people who come and calmly tell you,—There will be no remembrance in heaven.

I have said that, without personal identity, I could conceive neither heaven nor earth. Can you conceive of them without memory?

As for the earth under such a condition, it is palpable that it would be but a madhouse.

And heaven?

I am there in the celestial regions. *I* am there! This is easily said, but who is this individual whom you affirm to be me? he is a perfect stranger, for I have no recollection of him. *Me?* oh, where, at what time, in what place? While you leave me ignorant of those details I cannot proceed a single step.

Never mind, I must, you tell me, advance, and you lead me to judgment.

To judgment!—for what cause, and who is he that is judged? I hear it said—Thou hast committed such an action, neglected such a duty; thou hast believed my word, denied it; thou hast loved Jesus; thou hast rejected Him. Truly all these charges alike are enigmas to me; I seek and cannot find any answer to them.

But this is not by any means all. According to these very charges, I am placed on the right hand with the blessed, on the left hand with the condemned.

Oh, my whole nature rebels against such a proceeding!

It is written that God shall be found just. But as for me, I declare Him unjust, for I can remember nothing.

Do not talk to me any more of justice but of arbitrary power! Memory once destroyed, the solemn scene of the last judgment is reduced to certain blows or certain favours, falling here and there like a hail-shower on a stormy day; sparing these, crushing those, according as they are impelled by a mysterious will to which I have no clue.

You wished to preserve personal identity, and you take away memory—both fall together. I am only consciously myself so long as I remember. Annihilate the last vestiges of memory, and you annihilate the last remnant of identity as well.

And, if you dispute the fact, I point you to the old man in his second childhood. So long as a little memory is left him, he remains himself; when all remembrance of the past is darkened, absolutely darkened, he loses his identity, loses it to such a degree as to believe himself some one else. His poor mind is like an empty house, passers-by go in and out, the true master has disappeared.

Men have thought to make God's work easier, by conjuring memory away. They have only destroyed a prime element of order.

The world to come peopled by a race without a past; a future existence entirely built upon an anterior existence, with its very conditions only consequences of the acts, thoughts, and sentiments of that said anterior existence, and yet all memory of it done away,—why, I say it is a mere chaos! Cut the ropes which hold a balloon fast to the ground, send it rolling through space, without ballast or compass, and you have an image of your world to come: more fitting home for the insane than the redeemed.

Again, what a singular hypothesis; how little worthy of

God this which degrades man by way of elevating him. Here below, he had a complete individuality, possessing the past by memory; the future by hope; he exchanges time for eternity, and straightway his mind grows narrower, his sight shorter; the perspective of the past closes behind him. Truly, he was richer on earth, he was greater, he was at least conversant with his own life, and could measure the amplitude of ages past.

If you would mutilate our moral being to make God's work of judgment easier, know that God refuses such facilities; that He will have to do with man in his entirety. It is with his personal identity and his memory that man will have to appear before God. In the heavenly country, a man will assuredly encounter men whom he has known; known by hearsay, known by sight, and nations of men, whose history he has read.

Remember! says the Scripture.

"Remember that thou, in thy lifetime, hast had thy good things."

"I was an hungered, and ye gave me meat; naked, and ye clothed me; in prison, and ye visited me." And when the redeemed of the Lord cry out, in amazement, "When did we any of these things to thee?" Jesus clears up the difficulty by an appeal to their past recollection, "Inasmuch as ye did it to one of the least of these, my brethren, ye did it unto me."

They understand Him.

It is from our past that the witnesses for or against us are cited.

The rust of our silver and gold testifies against us; our alms, fruits of our faith, plead on our behalf. There is a most absolute solidarity between the time that was and the time that shall be.

Thou hast confessed me before men: I will confess thee before God. Onesiphorus, thou hadst compassion on my Apostle Paul, when he was chained in a Roman dungeon: at the last day thou shalt find mercy at the hand of thy God. Martyrs, ye died with me: ye shall also reign. As for you who said Lord, Lord, and who would bring forward the evidence of your pious talk, your fine-seeming actions, nay, your miracles wrought in my name, remember more accurately: Words, outward conduct, these, indeed, you gave me, but not your heart. Depart from me, all ye workers of iniquity!

We know the name of those who played a part in memorable events; we know their history, can recognise their character.

Men in presence of other men, town against town—Jonah with the inhabitants of Nineveh, the Queen of Sheba, Moses, —all have a clearly-defined and unalterable individuality. Even when cities are treated of, it is Sodom or Gomorrah, Tyre or Sidon, with their respective annals, their impersonal but specified character and conduct; actual cities, in short, not abstractions.

Thus memory and identity have a permanent existence, are the immutable basis of the future life.

The doctrine of the soul's sleep benumbed our conscience; the annihilation of our identity destroys it utterly. From the moment that I no more believe myself responsible for actions, I take no further thought about them. Such or such a wicked act may indeed appear to me in an ugly light —I grant you that; but, nevertheless, I contemplate it from a stand-point external to myself. I blame it in my own conduct, just as I might blame it in the vilest of men, neither more nor less. It does not interest me; I might almost say it is no affair of mine; and were it not for the reprobation of society, which I shrink from braving,—the fear of incurring the penalty of the law, I should give the reins to my every passion.

You speak to me of development, perfectiveness. I protest to you that I am indifferent to them. Let me grow ever so perfect here below, it will be labour lost when I find myself on high. It is a mere stranger, for whom I care very little, that is to get there. As for taking any particular trouble for him, incurring sacrifices, acting or not acting, the thing is absurd. There is only one individual in whom I really take much interest: the one who on this our planet is called *me*, me myself. I will procure for him as long as I can, all the pleasure and satisfaction possible here; after—why, hereafter is the affair of that other being with whom I have no connexion.

The same order of minds, who used to deny first personal identity, then memory, in their constant desire to simplify all problems, have now come to allow man to continue himself indeed, but still they must needs mutilate him; to leave him complete would be too great a complication; there would be no end to difficulties. Therefore they decree that he shall indeed remember, but only in part; shall retain the memory of events, but not of persons. In heaven, say they, we shall recognise ourselves, not others. Here is a fine invention, indeed, for simplifying matters!

I have a name of my own, it matters not what. On earth, I had a mother, a husband, children; I was surrounded by friends; I lived in town or country, and near me lived other human beings, rich or poor, happy or unhappy. Towards each of these, father, child, neighbour, I had certain duties to perform. My very life, indeed, was so intimately interwoven with theirs, we breathed so completely one common air, that, in a moral sense, I could not move, nor they either, without their existence and mine being modified. The elements out of which our past was made were just our mutual relations, our reciprocal conduct, our feelings for each other. My soul bears the impress of their actions; their soul has undergone the influence of my character. My life which is about to be judged, is part and parcel of their lives; that which stands written in the books about to be opened, is written in the mingled blood that flows from their veins and mine.

Now, it is just all this that you want to do away with. The world is to be suppressed with the exception of my solitary self.

I find myself before the throne of God; myself, it is true, but standing all alone there. Family, friends, neighbours,—a breath has blown them all away. I see myriads at my right hand and at my left, strangers all,—mere ciphers, such as we spoke of. I alone; I known only to myself and to God, I stand upright amidst the ruins of the world.

Absurd, immoral, as was the doctrine of a lost identity, a lost memory!

In point of fact, it is only the old empirical practice under another name; only the scalpel and the cauterising iron.

Let us amputate, burn, annihilate; nullity is more easily managed than life.

Do you think so? I do not. Heaven thus peopled with creatures half-living, half-dead, with one half their consciousness paralysed, one half their affections frozen, looks to me but like a vast hospital and abode of suffering

Or if there be not suffering, it is owing to the cautery. To mutilate, is not to heal. I see mutilated beings. I do not see men there.

Is that indeed a state of glory? Is that the perfection promised to the children of God?

Let us breathe the pure air of the Bible.

A slave, Onesimus, has run away. Paul teaches him the way of salvation, then sends him back to his master. "For perhaps he therefore departed from thee for a season, that thou shouldest receive him for ever." A strong expression this—*receive him for ever.* But if Philemon is not to know Onesimus again, what meaning can it have?

"Ye shall see Abraham, and Isaac, and Jacob, sit down in the kingdom of heaven." If you see them without recognising them, what does seeing them signify to you?

A crown of rejoicing is prepared for the Apostle of the Gentiles; his converts are that crown. But if he does not know them again, what becomes of his triumph? "Make to yourselves friends of the mammon of unrighteousness, that when ye fail they may receive you into everlasting habitations." *Friends*, the very same whose trembling hands your hands have pressed; whose tears you have dried here below. If they are merely x, y, or z, why they can no longer be friends, and Scripture testimony is overthrown.

On the morning of the Resurrection, many saints left their graves, and showed themselves to many. Do away with the recognition of individuals, and you destroy all proof of the miracle.

Upon the holy mountain there appeared two men in glory, one on each side of the transfigured Saviour. Who has announced their names to Peter? No one; nor had Peter ever seen them, yet he knows them. "Master, it is good for us to be here; let us make three tabernacles, one for thee, one for *Moses*, one for *Elias*."

I will not remind you of Samuel recognised by Saul; nor of Elijah, who, as he rises high in air, does not become unfamiliar and unknown to Elisha. "My father, my father!" Thus he continues to cry, till Elijah has vanished out of sight. I should have to quote the whole Bible.

The first shall be last! Why, according to your theory, I know neither the one nor the other—know not what this means.

The patriarchs, the prophets—are they indeed monuments of the faithfulness of God? I cannot tell, and I might pass a thousand years in the presence of these sublime forms without being any wiser.

Those Colossians, those Philippians, those converts of St Paul! who are they, and who is Paul? I never heard of him; let us pass on.

"They who pierced shall see him," I hear it said of the Jews and the Lord Jesus. Were there Jews? Was there indeed a man called Jesus? How can you suppose the Jews will know Him again if there be no mutual recognition hereafter?

I thank Thee, my God, the river of Lethe may indeed flow through the Elysian fields, it does not water the Christian's Paradise.

Before the sun has climbed above the horizon, all objects on earth are blended in one common, indistinct, grey hue; you can just discern their difference of form. The sun rises, colours appear, outlines define themselves, variety and tune are born at once. Before, there was only a dull monotony; now, there is harmony.

The life to come has a similar marvel in reserve. At

the first ray of its light, our true characters, purified but preserving their identity, will more fully expand, and the result of the infinite diversity will be a complete unity.

Have no fear. God will open out a way we cannot foresee. His wisdom, His will, will have as free scope amidst multitudes of separate personalities, as amidst bewildered myriads of beings without identity or memory, to whom everything is new, everything unaccountable, and who are appalled at the unknown region into which they have been plunged.

It is I myself. So said the risen Saviour to His disciples. *I myself.*

Those with whom I have lived, with whom I have suffered; you, my children, for whom I have so often prayed; my friends, whose faces are so familiar to me, you too, whom having not seen I still have loved. *It is you yourselves.*

Blessed be the Lord for this expression of His!

We were being very gradually and gently brought to the verge of final annihilation; God has stretched out His saving hand. Once for all, and for ever, we have escaped from it.

THE ETERNITY OF LOVE.

HAVE we indeed escaped?

Alas! no.

The power of God rescues our personality from the tomb: so much has been granted; but it leaves our affections there. Individual love is to be absorbed in universal. It is this latter love alone of which it is written, "It never faileth."

If this be so, then we have returned to the belief in annihilation; for to lose ourselves is virtually to perish.

I apply the term, destroying agent, to the flood that covers the whole country, and replaces its varied undulations by an immense sheet of water, which only reflects the sun.

Death shall be destroyed. This wondrous sentence closes the prophecies relating to our earth. But if you kill my affections, death triumphs; for death has swallowed up the noblest portion of our being.

If in this life only we love, (I extend the application of St Paul's words,) we are indeed most miserable.

What! I shall have given myself away; I shall have received that ineffable gift, a heart; our thoughts shall have become so intimately united as simultaneously to rise within us, by those secret affinities which we cannot explain. I shall live in him, in her; love shall have wrought the miracle of taking away all my selfishness; a smile on those lips shall irradiate my heart; a cloud of sadness on that brow shall have power to cast me down; nay more, we shall have bent the knee together; shall have ardently sought after God; mutually lived that noble Christian life with its agony of strife, its joy of victory; and when death comes, we shall have to say, All is over!

An absorption into the ocean of universal love will be the end of all. The first soul I meet will be as dear to me or as indifferent (it is all one) as that soul; any other individuality will be as precious to me as that beloved individuality which has vanished for ever. Oh, my heart protests against such a doctrine as this! I say now, as I said before, of memory and identity,—If I cease to love them whom I once loved; if I cease to love them with a definite, positive, special love,—I cease to be myself; and, moreover, while in this world, I am the most miserable of creatures.

I am, at the same time, the most degraded. Take away the immortality of love; give me children, a father, a husband to love, under this condition, that it is only for time; prove to me that the coffin-lid closes upon our affections as upon our bodies, with this difference, that earth will restore me my body and not my affections,—I declare to you that I shall love them with the love of an egotist, a materialist, nothing more.

Even if you set before me a career of Christian activity, souls to be saved after this manner, with a sort of wholesale interest in which the individual goes for nothing, I declare to you that my work becomes lowered in character, and that I shall get through it mechanically; the intimate, personal love of souls will come to little more than the placing one stone upon another, having hewn it out, as well as one can, with the least possible trouble.

It was not thus that St Paul felt when he exclaimed,

"Ye are my joy!" (you whom I have known, for whom I have suffered;) "ye are my joy in that day." The converts made by Peter, by James; the heathen that in future ages other missionaries will win over to the faith,—all these I shall doubtless love; but my crown, the delight of my eyes, the thrill of my heart, will be you on whose face my eyes have rested; you with whom I have prayed; you who wept at the thought that you should see me no more; you who caused me sorrow and joy; you, my own personal friends!

Who is it who has created our affections? God or the devil? Excuse so downright a question. If it be God who gave us these affections, and pronounced His own work good, will He one day suddenly change and pronounce it evil? He who dowered this earth with such strong and sweet attachments, will he denude heaven of these? It would have been easy to have placed us from the first in an atmosphere of uniform and insipid affection, felt by and for all alike; in an ocean without islands and without shore. But this is not the Divine idea; it is the vain imagination of man.

Man considers that there is grandeur, God that there is poverty, in monotony.

Try, for a moment, to picture to yourself a man who has no preference. Behold him loving everybody with exactly the same sentiment, his father neither more nor less than all other old men, an unknown child quite as much as his own. As for friends, he has none; or rather you, I, any stranger, the Grand Turk if you will, are all equally his friends in degree and kind. Why, such a man is no man; he has, I can see, arms, legs, but I do not discover a heart in him. If he really be living man, and not an automaton, I say that, loving every one, he virtually loves no one, that

I care not for such general tenderness, and that I would rather be the cat of such a one than his wife or his son.

If this earth, deprived of special and particular affections, seems to crumble away beneath our feet; if it presents us with nothing better than isolated creatures, wandering about, each in his own dim personality, equally attracting, equally repelling all the rest; if the result be a chaotic vortex, cold, indefinite, sad, and unspeakably tiresome, what would a heaven be on the same plan?

I know, indeed, that you make the Deity the centre of your heaven; that all affections are to converge towards that central point and be absorbed there. This is mere chemical action; no life, no soul here—annihilation again.

And yet this is how the human mind sometimes orders and peoples heaven.

Oh, how differently has God created man!

God created family ties, which man could never have invented; which, in his savage state, he often does away with altogether; which, in the excesses of a corrupt civilisation, he too much ignores; which the greater part of our false philosophers tend to dissolve. God has strongly bound us together,—the man to his wife, the father to his child; and when Paul seeks to depict, in one word, the moral degradation of the Romans in his day, he says—without natural affections.

What does that ark that floats over a submerged world, contain? A family: father, mother, sons, and daughters.

Why that scarlet thread on the walls of Jericho? It is there to save a family.

What said the avenging angels to Lot,—Hast thou here any beside—sons, or sons-in-law, or daughters? bring them out of this place, for we will destroy this place.

To whom did the Lord send his apostle Peter; to the

Cæsarean centurion alone? No; to his family, his household; the whole household believes, the whole family is baptized.

Nothing is done by constraint. God forces no one; yet it is the will of God that man should not land alone on the eternal shores. What appeals He addresses, what secret attractions He exercises; what prayers He puts into the heart of mothers, of wives; these we shall never know till the day of the revelation of all things.

Yes, there are families on high, united with indissoluble ties, loving each other with a firmer, stronger love than earth ever knew. No egotism diminishes; no infidelity sullies; no ambition chokes; no love of gold petrifies it; it is constantly re-baptized in the adoration of God, and this adoration, far from extinguishing it, only imparts its own eternal glory.

And yet, Jesus has told us that in heaven there is neither marriage nor giving in marriage.

No doubt. Under new conditions, there must be new relations. Our terrestrial marriage has consequences which are incompatible with the future life. That which is temporary ceases; that which is immortal lasts. True Christian love is immortal.

To be fully convinced of this, assume, for one moment, the contrary hypothesis. Picture to yourself Abraham—that marked, that impressive, personality—without Sarah, without that other personality so closely linked with his. Take a further step, imagine Jacob indifferent to Rachel. He meets her, his gentle love, the companion of his wanderings, meets her in that Paradise. No more loving names, no more pathetic memories, no more tenderness. He meets her, and with unkindled eye, unmoved mind, glides by her. Any other soul taken at hap-hazard would inspire him with equal interest. For the mother of Joseph and Benjamin he feels nothing more than for any other inhabitant of heaven. Alas! she whom, weeping, he buried by the way of Ephrath; she has remained in that grave. Both are dead.

The beings whom in the heavenly regions you still call Rachel and Jacob, have nothing in common with those hearts which burn here below with a love at once so human and so divine. I know them no longer. Not a single feature remains of those characters traced by the inspired pen. They are for ever lost to each other, lost to us.

For, in order to love no longer, mark it well, you must no longer remember. Love is no less intimately connected with memory, than memory with identity. No memory without love, no identity without memory, no human being without identity. Prevent a man from loving on the other side the grave, the soul that he loved on this; you can only do so by destroying his past, and in destroying his past, you destroy the individual.

The great poet of the middle ages better understood the dignity of the human soul, when he maintained intact the immortality of love. Even in hell itself he jealously maintained it. With equal flight, driven to and fro by the same wild wind, sighing out one same sad complaint, pressed, shuddering, one against the other, the two shades once united by a guilty love, remained faithful still. And shall not chaste affections last? while unsanctified ties thus defy death, shall the holy ones, into which God himself breathed immortal life, shall these be destroyed?

Have it your own way, then, methinks I hear it said. But with the endurance of individual affection, you introduce sorrow into heaven. Will all those you love have indeed a place there? Are you very sure to meet them all again? A father, a child. . . . .

I fall at thy feet, my God. I fall there with a cry which is an act of faith. Thou wilt save them; Thou wilt seek them out; all obduracy will melt beneath the ardour of Thy Divine love. If it were not so indeed!—my God, take pity on me! I know that Thou lovest them; I know Thou wilt wipe all my tears away; I believe from my inmost soul, that Thou wilt not wipe away my tears by narrowing my heart! Thou consolest by giving; Thou wilt take away nothing that is good, that Thou thyself hast pronounced very good. And then behold a mystery: Thou thyself, O God! from out thine immutable felicity dost look upon the lost. Nevertheless Thy love and pity endure; Thou hast not sacrificed them to Thy blessedness. These are muffled harmonies, but I can hear their distant echo.

What Thine omniscience does for Thee, Thy compassion will do for me also.

My love will not die. Struck at throughout my whole journey; covered with wounds; bleeding and mutilated, it is not thus that I shall enter the kingdom of heaven. The God from whose presence despair flies away, will not banish it by scattering the dust of my memories to the winds. Indifference will not be my cure for grief. My God has other remedies for the suffering that springs from love.

My tenderness will survive, Lord, like Thy tenderness. Thy love, Thy heart, my risen Saviour, guarantees me the vitality of my own.

There is one other objection to the identity of our affections.

"Though I have known Christ after the flesh," says the Apostle Paul, "I know him so no more."

And the inference is this—On high our attachment will be so modified as virtually to be done away with.

But a different way of loving is not by any means a forgetting.

Let us look a little down to earth.

While I lived without God and without hope in the world, I loved. How? Idolatrously, that is to say, selfishly, possessing, possessed, in reality seeking only myself in my love. This love was full of caprice; a word could change it, a look turn it to torture; tormented itself, it grew cruel in its turn. Often, without visible cause, it would diminish, grow cold, almost die out; or else the prosaic influence of long habit would threaten to smother it. A change is wrought in me; my soul finds a Saviour, I am born into a new life, and the mighty hand which has raised me, has, at the same time, raised my affections also.

Will you say, then, that I love no longer? I love better than ever. I love with a solicitude till then unknown; I love with inexpressible delicacy and refinement; I really and truly no longer love myself, but love another. I cherish His soul; it is His soul that I crave; it is His soul I would serve; I must have it immortal, must have it happy. Before, I loved for a day; now, I love for eternity.

This is what God makes of our love even here below. Will He do the contrary, think you, in heaven? After having built up in this life, will He overthrow in the next?

To sanctify, is not to destroy; to annihilate sin, is not to efface human affections.

He who vanquishes Satan, immortalizes all true love.

Although God has not seen fit to reveal to us all the mutual relations of the future state, yet some of the words that He has inspired are radiant with glory.

Does He see us prostrate beside some tomb? "Sorrow not," He says, "like those who have no hope. *I will bring them back;* when I return they shall be with me. At that solemn hour you living ones shall not prevent them that are asleep. In a moment, at the voice of the archangel, your beloved ones will rise again; you will come together to meet me. Comfort ye one another with these words; do not be comforted like those who have no hope."

Have you listened attentively to these sweet and subtle words; have you gathered this promise to your hearts; fully appreciated its considerate tenderness?

Oh, be sure He who Himself thus loves, will never break our hearts! Sadness! yes, that is natural; but let our sadness be fraught with confidence; Jesus will bring back our lost ones with Him.

A long period of waiting would distress. The living shall not prevent them that sleep.

But where? How? Be not afraid; the shout of triumph sounds from one end of heaven to the other, and we shall be all assembled—all together with Jesus.

"*Together!*" exclaims St Paul. "Risen *together; together* seated in heavenly places."

See David, before prostrate in the agony of despairing prayer, suddenly arise, wash his face, anoint his head. What doest thou, O king? Thy son is dead; he will not return, and yet thy tears are stanched.

"He will not return to me, but *I shall go to him.*"

But I desire to contemplate my Saviour in the exercise of His most Divine prerogative; at the moment when, with His sovereign hand, He loosed the bands of death.

His preaching demanded the support of miracles; but what His heart demanded was that He should wipe away our tears.

When at the gates of the city of Nain, He stops the corpse on its way to the grave; was it to display His power that He did this? The procession comes on, a sorrowing woman accompanies it—a widow. Jesus sees her, *is moved with compassion*: "Woman, weep not!" His hand has touched the bier: "Young man, arise!" And He gave him to his mother.

He gave in like manner the servant to the Centurion, his little daughter to Jairus.

"Trouble not the Master," said the servant; "thy child is dead."

And others thought, perhaps, What is dead is dead; the flower has bloomed and faded; thou wilt see her no more on earth or in heaven. In heaven, a mere fraction of the great whole, a unit midst myriads of similar units, thy daughter will be thy daughter no longer. Therefore, make up thy mind to it. Forget!

Not so Jesus. "Maiden, arise!" and He gave her to her father.

Let me seat myself awhile beside Mary, while Martha, who has just run in, is saying to her, "The Master is come, and calleth for thee."

"My brother is dead. By this time the prey of corruption." Such are the terrors under which our faith falters.

Then Jesus breaks in—"Said I not unto thee, that, if thou wouldest believe, thou shouldest see the glory of God?"

And Jesus was troubled in Himself, and Jesus *wept*.

"See how He loved him!" cried the Jews. They are not deceived, those eye-witnesses. Where over-strained, superfine intellects can only see a vague humanitarianism, the Jews recognise the presence of a strong affection. How He loved him! And He who loved Lazarus said, "Take ye away the stone;" then cried, "Lazarus, come forth!"

It is no person hitherto unknown who comes forth at this call. Jesus has not evoked a new and different being, a stranger, indifferent to those around. No. It is Lazarus who arises; the Lazarus whom Martha and Mary love, whom Jesus loves, and He gave him to his sisters.

I told you before that it was the very joy of this that hindered our faith. The apostles gathered together on the morning of the resurrection, were like us, they believed not for joy.

We have been wont to descend into the depths of sorrow, but hitherto we have never been equally flooded by bliss. Eternity reserves this experience for us.

Do our beloved dead see us still, take part in our struggles, lend us help? This is a mystery.

The things that are revealed alone belong to us. I find them sufficiently beautiful to satisfy me.

By faith, women received their dead again! I thank Thee, O my God.

Fear not, only believe. I will believe, Thou wilt not deceive me.

"*A general assembly,*" "*caught up together with them,*" "*together with the Lord.*" I will constantly repeat to myself these words, all vibrating with hope.

My heart salutes you, ye eternal shores! Amidst your radiance I recognise my beloved ones. The dying eye of a father was fixed upon them; they were their greetings that reached his ear, and that Divine smile that rested on his lips, that last sublime light, was kindled by their glance, their love, as well as by the Saviour's ineffable love. At that last moment those he had loved were still his own.

THE RESURRECTION OF THE BODY.

THERE are some who make light of the body. I am not one of them.

It is an easy resignation, indeed, when it concerns ourselves; a bitter grief when some beloved being is in question.

There it lies, that poor body; there is that face that I have looked at so much, the eyes which rested gently upon me, the mouth that spoke to me as no other will ever speak more; there is the whole aspect—I knew not whether it were beautiful or not—which was my sun, which was my life.

If my lips touch that brow ever so lightly, they meet a marble coldness there. Have you ever felt it sink down from the lips to the heart, that piercing, unnatural chill, unlike any other, that chill upon the forehead of the dead?

That body so sacredly cherished; that poor body, heretofore the object of such tender care;—they take it from me now! Strangers come, who bear it away, dig a grave, and lay it there; the earth is heaped up over it. The dust, the rain, the winter winds will all sweep over that grave; and while I am sitting, sheltered, beside our hearth, while I am warming myself—he—he is lying low out there, alone, forsaken.

Oh, this cry that eloquent lips have uttered!—every funeral procession has extorted it from some heart in its distress. It is not the cry of madness, it is the protest of nature and of reason.

We were not made for this; God had not created us for this; the image of God was not destined to moulder into dust. We may be submissive, may check the rebellious words that rise to our lips, but our thoughts will follow those remains, will glide into that tomb, will open that coffin, and return with tidings which will tear our very vitals.

During that last illness, while I possessed it still, one of my deepest sorrows was to see that poor frame decline. When my anxious looks encountered those altered features; when one of those ominous changes that one will not allow to one's self, suddenly burst upon me, I felt my heart sink. At such times, my face buried in my hands, my knees giving way under me, I fell down somewhere out of sight, more truly dying than that loved one in his very death-agony.

The destruction of the body! There lies the curse, the anguish of one who watches by a deathbed.

And now that years have worn away, with their good days and their bad, do you know what it is that suddenly lights up the widow's faded face? do you know why she sheds these happy tears? She has seen again—yes, like a lightning flash, some smile, some trick of feature, has appeared before her; some gesture, some intonation, a stray note dying away as suddenly as it rose. With passionate energy she clasps one of her sons in her arms; he has looked at her in the way his father used to look; he has said, as he used to say, "I am cold;" he has shivered as he used to shiver. Or else it is some dream, a ray of light from Paradise which has visited her in the darkness of her night. Yes, it was his very self; they were both walking along some familiar walk in their little garden. There was nothing extraordinary about it, no transports. In fact, it was as if they had never been separated at all. They chatted about one thing and the other, with a smile, a jest, as they might yesterday, as they might to-morrow. And when the widow wakes; her lips do not part with a groan of desolation; no, she has re-possessed herself of her loved one's image; she will meet his own self again ere long: she has gained strength to go on her solitary way.

You call us Materialists. 'The flesh!' you disdainfully murmur. These remains that our heart so follows, you return them to their dust without a regret; no place for them in your heaven tenanted only with wandering and impalpable shadows.

If we have God on our side, we are disowned, we are well aware, by a lofty philosophy. This divides man into two parts: the one full of sin and misery rose from the earth and gravitates thither; the other, immaculate and heaven-descended, returns of necessity to heaven. The two have nothing in common. Their very essence decides their destination. There is no longer need of a God to raise us, of a Christ to redeem; the fire takes what belongs to it, dust to dust, the soul to glory.

This is the reasoning of many a philosophic system many a heathen religion.

God speaks a different language. He who condemns also absolves. He who pronounced that fearful sentence on our body, has redeemed that body. Men give it up to corruption, God raises it in glory.

What is it that Jesus taught? The resurrection of the body. The Sadducees ridicule the idea, and put a hypothetical case to Him, in hopes of demonstrating its absurdity.

What is it that the apostles announce? The resurrection of the body. An immortal soul is still granted to us, it is considered admissible and generally received. And yet it is but a sad sort of immortality; now mere nothingness, now a headlong rush through a succession of varied existences; but at least it implies a soul, an immortal existence, we are told to be contented with that.

"What!" say our opponents, "does not that satisfy? Will nothing do for you but the resurrection of the flesh, the eternity of matter? Down with such madmen; lock up these publicans and sinners; these men of nought, in love with such low and vulgar notions!" The Jews threw such dreamers into prison; the Athenians of the Areopagus, with their polite, refined culture, merely shrug their shoulders. Festus, in presence of Agrippa, cannot contain his contempt;—"Paul, thou art beside thyself; much learning doth make thee mad."

Such a deliverance as this could not spring spontaneously from the heart of man. Man could harden his heart, but he could not grasp so great, so simple an idea as this; entirely lost, entirely saved. Man will not stoop to identify himself with the instrument of his sins; man will not accept a solidarity which proves to him his fall; prefers rather to annihilate the creation of God. To leave one's own body a prey to worms; to give up to them for ever the body of relatives and friends! Yes; tell him of that. He is strong-minded; he will not wince.

But to resume a body, his own body, in eternity! Pshaw! It is a low, vulgar idea; it revolts him.

Nevertheless, what man could not even imagine has been done by God. God, who saw us completely degraded, has completely restored; restored the whole man, body and soul alike. It is for this reason that the Lord Jesus rose.

Such, too, is the expectation of the saints. Paul sighs, waiting for deliverance; *to wit, the redemption of the body.* He strives to attain to *the resurrection of the dead.* His full conviction is, that the same Spirit which raised Christ will also *quicken our mortal bodies.* And it is this very Paul, whom certainly no one could accuse of self-indulgence, or idolatrous tenderness for his own person, who proclaims a new and startling truth, which many would be disposed to treat as blasphemous: "The Lord is *for the body!*"

Would you know the secret of this problem? It is contained in one word—Holiness.

While in the eyes of many the body is a mere vessel of dishonour, St Paul views it as the temple of the Holy Spirit.

"Mistake of nature," say the wise of this world. "Perfect work of God," reply the Scriptures.

The body has sinned, has been punished accordingly. Punished! Yes, but not cursed.

In point of fact, were we disposed to argue, we might ask which is the true culprit, the soul or the body? Where is it that the sinful idea arises? Would the soulless body be guilty of any excesses? Ask that corpse stretched out yonder!

But take the bodiless soul, on the contrary, or the soul in a body rendered completely inert, would it be of necessity immaculate? Would it be free from all pride, all hate, all falsehood, all covetousness; because independent of its fleshy tabernacle, would it, as a consequence, return to the innocence of Eden?

The folly of such a supposition becomes at once apparent.

You call those Materialists who honour the body I hold those who despise it to be far more deserving of the name. Ceasing to view it as a temple, they use it as a tavern.

We whom they call carnal respect it. Those members for which Jesus died, which will live again with Him, will again serve God on earth, must be kept pure from taint. You so-called spiritualists leave such humble anxieties as these to others: a dwelling so soon to be utterly destroyed does not, in your opinion, deserve so much care; the lowest reptiles are welcome to it; each passer-by may insult it,—never mind; nothing will remain of it in any case.

Oh, the coarseness of such a refinement as this! Oh, how noble, how supremely holy, the simple plan of my God!

The resurrection of the body strikes you, you tell me, as unseemly! I feel it sublime. It not only makes my heart beat with joy, but perfectly satisfies my moral sense.

The annals of past ages shew me Christians who suffered in their body for the sake of their faith. I see martyrs steeping the Roman arenas with their blood; I see the fearful torches that lit the feasts of Nero; I see funeral piles, and on them human forms slowly consuming; from out the torturing flames I hear hymns of joy and praise to God; nay, at the very moment I am writing, the veil of obscure circumstance cannot quite hide the privations, the watchings, the long journeys, the hard labour, that humble believers cheerfully undertake for the love of God. And shall the body which has suffered, sacrificed itself thus, have no portion in the kingdom of heaven?

Oh, yes! Its sure place is prepared there; no power can reverse the decree.

He who will raise the whole creation, will raise the body.

Resurrection! Admirable word. Any other would

have left some anxiety undispelled; this word meets my most secret fears.

Who is it that rises? The dead man they laid in the tomb.

However dark, however suffering my night may have been, each morning I rise.

That morning my beloved will rise, he himself, and not another. It is not a new creation, it is a resurrection. In the place of the beloved departed, whose image my heart keeps so faithfully, God will not give me some unknown being; no, God will raise up the one I love; my hope will not be deceived. Amidst that dust and ashes—oh, omnipotence of the Divine compassion!—a germ, visible to my God alone, encloses the vitality I believed for ever extinct. As a grain of corn, buried deep in some furrow, rises as a green fresh blade to cheer my eyes and heart; so, clothed upon with a body, glorious, incorruptible, like to that of Jesus, who rose long before—so will the body of my loved one rise.

April is smiling at the earth. Come, stoop down. Close to the old wall, do you see a broad leaf spread itself out like a canopy, beneath it a blue vase filled full of spring-tide fragrance? It is the violet. Take hold of that branch, and break it: wood, mere dead wood, you say. Look closer, it reddens, it swells; here are pink petals, crests of balmy stamens, it is the blossom of the apple-tree. Take that other branch, dead too, like the other; a cluster springs from it, golden, butterfly-winged—it is the laburnum. This other is burst open by a white candelabrum, with scarlet touches—it is the horse-chestnut. Death made all these branches much alike. Infinitely varied in life; each with its own special scent and sheen, they open out full to the sunshine, and cast their sweetness on the merry breeze.

During one night, one shower, the brown field is transformed into a meadow, rifled by the bee, the butterfly myriads of lately tranced and crawling things have changed into the winged hosts of the air.

What do these miracles say to you? To me they say that a God of love will raise up our dead.

"But how? with what semblance?"

St Paul will tell you. "Sown in corruption, raised in incorruption; sown in dishonour, raised in glory."

It was fragile and abject once; now Jesus clothes it with immortality and beauty.

Beauty! But those who were ugly, irredeemably ugly. And at once some luckless face comes and grimaces before our mind's eye.

Yet, when we come to think earnestly about the matter, is there indeed such a thing as irredeemable ugliness? Do features only make the face, or is it not rather the soul that shines through it?

Take for example any misshapen face you will. Deprive it of mind, it is hideous, you turn away from it at once. But let an idea shine through that ugly mask, you look at it without repugnance. Let it be animated by a noble sentiment, the flame rises, lights it up, you are irresistibly attracted, you contemplate it with pleasure. Let love, a pure, generous love, cast its radiance over that face, (do not smile,) I tell you that face will become beautiful.

You must surely have seen this wondrous transfiguration of which I speak. Yes; there comes one hour, the only one, perhaps, during a whole lifetime, when the ugliest man or woman among us grows beautiful. An hour of strong passion, elevating excitement; an hour when the soul reigns supreme. And if that soul be beautiful, why, the face is beautiful too. You read eternal redemption on the brow, in letters of sacred fire.

Again, death has revelations such as this. You who have seen a beloved one die, you are familiar with a transformation that yet did not interfere with his identity, that left him still your own.

You remember well, do you not? the serene radiance of his expression. You beheld his face as it were that of an angel. Such was the aspect Stephen wore, when they stoned him as he knelt, and in the open heavens saw Jesus standing on the right hand of God.

But when the last breath is drawn, what dignity, what ineffable serenity! The body had suffered much. It was old, perhaps infirm, very wretched in every way. Death comes; and an ideal youth, the youth of immortality descends upon the brow.

There are flowers which only yield their fragrance to the night; there are faces whose beauty only fully opens out in death. No more wrinkles; no drawn, distorted lineaments; an expression of extreme humility, blended with gladness of hope; a serene brightness; and an ideal straightening of the outline, as if the Divine finger, source of supreme beauty, had been laid there. You cannot take your eyes away. Dead, your loved one consoles you for the agony of having seen him suffer. His face, his inexpressible grandeur, his smile,—all say to you, "Believe; yet a little while, and thou shalt see me again."

I am about to relate to you one of the strong emotions of my life. I found myself in the crypt of a church at Palermo. My friends and I had gone down into it without exactly knowing where we went, and walked, with more of surprise than terror, between a double line of skeletons. And yet the spectacle was ghastly enough. Those perpendicular dead bodies, dressed in brown garments, that hung loosely around their bony limbs, with crossed hands, holding some sort of shield, with their names written on it; had fallen into dislocated attitudes, even more grotesque than horrible. The portals of our Gothic cathedrals have no representations that equal this. And yet we were not conscious of any terror. Death presented us, indeed, with his material aspect, his sad repulsive aspect, but the likeness of humanity was still there.

With one word, we felt God could call those dry bones to life again.

The next chamber had a more appalling spectacle in reserve. All along the walls—as in the cabin of some great ship—were ranged berths of equal length, and on these, dressed in gorgeous attire, hands gloved, lay the corpses of women,—with discoloured faces, empty eye-sockets, sunken features, hollow mouths, and wreaths of roses on their heads. There were hundreds upon hundreds of them, in all the pomp of their court dresses, and a nauseating smell, the cold, faint smell of death, rose from the vaults where the bodies were drying.

In the presence of these faces with their beauty so inexorably destroyed, of this ghastly satire on worldly vanities, I felt my blood congeal. But when at the end of the passage, lit by our guide's torch, a well yawned before us, and he lowered the red and smoking light he held to shew it better; when I saw that nameless *detritus*, damp, pestilential, which overflowed the well's mouth, and when our guide said—"This is the dust of those yonder; when they have lain there their time, we throw them in here," I remained almost lifeless with horror.

With my hand half plunged in those ashes, looking at what they had left on my fingers, a despairing doubt flashed blightingly across my soul.

As I fled in haste from that fatal crypt, and mounted with unsteady step the stair that led us back into the nave, just where the daylight began to appear, I suddenly saw four letters carved on the wall, I. N. R. I. Then a voice sounded very near my heart—"*Believest thou that I am able to do this?*"

Jesus of Nazareth, King of the Jews, yea verily Thou wilt do it!

From that day I have never for a moment doubted of the Resurrection of the Dead.

PART THIRD.

THE WHOLE CREATION SIGHETH.

SIGH! You all know it well, this sigh of sadness; this sigh of expectation. Not a breast that has not heaved with it; no lips from which it has not often risen to heaven.

We are ill at ease. All of us, whether we be happy or unhappy, have a burden to bear, the burden of human woes. There is no escape from one deep consciousness, intensified perhaps by the breathless hurry of our age,—that of the short duration of all earthly things. The best are soonest over, but all pass in exceeding haste, and we ourselves seem as though a mighty and resistless wind were sweeping us away.

Formerly, tidings, whether good or bad, were slow of step; we hardly knew what was going on at the other side of the globe till a year after the event. If blood had been spilled, the earth had had time to drink it up; if tears had flowed, the sun had had time to dry them. The griefs that spoke to us from afar, left the heart comparatively unmoved. That is perhaps the reason why our grandmothers' laughter rang so freshly despite their fourscore years.

Things are changed now. The tree of the knowledge of good and evil has bent its branches more within our reach, and each moment our greedy hands are raised to gather its fruit. And the result is not only an anxious restlessness, but a fund of bitter melancholy.

Formerly, the general tone was one of gaiety. The note that an attentive observer would have heard prevailing over all others, was a crystalline serene note, echoing from the cottage to the palace. The note that vibrates over our earth at this present hour, in the village, town, or quiet country, is a wailing note, akin to tears,—is an immense sigh.

Regret for blessings lost, sadness left by past suffering, craving and quenchless thirst; all these are included in it. But in many who are unconscious of it, there is also a latent aspiration after good things to come; an inextinguishable need of deliverance; an intense desire for permanent light. And when I represent to myself men of this class, I seem to see noble but chained beings, who stretch out their arms to the skies, whence the Redeemer is to descend.

You think me gloomy. Among you, I see some who lay claim to high spirits, are given to laughter, who feel no discouragement, no weariness, who protest that they are comfortably settled on this sad earth of ours, and not by any means in a hurry to leave it.

Yes, I know that there are two ways of looking at this world. Believe me, I too have hours in which earth seems to me young and beautiful. Spring days, when the spirit of life breathes upon the fields, when the sap mounts to the branches, when the foot treads half unawares on new-springing grass; when each nook and corner of the old wood is carpeted with periwinkle. There is a sudden efflorescence; the bushes are great nosegays, placed here and there in the dingles; the branches unfurl their leaves, not yet browned by the sun, or spotted by the fly. There are still indeed a few shabby weeds of last year which linger on by the brook; a few dry, angular branches standing out from the young foliage, but who notices them? Winter and death are fairly put to flight by spring.

How delightful to inhale the aromatic perfume of the pine-trees, the breath of the primrose! Sometimes a breeze comes to us from the gardens below, blending with all the rest the fragrance of the lilacs in flower.

Let us stop a while, if you will, on the border of the wood. Stretched out at full length, there I listen.

Who spoke of sadness? The coppice is full of woodland melody. The nightingale defying the sun, and when it pleases him to be silent, other strains are heard, other warblings of quieter character, simple symphonies, little hops from branch to branch, and two or three strokes of the wing that bear the songster to some more secret shelter.

There, under the apple-tree, is a buzzing as of a hive, on the hawthorn-starred hedge are myriads of insects, in red attire, blue attire, some perfect mosaics, others gemmed like a royal casket. Amongst the grasses, with their delicate plumes, other treasures again, and the air is full of busy, winged swarms, brilliant as lightning. And all so happy, so healthy; all celebrating in their own way the festival of life.

Yes, but they all die, and when that thought strikes your heart, the festival is over.

Then the woes of all the earth begin to rise like mist; gradually they spread over the magic of the scene, they put out all its glories one by one.

Oh, short duration of all things here below! Of the spring freshness, soon consumed by the drought of summer; of this May morning, that a return of cold winds will blight; of these poor insect swarms, of which not one will survive to see another April; of that labourer working there; of this young girl; of the dwellers in that village, with its peaceful smoke from cottage chimneys; the dwellers in yonder town, with its ancient towers. Fifty years, sixty, eighty at most, and all, from the rosy infant just learning to steady its little feet on its mother's knee, to its grandmother, whose head shakes, as leaning on her staff she slowly moves along; all will be laid in the dust. On earth, in the place that knew them once, a new generation will rise, with its nurslings and its graybeards in their turn. That generation, too, will be cut down and laid low; and the next, and the next; and death will be always, always the same strong reaper, rising early, the only one who sees others pass away, and himself passes never.

Do you remember that story of Musæus, so sad beneath its playfulness, full of such bitter irony under the disguise of mirth?

The genius of the Hartz, Rübezahl, a monarch whose kingdom extends to subterranean depths, met, one fine day that he wandered through the woods, with the daughter of the prince of the country. To fall in love with her, to seize her as she slept, to dive down with her into the bowels of the earth, to place her gently in the fairy gardens there, beside the fountain which sparkled in the gas-lights burning all round,—this was the work of a single moment. The princess awakes, a little startled, of course, at first; walks about, admires as well as wonders. Everything is splendid; a novel kind of poetry broods over the whole region. Soon she discovers that she is loved; and for some days this new feeling—which she, however, does not share—suffices to divert her. But one morning she chances to remember the sun, to remember her father, her mother, her young companions. She begins to weep; an unbounded *ennui* takes possession of her; a little time, and evidently she will die. Here is our genius in a pretty dilemma! He is too selfish to restore the princess to the place from whence he took her. To carry off the king, the queen, and their court would be too troublesome a measure; and, moreover, subterranean genii are very solitary in their habits. What is to be done? *Eureka!* Our genius has hit it; and while the princess sits in her apartments, her head buried in her cushions, breaking her heart, and insensible to all that so lately pleased her, Rübezahl appears before her with a basket of turnips in his arms. He places the basket at her feet. The princess, who has been slyly looking at him the while, finds the present a very homely one.

"Princess!" says the genius, "wave this wand."

He bows low, and retires. The princess carelessly passes the wand over the turnips. Oh, prodigy! Her father, his majesty the king himself, sceptre in hand; her mother the queen, crown on head; and her brothers, sisters, the court ladies, the chamberlain, the maids of honour; even the grooms, even the turnspits;—every one, in short, except a certain handsome young knight, whom Master Rübezahl had his own reasons for leaving in the lurch!

What embraces, what narrations, what festivals, in the enchanted gardens! Only, about midday the king, the queen, the ladies, young and old, seem to grow a little languid. Let us rest. They all go in, and luncheon is prepared. But, strange to say, instead of being recruited by it, the august personages grow more and more exhausted. You would say that years are suddenly heaped upon their brows; every moment wrinkles deepen; voices become cracked; steps grow slower; forms shrink; backs arched; old age is coming on. A few moments more, and the whole court, so brilliant a while ago, will be nothing better than an hospital for the aged ; tottering steps, little quivering coughs all round ; and when the needle has completed its circle, all turned again to turnips,—poor, withered turnips, will lie scattered on the floor.

As to the reception the genius got the next morning, when he came running in, basket in hand, the bursts of tears, the indignation,—we have nothing to do with these. We stop at the turnips, striking image of our short duration. I find it terribly, poignantly true.

Everything dies, and on this spring morning, if I lay my ear to the ground, I seem to hear, from every point of the compass, the heavy step of men who carry a corpse to its burial. Cries of pain rise from this Eden of ours. They come from the forest glade, where the hawk pounces upon some quivering thing ; from the village, where the peasant takes the new-born lamb from its mother ; they come still more from cities,—clamours, sinister laughs, slaughtered cattle, sobs, threats, men who kill, who are killed ; tears of those who refuse to be comforted ! And those who do not cry out, whom we do not hear, are those who suffer most.

Have you ever travelled rapidly through the country on a summer night? The cool breeze played round you, laden with the perfume flowers give out after sunset; your glance was raised, was lost in the infinite sky, amid its numberless stars. Half dreaming, you hardly seemed an inhabitant of earth ; and yet the earth was exquisite, ideal in its beauty. All at once, as you pass through a village, you see one little window with a light burning. The other cottagers are asleep,—here there is watching. What is it that watches ? Happiness ? No ! A mother bending over the cradle of her sinking child ; a wife standing pale by the couch on which her husband is dying ; two men cower ing over the hearth, and on the bed a body stiff and cold, which they will carry to the graveyard to-morrow.

Even the happy have secret griefs which their lips will never utter. Corroding anxieties, hidden terrors, fatal discoveries made in the nature of their loved ones,—all these dumb sorrows, but not the less devouring.

Fly from our civilised countries; go to the centre of Africa, what do you find there? A sandy desert so steeped in blood, such wholesale massacres, that travellers of every creed call those negro-lands the kingdom of Satan.

On their coasts, caravans of slaves, with halters round their necks, beaten, bartered, piled on one another between decks, exposed to sale, dragged off to plantations, married, unmarried, at their master's will, dying under the lash. In Pagan isles, wars, massacres, cannibalism. In China, Persia, India, refined cruelties, of which our nerves cannot bear the recital. In every latitude, human brutality, taking advantage of the helplessness of dumb animals, cowardly cruelty, or cruel kindness!

This is our world.

But there is something more heartrending still, because concerning us more closely, and that is our own inherent selfishness. Night and day, it poisons our souls, taints our affections. We are selfish, proud, envious, covetous. Cold to others, even to those we believe that we love; we are vitally interested only in ourselves; and even this interest is unwise, for we are often guilty of our own ruin.

Alas! who has not felt a keen self-abhorrence, who has not had cause for it? Do you know that shame that comes over us when we see ourselves as we are, and that unspeakable sorrow at finding that year added to year leave us but what we were, having gained no virtues, lost no faults?

Or have you duly measured your own powerlessness? Have you felt how narrow the walls of your prison? Have you wrestled with your thoughts, and been bruised in the encounter? Do you know what it is to touch without grasping, to be strong enough to combat but not to overcome, capable of feeling, but not of expressing what you feel?

And yet you do not sigh, you want nothing more!

As for me, from my heart there ever rises an unutterable groan. The world, as it is now, does not satisfy me, still less do I satisfy myself. Creation suffers and laments with me. St Paul expresses this mighty woe in one strong word—"travaileth with pain."

What is that we are looking for—Death? It is here, taking us all away at our appointed hour. Death is a curse, it sweeps the earth bare, but cannot transform it.

Is it the last judgment, the awful hour, that even the redeemed of the Lord cannot contemplate unmoved?—The judgment crushes the guilty; but creation is not saved.

Is it the final destruction, the devouring fire predicted in Scripture?—This will destroy the earth, but will not restore its innocence or its beauty.

Is it the new heaven and the new earth?—But it is this world that has suffered, and to it special promises have been made. The whole creation plunged in misery, the oppression of the poor, nature fallen from its first estate—all ask for something beside, claim some other promise, wait for something more!

What is that creation hopes for?—For its deliverance. For what does it sigh?—For its restoration. What does it wait for?—For Jesus, the King!

He will come again! This cry echoes throughout the Scriptures.

He will come again; He who publishes liberty to the captives, and crushes Death beneath His foot. He will come again. With Him will come purity, love, the era of perfect blessedness foretold by the prophets.

The messengers of the Lord in all times speak to us of a sanctified world singing praises to God; we only know a sinful world, hurling complaints and blasphemies against Him. Happiness overflows the earth of which they speak. Our earth is the seat of desolation. They tell us of times of refreshing; our times are times of exhaustion. Peace, love, exceeding great joy here on earth, both with God and our fellow-creatures; these are promised; and, behold, wars ravage, tears inundate our world, sorrow for the dead draws her dark veil round it, the angels as they pass it in their heavenward flight hear a murmur of plaintive cries, angry voices, and mad laughter, sadder still than tears.

From age to age generations of believers have been laid in the grave, their faces turned to the east; and each, in dying, has left behind the sublime watchword, Thy kingdom come!

Yea, Lord, Thy kingdom come! Scoffers, indeed, may laugh. Where is the promise of His coming? they say. "Since the fathers fell asleep all things have gone on the same."

Thy kingdom come! We have nothing else to answer, nothing else to ask.

Thy kingdom come! It is at once a prayer and a pledge. He who told us thus to pray is He who will surely come.

If, hearts big with love, hands clasped, if with strong crying and tears, the whole earth were to raise this burning aspiration to the skies—oh, I believe that the Lord would hear, I believe, indeed, that the Lord would come.

THE COMING OF CHRIST.

THE whole primitive Church expected the coming of Christ, and believed in His temporal reign. This belief, so strong and firm in apostolic times, faded in proportion as faith lost its early simplicity. Men took to materialise precepts and spiritualise prophecy, and thus truth got modified on both sides.

I am one who take the promises in a literal sense. I believe with all my soul in my Saviour's coming. I believe that our earth will witness the scenes described by the prophets, and I have drawn my conviction from the study of the Bible.

The Lord comes! As the lightning shining from the east to the west, so is the shining of the Son of God. He comes surrounded by His redeemed, by myriads of angels, comes as conqueror to claim His crown.

The hour has struck, the souls of the elect have put on their glorified bodies. God's power has done this. In the same moment the faithful who still live have been conscious of a marvellous transformation. It is not death; it is rather the casting off of a chrysalis covering. In the twinkling of an eye, incorruption has triumphed over corruption.

Do you realise this moment, this coming, this object of faith, now beheld from far, as actually come to pass?

Yes, it is true; my imagination is not at work, my eyes see. It is indeed Jesus my Lord. This is He who had pity on me; who suffered for me; whom I love with all the strength of my soul. My breast expands with a divine breath, each moment I love more, and feel that I am more beloved. My God! oh, to prostrate myself before Thee! to adore Thee! It is as though a sun had risen within my heart. At one glance my eye has taken in the thousand thousands in Thy train. My dear ones, there you all are; you indeed, you living, you for ever mine—all of us the Lord's. But yesterday, I laid your bodies in the earth, but yesterday I wandered alone, losing myself in the immensity of my sorrow, and now you are here, my hands touch you, you will not die any more. If God's arm did not sustain, surely man would founder in this ocean of bliss.

The rest of the dead live not again, says the Scripture, till the thousand years are over. Christ's risen elect, together with the nations living at the time, people our regenerated earth.

Israel has seen the One that hung upon the cross, come down from heaven; Israel has beat his breast and gathered round the King of Glory, his King.

Then an act of incalculable importance is accomplished. The angel who has the keys of the pit seizes upon Satan, throws him into the gulf, and sets a seal upon him.

Peace is made on earth. No more wars, no more wrongs; a law of love easily obeyed; a *hosanna* of all creation.

Let us pause for a moment. I want to breathe this new air, and to open out my soul to this light.

Satan bound. Do you comprehend the importance of the fact?

There is in the Bible a narrative which gives a lively representation of Satan's work among men.

Joshua, the High Priest, is standing before the Lord On his right hand a dark form rears itself, standing too—Satan—to *resist him.*

I know it well, that intercession which Satan resists. Witty men have ridiculed it; they have described that grotesque medley of serious and frivolous thoughts; have held up to us in raillery,—that cry of disquieted hearts, disguised by the verbiage of vanity. Possibly Satan does not resist *them* when they pray. But we poor creatures whom he tortures, we who would fain believe, and who hear him whisper sceptical words in our ear; we who would love, and feel his arid breath pass over our hearts; we who want to concentrate our minds on God, and before whom Satan displays the most paltry of earth's toys; we who wrestle unto blood, torn, often overcome by him; we who rise battered from our fall, and lift to our Father maimed and trembling hands; we who know that our enemy is there, always there, even to that death-bed by which He stays to watch us; why, to be freed from Satan, the great resister, the unpitying adversary—this for us is the crowning deliverance.

No more barriers between Jesus and the nations; no longer an accuser between the soul and God.

If original sin remain, the tempter no longer aggravates it; if the old leaven be still there, Satan is not there to make it rise.

We had need of faith; those happy ones have sight, joy, harmony, everything to lead them to give their heart to holiness.

Oh, I can understand that hymn of rapture which marks our earth's course through the skies. The ground is moved. the forests clap their hands, the streams fertilise the sandy wastes, the rose blooms in the desert. No more desolate places, no more broken hearts, we hear no longer the lion's roar, the shrieks of the slaughtered are changed to songs of thanksgiving. The Lord's alliance with His creatures glorifies the universe.

You are shocked at this! Such a scheme seems to you unworthy of God who is a Spirit. For my part, it leaves me penetrated with reverence, admiring reverence. Without this restoration of all things there lacked one ray of my God's perfect glory.

It well beseems the Creator to re-establish His work in its pristine beauty; to restore to it the lustre it possessed when He spake the word and it was made. It becomes His power to snatch it entire from the grasp of Satan. It befits His glory to display it radiant once more; more touchingly beautiful, because it has known suffering; more precious, because Jesus has died for it; more firmly rooted in holiness, because it has struggled to recover it.

You would have this earth in which God has taken delight, left by Him to perish under the curse; you would have Him to leave this triumph to Satan; not so, the rebellious angel shall not occupy it. From the depths of the abyss he will see the earth renewed, the true Monarch govern the kingdom he, Satan, had for a season usurped; the child of God serve Him in this enlarged Eden; the delivered creature willingly obey man; murders and lamentations cease; the restoration of all things be accomplished. Satan will see all this. If he did not see it, if we did not see it, Satan would have gained some advantage in the conflict; he would have successfully resisted God.

And now, tell me, do not you find such a restoration sublime? Does it not seem to you worthy of the Lord, this restoration of a world lost by the madness of man;

tormented by the rage of the great enemy, saved by the very Son of an offended God?

The mountains of Judea have beheld Thy cross, Jesus, Thou Holy of Holies; the walls of Jerusalem have heard the shouts of the maddened crowds that dragged Thee from Caiaphas to Pilate; Gethsemane has drunk Thy blood; Golgotha has echoed with the mocking laughter of the Roman soldiers; the sighs of Thy agony have passed over this land. Thy own country, Lord, the land of promise, shall see thy triumph; and stirred to its inmost depths, shall break forth in a cry of love and welcome.

In east and west, the children of this land have led a painful life. They have been mocked, trampled upon, till at times even they doubted, despaired of themselves and Thee. The earth that saw them so wretched, so prostrated beneath the hatred of the world, shall see them humble still, but radiant with joy, surround their God who reigns in the midst of them.

Oh, the tears of thy mourners, Earth! the lonely steps of those who walked among thy tombs! Thou who hast swallowed up generations of cherished beings; and to those who asked of thee their dead, hast shewn thy dust as sole reply. Thou wilt restore them all, eternally young and happy; they will deck thee like a burst of new flowers; two and two, in families, in companies, they will walk again, singing with joy, on the sites they loved.

The beasts of thy forests; all that move in solitudes unknown to men; all that swim in the abysses of the deep,—used once to tear each other to pieces. A sound as of some pillaged town; a nameless sound, which, as we listen to it, fills the soul with terror, rose incessantly from thy whole surface. Then they who listen will hear a hymn of deliverance burst forth from mountain and plain, and the waves of ocean will repeat it to their shores.

Thou thyself, curse-stricken Earth; thou whose breast cracks at the equator beneath the breath of the simoom; whose barren poles are crushed beneath icebergs,—thou shalt blossom out fair and fresh, younger than in the days of Eden. Thou hast borne our rebellion and our woe through the immensity of space; thou shalt then march in bridal beauty through a tranquil sky; blessed among worlds, bearing on thy surface the redeemed and the Redeemer.

How will these things be?

I know not, but God knows. The least moral contradiction troubles me more than mountains of physical impossibility.

How will the dead rise? how will the earth, at the coming of the Lord, contain both the generations of risen saints and the generations of living men? how will the strange change of which St Paul speaks be effected? in what way will death, powerless over the former, still continue its sway over the nations that are to exist at that marvellous period? in what way will Jesus govern? where will His children dwell? will there be some easy method of communication between earth and heaven? a marvellous ladder like that which Jacob saw?

Of all this I am ignorant. All this is my Father's business; I am not at all uneasy about it.

Nothing is too hard for Him whose seven fiats created the universe.

He will come soon! Watchmen lost in the darkness, we send this cry of hope one to the other.*

* Let me here quote an anecdote, related by the Count de Maistre. "Some one once said to Copernicus, 'If the world were constituted

Yes, the morning stars will soon sing together the hymn which greeted the dawn of the seventh day; the bones that strew the ground will soon rise; Jesus will soon return.

I shall see thee again, thou holy city, no longer depressed and trodden down by unbelievers; I shall see thee glorious, I shall salute thee, queen of the world. Thy fountains will gush forth anew, O Judea! Under thy oaks, O Carmel, the turtle-dove shall fly in peace, not fearing the cruel sportsman! Desert, thy wide swamps shall change to gardens; thy swords, turned to ploughshares, shall prepare thy rich harvests, O country, everywhere called blessed!

You who weep, say, Are not your tears less bitter? You who are tossed upon the open sea, do you not begin to discern the shores of the land of life?

as you say, Venus would have phases like the moon; she has none, however. What have you to say to that?'

"Copernicus answered, 'I have no reply to give, but *God will be so good* as that an answer to this difficulty be found.'"

In fact, *God was so good*, that Galileo invented the telescope with which these phases of Venus were discovered; but Copernicus was dead.

God will be so good, that we shall see the prodigies of His power; but we shall then be living an eternal life, and shall only wonder at one thing: our own former difficulties, when we could depend upon the great God of heaven for their solution.

NEW HEAVENS AND NEW EARTH.

THE destinies of our globe are accomplished. The world that we knew has finished its course. Satan, loosed for a season, has waged his last war. Jesus has for ever vanquished him. Heaven and earth have fled away. There is no more time. The dead of every age are gathered together.

The grave has given up its prisoners, the sea restored those it had swallowed up for thousands of years. Those who believed God, and those who blasphemed Him, those who supremely desired, and those who rejected Him, those who lived delicately, and those who ate the bread of affliction, are all there, gathered before the Lord. Jesus has given up the kingdom to the Father. The Father, the Ancient of Days, has given all judgment to the Son.

His eye reads the most hidden thoughts of the obscurest creature there. The past lives and speaks. Distant ages are present. Forgetfulness—that infirmity of our nature—is annihilated; all that man has ever felt or done, all that remote centuries had folded up in their veil, all is exposed to fullest light.

I know no word in our human speech that can express the solemnity of such an hour.

And it will surely come. You will be there, so shall I, so will those we love. A shudder passes through my whole being. Jesus, Thou hast saved me. Thou, my Judge, Thou hast shed Thy blood to save me. Self-lost, by Thee redeemed, despite much faithlessness, I have sought to serve Thee. Nay, more, I have lived with Thee upon the regenerated earth; I am Thine, so much is certain. But, beholding Thee so awful, Thou whom I knew so meek,—I feel my courage fail. And then my sins rise before me, not one is omitted; I see them as clearly as though I were God himself. There are more, many more of them than I thought; they are uglier than I knew—I abhor myself. And they are all written down, and nothing that is defiled shall enter the kingdom of heaven.

Then a voice, that awful voice which, in the forest, maketh the hinds to bring forth their young; that terrible voice which drives far from the presence of God whosoever has rejected His pardon; that voice, the very same, fraught now with inexpressible tenderness, exclaims, "Come, ye blessed of my Father!"

Does not a hallelujah burst from our breast,—Glory to God in the Highest!

The supreme joy of paradise will be to adore. It will be to tell over, with a boundlessly expanded comprehension, the sacrifice of Jesus, the love of the Father, the merciful action of the Holy Spirit.

The last judgment is over.

Behold the new earth, the new skies!

Death destroyed for ever, Satan for ever overthrown. If one may so speak, eternity now begins.

You do not expect a poor human creature to reveal its secrets. But there are some shadowy features, some faint sounds, which have reached our latitudes, and these I will endeavour to describe.

Heavens and an earth.

That there should be heavens surprises no one. Heaven, purity, light, the dwelling of the Most High, every one understands that in a measure, and anticipates it with confidence.

But an earth also! Who amongst the wise would ever have imagined that?

The beings whom the Eternal raised from the dust, those who have reigned with Him over the world, these were men, they are men still, they will always be so. God, who has decreed it, has supremely developed them, and placed them in conditions suited to their raised estate; a new earth.

What will it be like? I do not know; I know only that *God's tabernacle will be there*, that He will wipe away our tears, that joy will reign, and I know that it will be for ever.

When my eye, as it wanders over the country in summer, beholds it decked with so many charms, although destined to destruction, my thoughts take sudden wing to that promised land, before whose mysterious adorning will pale all that we now call beauty.

Oh, forests, with your fresh coolness; glades with tempered light, filled with winged creatures rejoicing in their life of a day; mountains with grassy summits, majesty of peaks of snow; ineffable charm of the valley; blue lakes, entranced, looking up to and reflecting the sky,—my God made you what you are. It is God who will make the new earth. Our low prose effaces your poetry; the hymn which rises from your solitudes is overpowered by our jarring voices; your flowers pass away; the flowers of paradise will be sweeter still, and will not fade.

But God has prepared still more.

Glory.

This is a sublime promise, and I would not be ungrateful for any one of God's gifts. And yet, if I may dare to say so, whether from feebleness of nature, or conscious unworthiness, glory dazzles me, does not thrill my heart.

A sweeter certainty, a more intimate happiness, fills it with emotion, that of loving.

To love my God. To have some lowly place in heaven, and from thence to see my God, from thence to love Him with enlarged capacities, delivered from all my coldness, all my insincerity. To love my friends in God, with an affection also enlarged, purified, bright, burning as the sun; no fear of idolatry, no envy to corrode, no selfishness, no deceit.

I have so poorly loved those I loved most. How often my affection has sunk beneath the weight of earthly cares, how often I have mourned my heart's powerlessness to cherish unqualifiedly. I have bruised myself against the limitations of my own love for others, as well as against those of the love of others for me. But now everywhere there is the Infinite,—in me, around me Infinite tenderness, and this co-existing with infinite purity.

I shall sin no more.

Holinesss is henceforth the air I breathe; if it failed, I should cease to breathe. I know no other now. I have left sin behind me; it will no more sully the ground I tread, no more stain my white raiment.

Oh, blessing of perfection! To sound my own heart, and find only purity there! To move at will in spontaneous obedience, as the bird floats, and traces wide circles in the luminous atmosphere.

Have I not long enough dragged my chain? have I not groaned beneath the blows of a detestable tyrant whom I abhorred? have I not spread out my captive hands to the Redeemer? Liberty! liberty! My breast dilates as with a fresh breeze from mountain tops. I feel myself a king; I am Thy child, my God; Thy brother, O Jesus! Yes, it is indeed for this that I was born.

Truth.

A great genius died exclaiming, "Light! more light!" His cry is ours. We believe, but there are moments when the truth that we have so abundantly received seems to melt away in our hands. The firmer we seek to grasp it, the more impalpable it becomes. We thought we had a strong hold of some solid thing; a mere smoke rises, fading out of our sight. This is only a nightmare indeed; we wake out of it, but we wake shattered.

At times, a terrible crumbling-away process goes on within us. Everything rocks to and fro, as in the countries shaken by volcanic fires. We want to lay hold upon God; He escapes from us. We utter a groan of despair; God hears that,—He succours us. But what a shock we have had! how it has aged us, as it were! We have, indeed, won the experience of our Father's faithfulness; but we have lost the simple confidence of childhood. We believe more firmly, perhaps, than ever; but we know that darkness may overcast the brightest day.

But there, under new heavens, on the new earth, the sun will shine with undisturbed brightness. No night, no eclipse; and our eyes will meet it undazzled.

To see truly, to think truly, to feel truly,—my heart beats high at such a prospect! This breathless pursuit to lay hold of truth; this desperate struggle to retain it; faith, that supreme effort, that combat where the life of the soul is at stake,—all this is over, left far behind. My eyes behold; falsehood is annihilated; error vanished away. Truth! thy radiance fills the sky; thou art the medium in which I live.

But thou shinest not for me alone; thou fillest the

universe with thy glory. And this is another happiness.

There are truths, my God, that I have believed on Thy word. Others denied them; I obeyed them. I was ridiculed, but I remained faithful to them. Perhaps for a moment I hesitated; my heart sank. Nevertheless, knowing whence they came, I took courage; and, such as they were, followed them, despite the hue and cry. Yet, while following them, a doubt would cross my soul,—was I, indeed, right against so many? That truth, so scoffed at, contradicted, dying out it seemed,—was it truth indeed?

And now, behold it shines forth triumphant, irrefragable. It was no phantom; it was indeed Truth.

Out of all my past confusion, one confusion only remains, the shame of having defended the cause of truth with so faint a heart; of having, I a believer, believed it so little.

The justice of my God will shine forth.

Do you remember those decrees of His that were wont to trouble you?

That God should punish *me;* that He should purify even to the point of mutilation,—does not surprise me. But others—that beloved son, that father! And then the iniquities that have been inflicted; the atrocities endured! And again, such and such a decree, which, by taking from a wife her husband, from a daughter her mother, delivers them defenceless up to vice, and vice takes its prey. Those poor lives which spring up in a corrupt medium, as though they were devoted to degradation, and so soon become of necessity degraded.

There have been seasons when I felt my mind darkened by a secret dread of finding God cold to our griefs; indifferent to our losses; an inexorable Destiny, himself subjected to I know not what fatal general laws. But, oh, I see now that this is not so! Before, there was a dark abyss, which made us giddy; now, there is light, and that light reveals the unfathomable love of God.

Thy compassion, Lord, blended with Thy justice; Thy justice throbbing with tenderness,—these we shall see, these the universe will see. Not one accusing sigh will rise up to Thy throne.

And that justice will illumine many an unappreciated brow. Many flowers, the exquisite beauty and perfume of which were unsuspected, will open to that heavenly day. Those who were reviled or unnoticed, will shine perfect in beauty, and as we see them, our hearts will glorify God.

Knowledge shall be done away.

Even so the dawn is extinguished by the sun that bursts forth in the east.

Nothing will perish that was noble, generous, full of holy grace and poetry. Let us prepare our souls like golden vessels destined to hold this nectar, the knowledge of the Divine perfection.

There will be music there. No harmony here below; not even those marvellous strains, chanted by instruments, repeated by our human voices, which make us weep as though coming to us from the land of the blest; not even those modulations spreading from sphere to sphere, infinite in sadness, infinite in joy; not even this glory of the ideal can give any idea of the harmonies with which heaven will echo.

The secrets of creation, the plans of God revealed; harmonies more touching still,—it is in these that our thirst of knowledge, ever satisfied, never sated, will at length be quenched.

We shall be active.

The angels are so; Jesus is so. Active without a struggle; active without exhaustion.

Have you not known rare and transient hours of work, when your mind moved freely amidst its own creations? As fast as the thought arose, it was shaped fittingly, and clothed, sometimes in a garment with graceful folds, sometimes in one of austere simplicity, but always the idea was ennobled by its expression.

That was done without difficulty. The angel, at Eden's gate, had lowered his flaming sword. You wandered—brow all light, heart all gladness—in a world where all activity was delight. What! there are men who sow in tears, there are ploughs which tear the earth's breast! You could not realise it.

A breath; Eden is closed, the sword is brandished, you lie prostrate. Darkness over your spirit, your nerves spent, your words powerless, your thoughts still more so, and, if you struggle, a bloody sweat.

Oh, then, how feelingly you remember the earthly paradise! But heaven has in store for us delightsome labours, easy as respiration, refreshing as dew, and to these there will be no end.

A permanent state.

This is the fulness of joy. My heart can rest in it.—*For ever!*

I have felt such bliss, that heaven, I have thought, could add nothing to it; lightning-flashes of adoration, love, truth, all combined; but it was only for a moment, and the certainty that it would end, cast its dark shadow over it.

But in the presence of my God, in His paradise there will be no end.

The light will not fade, the heart will not fail, the Lord

will not hide His face; nothing will pale, nothing will grow cold; no defection will be possible, the full cup will never break, our lips never turn away.

Eternal youth, eternal desire, eternal enjoyment. And the essence of this eternity—*love.*

We will go no further. I bow me down. Such brightness makes my eyelids droop. My voice falters and fails. Prayer alone, thanksgiving, the sigh of an humbled spirit, intercession for those who weep—these fill my heart, and rise from it without words.

Let us pause It is good to be here; this is the gate of heaven.

THE END.

NEW BOOKS.

Melbourne House. By the Author of "The Wide, Wide World," etc. 2 vols. 12mo, ...

A most touching and beautiful Story, in which, through the history of a little girl, most important truths are taught in a very interesting way. With most readers, Little Daisy of Melbourne House will be as great a favorite as Ellen Montgomery of the "Wide, Wide World." This Story has all the freshness of her first work.

Ellen Montgomery's Book Shelf. By the Authors of the "Wide, Wide World," and "Dollars and Cents." 5 vols. 16mo, illustrated, in a neat box, ... 6 00

The Volumes are also sold separately, as follows:

Mr. Rutherford's Children,.................... 1 20

Sybil and Chryssa,.............................. 1 20

Hard Maple,.. 1 20

Carl Krinken's Christmas Stocking,......... 1 20

Casper and His Friends,........................ 1 20

This interesting Series of Books has long been out of print, and frequently called for. This new and handsome edition will be hailed with delight by youthful readers of various ages.

Egypt's Princes. By the Rev. G. Lansing, American Missionary at Cairo, 12mo..................... 1 50

A most interesting book—giving life pictures of Egypt as she now is. Equally well adapted for the Sabbath School Library, or the Christian Fireside.

Sea Drifts. By Mrs. Georgie A. Hulse McLeod. 16mo. illustrated,.. 1 25

A beautiful religious Story of Boarding-school life, the scene of which is laid near Newport, R. I. It is well adapted for girls verging into womanhood, and will prove alike entertaining and instructive.

The Martyrs of Spain, and the Liberators of Holland. By the Author of "The Schönberg-Cotta Family. 16mo,.. 1 25

It has been well said, that the charm of this lady's writings consists in their truthful adherence to the spirit and customs of the olden time. We have here those qualities applied to Spain and Holland. Few religious writers are more favorably known to the reading public, than this attractive writer.

Good for Evil, and other Stories. By A. L. O. E., 0 90

A series of Short Stories by this eminently popular author, which possess all the interest of her longer stories. It has six fine illustrations.

Cortley Hall. By A. L. O. E...................... 0 90

Containing "The Straight Road the Safest and Surest," and the "Stories of Jewish History,"—the first highly entertaining, and the second very instructive.

Human Sadness. By Countess de Gasparin. 16mo, 0 90

The Countess de Gasparin's famous work, "The Near and the Heavenly Horizons," has rendered her name familiar to the lovers of good books. The present work will be found well adapted to those who are in affliction.

The Book of Animals. With numerous illustrations. Square, ... 0 90

A very pretty book for children, plentifully illustrated, and abounding in interesting Stories.

The Child's Bunyan, or the Story of the Pilgrim's Progress told for Little Children. 18mo, ... 0 60

The Cripple of Antioch. By the author of the "Schönberg-Cotta Family." $1 25

A fascinating narrative of Christian life near the beginning of the Christian era. A book which, when once taken in hand, is not easily laid aside till the end is reached.

The Cedar Christian, and other practical Papers. By the Rev. T. L. Cuyler. 16mo 90

"Genial, open-hearted and fascinating in his style, both spoken and written, Mr. Cuyler has made for himself a land-wide reputation, and written his name everywhere as a household word."—*Evangelist.*

Ned's Motto; or, Little by Little. By the author of "Win and Wear," &c. 1 25

This may be truly reckoned among first-class books for the young. Ned is the son of a captain killed in this war, who, though a child, manfully contends against the pressure of want into which the family are brought by the sad event; encouraged by the cordial sympathy of the neighbors, and acting patiently on the motto: "Little by Little."

Mabel's Experience; or, Seeking and Finding. 18mo 0 90

A capital Scotch story that will delight all readers and do them good.

The Straight Road the Shortest and the Surest. By A. L. O. E. 45

Paying Dear. By A. L. O. E. 0 60

Esther Parsons. By A. L. O. E. 0 60

Christian Conquests. A series of Stories by A. L. O. E. 12 cuts 0 90

Try Again, and other Stories. By A. L. O. E. 12 engravings 0 90

The Silver Casket; or, the Wiles of the World. By A. L. O. E. 8 illustrations.......... 0 90

Stories of Jewish History. By A. L. O. E. 0 60

The Bags of Gold, and other Stories. By A. L. O. E. 6 cuts 0 60

Falsely Accused, and other Stories. By A. L. O. E. 6 cuts 0 60

The Sale of Crummie, and other Stories 0 90

Maud Summers, the Sightless. 4 illus. 0 90

The Three Cripples. By the Rev. P. B. Power. 0 75

The Last Shilling. By the Rev. P. B. Power. 0 75

The Two Brothers and the Two Paths. By the Rev. P. B. Power 0 75

The Diamond Brooch, and other Stories.. 0 60

The Buried Bible and other Stories. 0 60

Faithful and True. By the author of "Win and Wear, "Tony Starr's Legacy," etc. 16mo. 8 illus. 1 25

A well-told story of Life on the Green Mountains—full of action and interest—fresh, and with an excellent moral to it. The main object of the book is to teach the importance of being "faithful and true," especially in the little things of every-day life.

The Safe Compass and how it Points. By the Rev. Richard Newton, D.D. 6 illus.... 1 25

Dr. Newton is one of the very best writers of juvenile religious literature in the land. He seems to have an inexhaustible fund of unexceptionable stories and illustrations, and knows just how and when to use them.

Claude, the Colporteur. By the author of "Mary Powell," etc. 16mo. 8 engravings.............. 1 25

A graphically told story of youthful labors, trials, and successes. It is a book that will be devoured with eagerness by the young reader.

The Post of Honor. A Story by the author of "Broad Shadows on Life's Pathway." 16mo............ 1 25

A well-told story of Missionary Life, suffering and triumph—all founded on fact.

The Jewish Tabernacle and its Furniture. By the Rev. Richard Newton, D.D. Illus...... 1 75

The Old Helmet. A tale by the author of "The Wide, Wide World." 2 vols.............................. $3 50

www.ingramcontent.com/pod-product-compliance
Lightning Source LLC
LaVergne TN
LVHW020223110826
845151LV00003B/803

* 9 7 8 1 4 2 5 5 3 2 7 9 6 *